Bets Wishs Doc

Bets Wishz Doc

Dr. Martin E. Cohen
with Barbara Davidson

A
Arthur Fields Books, Inc., New York 1974

Descriptions of the Frostig booklet test and the Beery-Buktenica test used by permission of the Follett Publishing Company.

Illinois Test of Psycholinguistic Abilities, by Samuel A. Kirk, James J. McCarthy, and Winifred D. Kirk. © 1968 by the Board of Trustees of the University of Illinois.

Michigan Language Program © Donald E. P. Smith and Judith M. Smith. New York: Learning Research Associates, Inc., 1971.

Rowland: *Beginning to Read, Write and Listen,* copyright 1971, developed by Boston Educational Research Company, Inc., for J. B. Lippincott Company, East Washington Square, Philadelphia, Pa.

Winterhaven Copy Forms Test © Winterhaven Lions Research Foundation, Inc.

Published simultaneously in Canada by Clarke, Irwin & Company Limited, Toronto and Vancouver
ISBN: 0-525-63002-3
Library of Congress Catalog Card Number: 72-94677

To

Carole

Jeffrey

Ricky

Steven

Michael

who make it possible each day

Author's Note

The material in this book is drawn from my experience over many years working in several schools and institutions. In the interests of readability, I have taken the liberty of telescoping various incidents that occurred in different locales into a single narrative. While all the events in this book are true, and all the characters based on real people, I have changed all names to insure privacy and any resemblance to living persons is purely coincidental.

There are a number of people without whose help this book never could have been written. Above all, I want to thank my wife, Carole, who gave me confidence when I needed it most. I also owe a lasting debt to Dr. Stanley Evans, an optometrist who introduced me to working with learning disabled kids. I am continually awed by his knowledge, energy, and understanding.

My kids' parents and teachers have been invaluable, too. But it's the kids themselves who have been the real inspiration to me. In spite of overwhelming odds and difficulties almost impossible for the rest of us to imagine, they tackle each day armed only with their own personality, intelligence, guts. Other books have described their lives from the outside, but if I have succeeded in letting the reader inside their world—permitting them to speak and act for themselves—I will feel my efforts have been repaid a thousandfold.

They have one hell of a story to tell.

Doc

Bets Wishs Doc

I

Joey Rich was a short, chubby kid with blue eyes and dark curly hair. He seemed the perfect Madonna's child—sweet-looking, always well-groomed. He looked as if nothing was wrong with him, but plenty was. At ten, Joey couldn't do a simple one-piece puzzle. He'd take a piece much too big and try to jam it in, force it, instead of looking for another that might possibly fit. He didn't know his alphabet. Obviously, he couldn't read or write. He couldn't even walk right.

Joey came from a welfare family in Queens, New York. His father spent almost no time at home and on the rare occasions he did show up he ignored Joey.

The mother, a soft, protective woman, had done her best trying to help Joey, but there he was, in the third grade in public school, going nowhere. Even Joey seemed to know he wasn't going anywhere. He kept walking around the classroom, disturbing the other kids, and often ran out of the room and the building. His teacher, with thirty other kids to look after, couldn't pay special attention to him. And she couldn't buy him off any more by saying: "Joey, if you just keep quiet and sit down I won't tell your mother, I won't tell the principal, I'll give you a passing grade. Just go back to your desk and sit down." No sale. Finally he was put on "home instruction"—a euphemism for getting kicked out of school.

I first heard of Joey when his guidance counselor, a friend of mine, called to ask if I'd take him in the special school I run for kids with learning disabilities (LD). He said Joey seemed to be an LD kid who would respond to our program. The new semester had started a week or so before, and normally I don't admit new kids; but Audrey, one of my teachers, had just lost a child whose father had been transferred to another state, and she was one kid shy. Besides, knowing Joey's home background, I thought Audrey would be great for him. She's this real protective mother-type who just loves kids. She ties them to her apron strings and fights for their every privilege. She screams bloody murder if someone cuts five minutes off their lunch hour or if they have to miss gym because of a trip.

Audrey may have been ready to take Joey, but the Board of Education wasn't—they needed some time to arrange transportation for Joey, so he had to come to school on his own. He lived only ten blocks away, so that was no sweat; and, sure enough, the first day he was Johnny on the spot at eight-thirty. But the next day he turned up at ten and then eleven and then twelve. So I took him aside.

"Hey, Joe," I said (if I was asking for grown-up responsibilities, he needed a grown-up name), "it's just not right for you to get here at ten o'clock. I'm not going to take it. From now on, if you don't make it by eight-thirty I'm not going to let you in. You can sleep, play in the streets, do anything you want, but unless you're here on time I'm going to lock the doors on you."

Laying it on the line like that seemed to work for a couple of days, but then he slipped back to the ten o'clock routine. I knew Joey's history. I had to let him know who was boss. And fast. So I said, "Look, Joe, if you're not here at eight-thirty, I'm going to come and get you."

"You can't do that," he said. "I'll tell my mother."

"I don't care what you tell your mother," I said. "I'm going to come and get you anyway."

The next day Joey didn't come to school. I drove to his home. His mother was fit to be tied.

"I can't get him out of bed," she said. "He won't get out of bed."

"What do you mean by that?" I asked.

"He just won't get out."

"Oh no?" I marched into the bedroom, yanked off the covers and dumped Joey on the floor. "I'll give you five minutes to get ready," I told him, "and then you're coming to school with me."

Joey started to cry and his mother was so upset I thought she was going to cry too.

"Look," I told her, "he can cry all day long at school and it won't bother me. I just don't want it bothering you. School isn't that bad. He's got to be in school."

Joey fought me all the way, but I knew I had no leeway with this kid. I had to physically carry him into the classroom by his belt and the seat of his pants. But when he saw the other kids, he got embarrassed and went to his seat. He didn't come late any more. We had won that round.

After that Joey had a couple of good weeks, so I decided it was a good time to get to know him better and find out his

3

deficits. There was no way we could give him a reading test or any other standard tests—he just wouldn't respond. So I took him down to the gym on his lunch hour and tossed a basketball around with him, trying to get my head down to where his head was so we could talk.

The basketball playing of course was a disaster. I'd already noticed that Joey's balance was poor. He couldn't move properly and he had trouble with such simple tasks as picking up a crayon. As we played I noticed he also had no real sense of concepts such as near or far, up or down, left or right. His judgment was so bad that he'd throw wide by yards. The kid had no frame of reference at all. And his coordination was so poor that often the ball hit him before he could make more than a slight move to grab it. But as we tossed it around and Joey relaxed and got involved in the conversation, he forgot about the playing.

"What do you do, Joe," I asked, "when you're not in school? Do you jump over hydrants, kick the can? What?"

"I don't do nothin'," he said, tossing the ball past me.

"What about your friends," I asked, retrieving it and shooting it back at him. "Do you have any friends?"

"No," he said.

Bit by bit over the next week or two, he began to open up. He began to talk about his life and we became friends. But I kept thinking, We've got to get a quick win with this kid. If he doesn't succeed, if he doesn't believe he can do things by the end of the term, he'll never be back next year.

Slowly I cut off the basketball and sent Joey back to class. I told him he should spend time with the other kids and start to work with them. Everything was fine for a few days and then Audrey told me that Joey had taken up walking again.

"He won't stay in his seat no matter what I say," she told

4

me. "He just keeps walking, first up to the board, then back to his seat, then to the windows, then circling all around the room. It's disturbing the whole class."

I went into the room. This was no new situation. We've had lots of road runners—it's one of the basic behavioral symptoms of the LD child.

"Hey, Joe," I said, "I hear you like to walk. Well, walking's good exercise. I want you to come out with me and show me how you walk. We're going to do two things—show you that walking can be fun and knock off a little weight at the same time."

Joey and I got out in the corridor and I showed him where I wanted him to walk, from one end of the hall to the other and back again.

"No," said Joey.

"Yes," said I.

And No and Yes.

"If I have to help you walk," I said, "it's not going to be pleasant."

Joey walked. But that wasn't enough. I wanted to make sure he ended his roadrunning once and for all. So I began making fun of him.

"Can't you walk straight?" I teased him. "Why do you walk with a waddle! You walk so badly that if you were a penguin not even a penguin colony would let you in. Do you have to look at your feet when you walk? Think how ashamed your mother would be if she saw you walk like that."

Joey's face began to get red, not really crying, but not far from it either. On about the twentieth turn he bolted out the door at the other end of the corridor and into the street. And I went right out after him.

Now, I was thirty-two at the time and not in very good shape myself. I chased this kid for sixteen blocks, keeping about five steps behind him and dying all the way. But I'd committed myself, so I had to go all the way. Otherwise, the kid was gone.

When I did finally catch up to him, all I had to do was put a hand on him and he stopped. I tried not to seem out of breath. Holding back the puffing, I said, "Now, Joe, let's go back and finish our walk." He did. Then I took him back to class. "If you don't want to do this again," I said, "you'd better get in there, pick up a book and work."

From then on, Joey really got going. He must have sensed that here, at last, was somebody who cared about him, who was willing to chase him to hell and gone, quite literally, to make sure he shaped up and was determined to see he made a go of it.

Joey obviously had been hungry for something—that was part of what all the walking was about—roaming around the room looking for something he *could* do. All his school life, people had been telling him to do this or do that—read, write, learn—all things he *couldn't* do. The natural reaction is to say, "Hell, I'm not going back to that place any more. And I'm not going to try anything."

I call this the "I can't, I don't want to, don't make me" syndrome. Most of these kids enter school hardly able to read or write. They may not be able to recite the alphabet; almost all are working several years below their age level. Yet instead of acknowledging these shortcomings, most of them decide that they don't *want* to read because they *can't* read and *nobody is going to make them!* It's an emotional out that many an adult will recognize. What is not so easily recognized is that kids like Joey lack the perceptual foundations for successful academic learning.

6

By this time, we had put Joey through a complete perceptual evaluation—my specialty and that of the school. And we had confirmed that, as suspected from the clues in class and in playing ball, he had enormous perceptual deficits. He didn't know left from right, he reversed letters, he couldn't handle oblique lines—"X" became " + "—he couldn't distinguish the whole from its parts, he couldn't write on the line and jammed up his letters in typical "Plan Ahea$_d$" fashion, he couldn't seem to match the sounds of letters with the way they looked on a page, he had no sense of size or form constancy—he couldn't grasp the concept that a square always remained a square or that things didn't actually get smaller when they moved away.

How can you read without these rudiments? The answer is that you *can*—to a limited and even acceptable extent—if you're highly motivated, highly intelligent and get enough experience thrown at you. You can learn to read with all these problems the same way you can get from Philadelphia to New York via California. Just because you're learning-and perceptually disabled does not necessarily mean you've got to be a total failure. It just means doing everything the hard way and coming in last when you should have been far up front.

But most kids—to say nothing of adults—with Joey's perceptual blocks would just give up. Joey was no genius. His IQ stood somewhere around ninety. And his self-image stood around zero.

We put Joey through his perceptual training paces starting at the bottom and kept him at it every day in an attempt to eliminate the basic perceptual disabilities that were bugging him. We also bombarded him with beginning reading programs, those that emphasized auditory and tactile input, where his perceptual abilities were highest.

And I leaned on Audrey all the way, using her as my foil. If I was the pusher who wouldn't let him run away, Audrey was the puller, the gal he loved and wanted to impress. A good mark or praise from her was real status—no one else's would do. In fact, at one point, when he had made substantial progress and Audrey felt she could turn him over to her aide for some of the simpler training, Joey rebelled. For once we gave in to him.

Getting going with Joey and keeping going were two different things, of course. We had broken through the "I won't" but there were years of "I can't" to peel away. Every time he refused to try something I was in there giving him the same old business.

"I can't. It's too hard," he would wail.

"Look, Joe," I would say, "everyone knows you can't. Your teacher knows you can't. Your mother knows you can't. Everyone in this room knows you can't. If you want I'll get a tape recorder and you can make a record of it and we'll play it for the whole school. But Joey," I would say, "there's one thing you're not doing that you *can* do—that you and everyone else knows you can do. You *can* try. Now let's try trying."

"OK, Joey?" Audrey would say. And back Joey would go to work.

After a couple of months of this, I wasn't too surprised to find a belligerent Joey Rich barging into my office. He slammed down on my desk the first Bank Street primer, designed for kindergarten, and said hotly: "There. I did it. If ya don't believe me, you can ask my teacher."

I was ready for him. "I'm not so sure. Sit down and read it to me." After a few sentences that he read perfectly, I stopped him. Now was the chance to motivate him all the way. "So?" I said. "You can read it. Big deal. What's so great about that? I have a four-year-old at home who can read that and you're ten."

The treatment apparently worked. Joey was far into first-grade reading by June and into second-grade reading by December of the next year.

He also progressed well in other areas. In gym and on his own he quickly became more oriented to structured action—shooting at the basket, jumping hurdles, joining in games—rather than resorting to the kind of aimless running around that a kindergarten kid tends to do and that many of our eight-, nine- and ten-year-olds still indulge in. And his perception and reasoning abilities began to grow by leaps and bounds.

About a month after Joey began his second year of school, I watched him in perceptual training class. Each child sat blindfolded holding a form in their hands. The assignment was to describe its shape, size, thickness and texture to the best of their ability. The first kid, Jimmy, was extremely slow with his answers and the other kids were on his back to hurry up so they could get their turn. Suddenly, just for kicks, I decided to throw in a mickey.

"What color is it, Jimmy?" I asked. While Jimmy and two other blindfolded kids sat there trying to figure out the answer, Joey, who is normally quiet, started to roar with laughter. I roared right along with him. Joey was going to do just fine.

2

Joey Rich is one of the lucky ones. He was spotted. His problem was diagnosed as a learning disability. And he wound up in one of the pitifully few schools that recognize these kids and try to help overcome their problem.

With so many LD kids still undiagnosed, it's impossible to come up with a firm estimate, but we can say with certainty that at least seven and a half million children in the United States are learning-disabled. Some estimates run as high as one out of four in every classroom. Recent studies suggest that eighty percent of all juvenile delinquents have a history of learning disabilities. And no one knows how many people with IQ's of 115 or 120 are forced to hack it as laborers, dishwashers or garbage collectors because they never were able to learn to read or write.

What is a learning-disabled child? ←

Some twenty years ago, professionals in various fields began to notice kids with no severe brain dysfunction like epilepsy, kids showing no obvious retardation and displaying no severe emotional problems such as schizophrenia—all known blocks to learning—who just couldn't seem to get the hang of simple schoolwork, particularly reading. Because reading was the most apparent problem, one of the early terms applied to such kids was dyslexia, or word blindness. Now it's a term widely used, and misused, to designate almost any otherwise average child who has trouble learning to read, who still reverses his letters in writing at the age of six, who doesn't know his left from his right, a kid with just about any learning problem. Dyslexia, as it is defined now, *is* a learning disability, but a very specific one. It is reserved for those children who seem able to learn everything else—math, games, puzzles, logic—except how to decode written symbols on a page. The kid's brain blocks out letters and word symbols so that by the time they reach the cortex either they don't register or they are received only as a faint blur. (Dyslexia, it should be added, has nothing to do with whether or not the kid needs glasses.)

But continued research with these children, particularly regarding their behavior, began to uncover a wider range of common symptoms than just poor schoolwork and non-reading. These non-readers seemed to be constantly distractible and inattentive, which often resulted in their being classified as behavior problems. They wouldn't sit still, wouldn't listen, fidgeted all the time, wouldn't control themselves, jumped out of their seats—and back in and out again—forgot what the teacher had said a second ago. Every little thing seemed to claim their attention; they were impatient, had no sense of time, constantly demanded attention, always seemed on the go. That is, until they turned the flip side and perseverated—sitting daydreaming or glued to one activity for hours.

So a new label was applied to these kids—hyperactive or hyperkinetic—a symptom, many believe, of neurosis or emotional disturbance, which psychological therapy could correct. But there were some neurologists who maintained that these hyperkinetic kids *couldn't* control themselves—that their hyperkinesis resulted from some injury to the brain, either inherited or contracted at or near birth. Though much less severe, their behavior seemed characteristic of many organically brain-injured children. And going back through case histories, the neurologists found these same children had displayed much the same unhealthy degree of distractibility and activity even as newborn children. Mothers reported they thrashed around in their cribs, grabbing everything—rattle, bottle, clothespin—and then throwing it away a minute later, screaming almost constantly but cutting off the instant they were touched (an unnatural reaction—most babies' crying subsides slowly as they gradually process the information that comfort is at hand).

Thus the term brain-injured or brain-damaged came into use for our LD kids, along with the concept that this was an innate condition, not one developed under emotional stress. But since the child's brain usually registered no observable abnormality on a neurologist's electroencephalogram, the best instrument now available for detecting brain lesions or injuries, the handicap was amended to minimal or chronic brain damage, minimal or chronic brain syndrome, minimal brain dysfunction (mbd), or some such similar label—minimal or chronic brain injury, non-organic brain injury, and even something called the Strauss-Lehtinin syndrome. The neurologists, who still have little more to go on than a close examination of the physical reactions of the child and a

12

detailed study of family and medical histories, believe that these innately hyperactive mbd children—as well as the true dyslexic—are suffering from some as yet unmeasurable fault in the electro-chemical impulses that govern their brain: somewhere, somehow, the right connections are not being made, or are being made poorly, only in bits and parts. Figuratively speaking, it's as though there is static along the wires that prevents the child from fully concentrating on learning, especially on more complicated levels—*no matter what his intelligence*.

Now the frustrating thing—and one of the reasons it's so hard to spot these kids—is that, once tuned in, they can display very sharp minds. In addition, their list of symptoms does not sound like—much less *look* like—symptoms at all, although they are suffering from them nonetheless. It's no wonder that too often the problem gets overlooked until it is just too late.

What makes these kids so hard to spot? One need only to look at the children in my school—eighty-five percent of whom, like Joey, have been diagnosed mbd or some variant thereof. These kids are only minimally handicapped—and in fact we are careful to screen out any children who are severely retarded or autistic, seriously emotionally disturbed, or who have a serious physical handicap like blindness or deafness. For the most part, our kids look and act like perfectly normal children. They don't drool and their heads don't loll. They don't stare blankly ahead like zombies. They tend to be klutzy, but so what?—so are many kids. They are often inattentive, but what child isn't at one time or another? They tend to be highly active, but so are most kids. They won't sit still, they are highly distractible, they often seem unreachable—and what parent doesn't have such complaints about any child? The list of "non"-symptoms for LD kids goes on and on.

Yet these kids go through private hell. Some can't hold a pencil, some can't tell a square from a circle, some can't color within the lines, some can't judge speed and distance well enough to keep from running into a wall. Most are severely limited in their abilities to coordinate and order themselves—even their own bodies—and all of them have great difficulty relating one similar experience to another— the ability to generalize, which is a prerequisite to any kind of learning.

Mainly, these kids can't seem to learn anything. And because they can't, neighborhood kids shout "retard" when they can't get the hang of a game and toss in "baby" for good measure when they cry after losing. Adults whisper grown-up equivalents; and their own parents fall into bed exhausted after one more day of unsuccessfully trying to get their LD kid to wash his face, dress neatly for school, clean up his room or go to bed—all to the tune of screams and tantrums. Teachers find them impossible as they walk around the room, constantly talk out of turn, don't do their work, and beat on other kids or throw things around. If things get bad enough, the school kicks them out. And if they stop just short of creating an intolerable disturbance, the school does something almost worse. It floats them along until they are old enough to try to make it on their own in the school of hard knocks.

And all because of problems that I believe can be overcome.

What causes mbd? Many believe it is inherited or else contracted at or near birth. Case histories on parents and mbd children, too often prepared years after the fact, seem to support this genetic theory since many of these kids' fathers, in particular, showed some of the same symptoms and learning difficulties in their youth. And the fact that, today, nearly eighty percent of children diagnosed mbd are boys would seem to support the genetic case.

Others, while not denying the genetic argument, feel mbd may be rooted in other factors as well. Some attribute it to poor nutrition and metabolic imbalances during pregnancy—and certainly we are seeing more and more children from child welfare agencies and the ghetto areas who are diagnosed mbd. And a surprising number of LD children are adoptees whose natural mothers have no plans to keep their child, and so are likely to neglect themselves.

Others blame mbd on certain modern obstetric practices: forceps delivery, which can injure the child's soft head; the use of anesthetics which enter the infant's system from the mother, slowing the infant heart rate and decreasing its supply of oxygen at birth.

There are those who believe mbd can be caused by natural birth difficulties: long labor, a breach presentation or the trauma of prematurity. A traumatic illness or shock in the early days and weeks of life also may be a factor.

Some psychologists and psychiatrists find the whole concept of blaming learning disabilities on mbd hogwash. LD, *they* say, results from emotional disturbance acquired at a very early age. And it is true that many children arrive at school not only diagnosed emotionally disturbed but determined to prove the diagnosis correct. They are bratty, infantile in behavior and generally divorced from reality. Their frustration threshold is so low that at eight, nine, ten and eleven they still throw tantrums and scream or cry at the least setback. And they are so inflexible about their environ-ment—another sign of emotional disturbance—that the least change in schedule will generate an argument. One wonders, however, which came first—the emotional disturbance or the learning disability that made it so difficult for them to cope with the world in the first place.

My position on all this has been somewhat heretical: Who cares? Who cares whether it's this cause or that cause, this dysfunction or that dysfunction—the main thing is that these kids, for whatever reason, are learning-disabled and need help. We're there to give it to them. In fact, recent studies have shown that we send twice as many kids back to their regular schools as the average program in the New York City school system. But then, I have a special *personal* interest in these kids—early in life I shared some of their same learning problems myself.

I was born in the Bronx of Jewish parents and pushed along toward the expected medical career. I didn't think about it too much. My IQ was well above average and I read voraciously as a child. I believed I would become a doctor.

The only trouble was that I was no student. I was every-thing else—teacher's pet, champion chalkboard eraser, number one bell monitor and later a professional musician, a fair artist and a pretty good athlete—but I was barely passing my courses.

But Lady Luck smiled on me and I managed to slip into college, where I cut every corner and every class I could. In the next two and a half years I failed an English course, four language courses and came near failing all my courses in bi-ology, physics, chemistry and math. By my junior year I was shocked to realize that not only wasn't I going to make it in

16

medicine, I might not even make it through college. The dean suggested that perhaps I'd be better off leaving school and joining the Armed Forces.

The message came across loud and clear. And my reactions were much the same as those of our LD kids, particularly the older and brighter ones, when they are kicked out of school. I was confused. I was hurt. I was sure I had tried. Everyone knew how bright I was. How could this be happening to the Boy Genius from the Bronx? The whole system was obviously unfair and stacked against me.

Luck again favored me and I was rescued by the same source that bails out many of our LD kids—the family. A relative pulled some political strings and got me admitted as a pre-med student in a school in the South. The world was right-side-up again, I went ahead with my plans, I even got married. Then the politician died, the deal fell through, and I was left with a new wife to support, no medical school in sight and the possibility of not even a college degree. Though I certainly didn't realize it at the time, it was the luckiest break of my life.

For the first time in my life, I faced facts. I hadn't worked. I had never been very interested in medicine. I was no genius and certainly no Superman, just a kid who had run away from anything that looked difficult.

Somehow I got back into college, and this time I buckled down. I majored in psychology and then decided to go into optometry. Which is where I first discovered Joey's world.

While studying for my doctorate at the Massachusetts College of Optometry, I began taking regular courses and clinical work in vision training—a traditional function of optometrists but one unfortunately practiced by very few—retraining eye muscles to correct strabismic, or turned, eyes and training them to focus and converge properly and work together as a team. Almost all the children in our clinic had some problem in this area and many were having difficulties in reading and school.

At the same time I began reading widely in the professional optometric journals and began to realize that, far from the popular conception of optometrists as those who just prescribed and fitted glasses and contact lenses, optometry had made a significant but largely unrecognized contribution to child development and education.

Optometrists began successfully improving the function of the visual system (what we call vision training) as early as 1900. In the process they began to realize that efficient coordination of the eye was as much a *learned* function as coordination of the body, and probably even more complex and important. Man has evolved as the most vision-oriented of all animals; the eyes alone transmit twice as much information to the brain as the entire rest of the body. In addition, the eyes direct and integrate much of the body's actions.

But optometry, I found, had not stopped with vision training. In the late 1920s and '30s, an optometrist named A. M. Skeffington had taken a leap from vision training into the still controversial field of visual perception.

Skeffington noted that there were people who couldn't seem to judge such visual concepts as speed and distance even though there was nothing wrong with their acuity. Others could not determine whether a substance was soft or hard without touching it as well. Some had to go through physical motions—such as raising their hands—to "see" left and right. Some had great trouble literally picking out the forest from the trees.

To truly "see" or *perceive* something, Skeffington maintained, a visual image not only had to reach the brain through the camera-like retina but be interpreted and reproduced by it correctly. Vision in this total sense was not automatic, *but grew as the child developed,* something later studies confirmed. Skeffington's subjects' perceptual abilities were not abnormal, just underdeveloped for their chronological age.

Gerald Getman, another optometrist, devised models for training children with perceptual difficulties that showed that the child develops perceptions in a predictable progression of touch, taste and smell, then motion, then hearing and finally sight. He found that by the age of six a normal child would grow from an almost total motor perceiver to a predominantly visual perceiver; therefore, with children who had visual perception problems, it made sense to retrace the process.

By the time I reached optometry school, optometrists had spent years successfully retraining such kids along the motor-to-visual path until they achieved perceptual proficiency. But despite this growing evidence indicating that visual perception was learned, the idea of perceptual training for kids with learning problems usually engendered snickers from doctors, educators, psychologists and even optometrists in the early 1960s. It still does in many quarters.

At Massachusetts, for example, there were no courses in perceptual training so, along with some friends I prevailed on the college to bring in outside experts to give us courses and clinical work. It was kind of a bootstrap education, but it convinced me that perceptual training was going to be my specialty.

I saw it work.

I saw kids who were poor readers become good readers after they went through elementary perceptual exercises such as creeping, crawling, rail-walking, matching and touching.

Not everyone made it to academic heights but their performance usually improved.

Besides, I really dug the kids.

In 1963, after getting my doctorate, I returned to New York to begin my practice. A year later I had some forty-odd kids coming in weekly for perceptual training. I had joined the staff of the Optometric Center of New York (now the clinic for the New York State College of Optometry, long a pioneering group in the field of vision research), and I was lecturing on the subject to PTAs, teachers' associations, college students, special education teachers, regular teachers, parent groups, community groups, anybody who would listen.

Soon I was asked by various schools for children with learning problems to supervise their perceptual training programs. I served as director of one school for LD children, age five to fifteen, who could reasonably be expected to return to regular school within a few years. And then I became director of my own school specializing in perceptual development. All this experience with LD kids has only reinforced my belief in perceptual training as the key to unlocking their world of learning disability.

What is perception? It's the ability to assign the proper meaning to raw signals received through one sense or another. It goes beyond acuity, although poorly functioning sense receivers—blindness, deafness, problems with tasting, feeling, smell or movement (kinesthesia is now recognized as an important sense modality)—of course will impair the development of good perception in those areas. And it stops short of intelligence and the ability to reason—although poor perception will impair intelligent performance. For example, your reasoning powers may be sound enough to tell you not to run a car into a tree, but if your speed and distance perception are off you may run into the tree anyway. Or if you have poor eyesight or focusing problems that prevent you from seeing the tree, your perceptual judgment of speed and distance may be thrown off, no matter what your reasoning powers.

Most animals perceive with all their senses and so does man. But the mature human being is much more eye-oriented, and as a result has developed the most sophisticated and efficient ocular system, to the possible expense of the other senses. Had we been less eye-oriented, we never could have communicated through abstract thought and visual symbols such as books or even TV (animals, for instance, can't "see" television). Man processes almost all the information in his world visually, with only secondary help from auditory cues. He relies on these perceptions every minute of his waking day.

Yet in school we have kids who, at age ten, can't judge distance and speed well enough to keep from running into something right in front of them. Or a boy who believes that it takes only two of his crawl strokes to swim across a thirty-foot pool; others will take off ten feet before reaching a two-foot hurdle, land in front and ask: "Did I make it?" These are the same kids who crowd their words together so that their writing is incomprehensible, or who don't leave enough space on a line. Their ability to play any kind of athletic game is severely compromised, they run into everything and everybody, and they just might end up being hit by a car while crossing the street.

Because of their blocks—neurological, emotional and, in most cases, both—my kids haven't learned as they should.

They haven't developed the perceptual arts that are taken for granted in a child their age. All the children we've chosen to work with in our school manifest some sort of perceptual dysfunction. The way they perceive, or fail to perceive, their world is not abnormal—something we try to impress on their parents—it's just that they have omitted learning some skills, gotten a shaky hold on others, and devoted their intelligence to learning compensations necessary to survive and appear reasonably normal in the world.

And since these kids often *are* bright, it is small wonder that they go undetected for so long—in the undemanding world of childhood, many of their compensations are not only workable but look clever and cute and are reinforced as such. One little girl, for instance, was discovered as barely a primer reader in the third grade. Her family, a highly bookish one, had thought it cute and funny that at age four she was "reading," out loud, close to the story line, but with the story-book upside down. (After all, from her vantage point, that's the way she saw the books her older sisters and parents were absorbing.) Using the pictures as an aid, along with her own good memory and listening powers when others read the stories aloud, she managed to complete almost three grades of school before someone discovered she had little or no idea what the printed word symbols on the page meant. And she also had no idea that this compensation for her lack of visual perceptual skills wasn't "reading."

It is hardly surprising that many of our kids behave like babies, in spite of their intelligence and chronological age. In almost every instance they *are* immature, at least as far as their physical, academic and even social perceptions are concerned. They don't "get" human relationships, leading to tremendous problems in the area of "social perception."

They overreact or underreact, screaming bloody murder at a small scrape or, just as likely, totally tuning out on a serious cut or burn. They will spend most of their time off by themselves, or play with younger children (who also tend to live in their own world) or reach toward older, less demanding adults, like grandma.

Too often our LD child ends up locked in his own world, perseverating away on the things he thinks he understands, unable to receive instruction from parents, teachers or peers, building his own distorted structure, imagining himself—as I did in college—as some sort of Superman. Even though he has all the wrong answers, the kid feels secure in his locked-in world. Believing he's Superman prevents him from facing the intolerable, miserable fact that he not only *can't* do most of what he is supposed to do, but he doesn't understand *why* he can't.

There is another way of dealing with his world of failure and frustration, and the LD kid usually discovers it quickly—often as early as six months. If he yells loud and long enough, if he makes enough trouble, other people will accomplish for him what he can't do for himself. They will pick up and hand over the rattle he can't crawl for, open the doorknob he can't turn, tie his shoelaces and button his shirt, even stay home every night so he doesn't embarrass them before the babysitter. He learns young to satisfy his needs by manipulating other people.

Lacking knowledge of any other kind of life, he can deceive himself that he's doing fine, that he's really great. And this is reinforced by parents who, out of secret shame, are spending a great deal of time deceiving themselves that nothing is wrong with their kid. Who wants to believe that their child is not up to par, particularly when that child started out

23

looking like the brightest and the best, with no obvious handicaps?

Therefore, it is little wonder that most parents wake up rather late in the day to the fact that something is wrong with *their* child. When they do, it is a painful, shocking and incredibly guilt-producing experience, made no easier by the fact that no one else seems to realize what is wrong, to say nothing of providing the right remedy. In the following chapters you'll meet Betty and Ed Wilson as they go through the experience common to hundreds of parents I've interviewed at our school. And instead of just reading a doctor's observations, you'll get a sense of how it feels to learn about LD as a family does—from the inside out.

3

Tim Wilson was eight and in his second month of third grade when the final blow fell. Mrs. Bell, the guidance counselor at Tim's school, phoned Betty and Ed Wilson, requesting they both appear at an emergency conference with the principal.

Ed's irritation grew to annoyance upon learning that his presence was required. As a rising young executive, he was under considerable pressure at work. He had also long since tired of the school's complaints about his son.

"They were all so nebulous and trivial," he recalls. "They would tell us that Tim was 'disturbing the class' or had a 'behavior problem.' They would say he wasn't paying attention or had badmouthed the teacher or left his seat. What kind of nonsense is that? But that didn't stop them from sending him to the school psychologist, who of course couldn't find anything really wrong. All I could think was, 'Christ, not only can't these people manage an active growing boy, they can't teach him. Tim was just moping along at the bottom of an average-pace class—even though everyone seemed

25

to agree he was quite bright—and all they could say was that he had 'to grow at his own speed' and 'mature.' And I had gone into a big financial hole a few years earlier just to move into the district because I'd heard schools here were so good.

"What a letdown!" he remembers thinking bitterly. *"I'd* been able to teach Tim to ride his two-wheeler the summer before, though most other kids his age could do it long before. He didn't ride it very well—he'd run into things and fall off—but he *could* ride it. And I could make him behave the same way I taught him to ride his bike—by really giving it to him. Tim *minded* when I was around. I didn't like the fact that he was afraid of me, but I figured he'd grow out of it when he appreciated what I was doing for him."

Most of Tim's discipline fell to Betty because, as Ed admits: "I guess I wasn't around as much as I should have been so I really didn't see how bad things were." That didn't stop him from being annoyed with her. "I remember when she called about the conference, I said, 'For Christ's sake, Betty, what is it this time? Can't you handle anything?' All I seemed to hear from her were complaints about Tim, either at home or at school; though, come to think of it, I hadn't heard too much in quite a while. I guess she stopped telling me about a lot of things when she saw it only made me mad. And I truly thought she let Tim get away with murder. She just couldn't seem to bring herself to give him a smack when he really needed it or to discipline him in any way."

"Well," asked Ed, when he and Betty reached Mrs. Bell's office, "what's the matter now?"

The guidance counselor had grown weary of these parents who parried every attempt to talk about Tim's behavior with an indictment of the school for failing to make a star pupil of their Einstein of a son.

According to Mrs. Bell, "Betty would say, 'Don't you think Tim's just bored?' And Ed was worse. At one conference last spring he told me that his taxes were paying my salary and we should just teach Tim and stop fussing with psychologists and the like." After nearly two years of teacher complaints about Tim's behavior, Mrs. Bell had begun to suspect the child might have emotional problems and had finally fitted him into the schedule of the school psychologist, who was responsible for over eight hundred kids in three different schools.

The psychologist's report was carefully phrased; to an untrained parent it seemed to give Tim a clean bill of health. Betty was relieved, Ed jubilant. They only half-listened when the psychologist told them Tim "seemed immature for his age," while listening fully to the rest of the sentence: "but otherwise he seems quite normal and very bright."

Mrs. Bell had sensed trouble in the report, but she had long ago learned that in dealing with parents—particularly parents so blind to their child's behavior—the less said the better. Then, in third grade, Tim had been assigned to Nancy Johnson's class. A newcomer to the faculty, fresh out of school with her master's degree, Nancy had all the makings of a great teacher, or so the principal thought. "He was almost as enthusiastic about Nancy as Nancy was about teaching," Mrs. Bell recalls. And when she was introduced to Tim's case and met his parents, she agreed with them on everything. She too was sure that Tim was just bored and she was certain she could bring him out. "Ed and Betty left looking smug as I've ever seen two parents," says Mrs. Bell.

"Even I was convinced things finally were going to work out for Tim."

But now a belligerent Ed Wilson was back in her office, and Mrs. Bell had to pick up where Nancy's enthusiasm left off and reality began. It wasn't going to be easy. She decided a little "show and tell" might be in order.

She took Betty and Ed into Tim's class and pointed out a boy with cracked glasses sitting at the desk next to Tim's empty one. Where was Tim? They looked and found him, face to the wall, exiled to a table in the back of the room with a kindergarten primer and some simple puzzles in front of him.

"What did he do?" Ed demanded as soon as they were outside again. "I was furious," Ed says. "How could they permit him to be treated this way, to be so humiliated? Also I felt—well, betrayed. This teacher, this Miss Johnson, had seemed so great. Sure, Betty had hinted that Tim still wasn't doing all that much better—at least, from what she could see of his homework—but that didn't justify sticking him in back of the room like some kind of dunce. I didn't know that was standard procedure with a behavior problem. I didn't even really believe he was a behavior problem."

"What did he do?" Ed repeated. "What made her do that to him?"

"He had a fight in class with the boy whose glasses are broken," Mrs. Bell replied. "When Miss Johnson tried to stop him, he started hitting and kicking her and screaming."

At that point, Betty's mind registered on a note of panic. "I had been through too many scenes like that with him myself," she explains. "Only about three weeks before, I'd caught him beating up another little boy on the street who was only three-quarters Tim's size and two years younger, and when I pulled him away he screamed and tried to kick me. Tim was angry because the other child wouldn't let him play with his ball. I understood why. The last time this child shared a toy with Tim, Tim refused to give it back. When I told Ed about it that night," Betty remembers, "he actually seemed pleased that Tim had done a man-type thing like get in a fight with another boy. All he asked was, 'Did Tim use his fists?'—Tim would use this sissy or baby-type slap and Ed hated it. And then Ed asked: 'Who won?' and seemed pleased until he heard how much younger the other child was."

Ed didn't like what he heard from Mrs. Bell about the kicking and the screaming. "It sounded too much like all those baby tantrums I thought I had knocked out of him," he says now. "He hadn't thrown one in front of me since he was five, and Betty *had* pretty much stopped mentioning that part to me. She'd stopped mentioning a lot of things," he continued, looking glum. "I guess I gave her a pretty hard time whenever I heard something I didn't like.

"Still, I wasn't convinced the guidance counselor wasn't exaggerating too, the same way I thought Betty was whenever she'd complain. Can't this damn school handle a little old-fashioned roughhouse without making a federal case of it? I thought, and asked Mrs. Bell who started the fight."

"Tim," the guidance counselor replied.

"But why?" Ed asked. "There must have been some reason."

"As far as I know, his teacher asked him to read."

"But that can't be all," Ed insisted. "Why would he get upset about that? He can read."

"We're not sure," said Mrs. Bell, pausing before the door to the principal's office. "We *do* know that he tests very poorly whenever we try to find out what he *can* do, and that now he refuses to read or do any work at all in school."

She opened the door. Nancy Johnson, Tim's teacher, and the principal were sitting there waiting.

"This cluck of a principal," Ed said, "started hemming and hawing. You could tell he hated any kind of scene—you know, a paper-pusher. Besides, this time he was going to have to admit that his great, almighty school system had failed."

Mr. Lieberman, the principal, reminded them how pleased the Wilsons had been with his choice of Miss Johnson as Tim's third-grade teacher. "So were we," he said, "but Tim has been causing a great many disturbances in the last month or so. He's been talking out of turn, leaving his seat, fighting, and using quite bad language . . ."

"Tim is a boy," Ed interrupted. "They all get in trouble. I remember . . ."

"Yes," said the principal, cutting Ed off, "but Tim has proved unusually unmanageable and immature. He also has problems with his schoolwork . . ."

"Did he ever!" was all Betty could think, remembering his sloppy homework. "The 'b's and 'd's were reversed; 'saw' came out 'was'; he never wrote anything on the line or spaced things out properly—all the words were scrunched together. And his drawings were stick figures with everything out of proportion—big heads on little bodies, if you could tell they were bodies. And he erased so much and crumpled and even tore the paper. Usually he wouldn't sit still long enough to finish. I'd come up to his room and find that he was daydreaming with his rock collection or that he had gone out, leaving this half-finished, messy stuff lying around."

At first, Betty had pushed Tim to do his homework neatly and correctly. But she had no more success here than in getting him to tuck in his shirt when it came out or tie his laces when they came undone or making him go to bed on time. "He just yelled bloody murder," Betty said. "Finally, just to keep the peace, I stopped making him do his homework and started doing it for him. I was ashamed of that mess, how it would make Ed and me look."

But as she listened to Lieberman recount Tim's school failings—his inability to read, write or do any of his work at his grade level—Betty not only began to feel more and more confused and frustrated, she began to share some of Ed's anger. "It was the school's responsibility to teach these things, I thought," she said, "so why were they bitching? Even they had said that Tim's IQ was high and, Good Lord, we'd given the kid every kind of educational toy, he'd been to one of the best private kindergartens, he'd supposedly had all the pre-school readiness anybody could want. With all that, why couldn't they just *teach* him what he was expected to know?"

"Ideally," the principal was saying, "we would like to place Tim in a special class for slow learners—at least try him in that kind of program for a while—it's possible he might respond. But unfortunately we have no openings at the moment and the waiting list is a long one—a year or more. Also, most of those children we do accept show some slight retardation and Tim, as you know, is not retarded. But because of his difficulties in school, I'm afraid we can't keep him here any more. So we're placing him on a home study program." He explained how a special teacher would visit them twice a week.

It took Ed a moment to absorb the meaning. "Are you saying," he asked, incredulous, "that you're kicking Tim out of school?"

"Well, no, not exactly," temporized Mr. Lieberman. "In a few months, we should have a placement for him where we think he'll do very nicely. Of course, he'll have to have an evaluation first, but our psychologist has checked him out again [this was the first Betty and Ed had heard of this] and feels now that Tim's problems are definitely emotionally based. He's recommended that Tim go to one of the special classes for the emotionally disturbed at the Collins school."

"But Tim isn't crazy!" Betty almost shouted. "That's a school for crazy children!" ("Ed and I already knew about the Collins school," Betty explained. "Sure, some kids there weren't so bad. But they also took kids who thought they were King Kong or Mother Goose—real psychotics. And a lot of them were known to be violent—one had stabbed his sister and set fire to the house. Mainly, neither Ed nor I could accept the idea that Tim, whatever else he might be, was *crazy*.")

"You can't be serious!" Ed said.

"I'm afraid we are," said Lieberman, looking more uncomfortable than ever.

"Are there any other alternatives?" Ed asked, slumping down in his seat. "I mean I just can't believe . . ."

"None that we can help you with now," Lieberman replied. "The psychologist . . ."

"Where is this psychologist?" Ed demanded.

Lieberman explained that it was the school psychologist's day at another school in the district. "The psychologist," Lieberman went on, "thought that Tim should go into therapy, that that might help. Mrs. Bell has a list of therapists in the area. But unless Tim shows really marked improvement, we won't be able to take him back here.''

Nancy Johnson mumbled something about being late for class and bolted out of the room. Mrs. Bell produced the list. Betty and Ed took it in silence. ''We were both too dumb-founded at that point,'' said Ed, ''to say anything.''

Lieberman ushered Betty and Ed out of his office where a teacher's aide was waiting with Tim, his left shoelace untied and his shirt hanging out, staring at his toes as if they might run away.

''Mr. Lieberman would never say anything, but I knew him too well,'' says Mrs. Bell. ''He never expected to see Tim again. He was just glad that he'd rid his school of his biggest headache—not a child with problems but a delin-quent, spoiled brat. I really felt sorry for Betty and Ed. But I really didn't know at the time what else we could do. There was no way we could handle Tim here any more and maybe the school for the emotionally disturbed *would* help. And I was convinced that he had emotional problems—it turned out he did—though I didn't know why. Looking back on that day I really feel miserable.''

But Mrs. Bell's misery was nothing compared to Betty's and Ed's. They had just entered a snakepit, with no exit except the totally unacceptable one of a school for ''crazies.'' And it didn't help that nobody, particularly Betty and Ed, had any clue that the reason they and Tim had landed in that pit was that their son was an LD child whose handicaps had led to emotional disturbances. ''How could this happen?'' asked Ed.

4

The clues were all there—and from the beginning—though Betty and Ed couldn't have been expected to pick them out. Their ignorance and gradual adjustment to Tim over the years were more than matched by the ignorance and evasiveness of many of the professionals who had dealt with them and their son. "We really couldn't see Tim as anything but a normal child," says Betty. "A handful, a problem—a child we often wished would be different—but still a basically normal child. I think, too, we secretly both blamed ourselves for the way he was and didn't want to talk about it. We avoided the whole subject, particularly in the last few years. Even the decision not to have any more children just happened."

One of the first signposts that went almost unnoticed by Betty and Ed occurred at the very beginning. Tim had not colored up fast and well at birth. He was gray, not really pink. Since this is one symptom of a possible heart murmur, a pediatric cardiologist was called immediately to check out the new baby. Later, when Betty's obstetrician told them about the emergency check-up—and forwarded the cardiologist's bill—he said that it was a routine procedure and Tim's heart was fine. "What he didn't tell us," says Ed, "was that this might have been caused by some slight neurological dysfunction in Tim's brain. Or that those seconds and minutes without adequate oxygen might have caused some slight insult to the brain."

Soon after this, Tim developed a strong allergy to milk and several other common baby foods. But the gruff, old-fashioned pediatrician said this was fairly common and that he'd grow out of it, which he eventually did. The pediatrician didn't say or didn't know that allergic reactions are common with LD children.

Tim had never been an easy child. As an infant he had developed a terrifying scream—one that seemed to erupt without reason and that cut off the moment he was touched, instead of trailing off, as is normal in babies who absorb the information that a comforting presence is near. He had been and still was a poor eater and worse sleeper, driving both his new parents nearly mad. "But, of course, we adjusted," says Betty, morosely. "We made Tim's hours our hours even though it meant only a few hours' sleep for us. But we couldn't help wonder, with the little he ate and the little he slept, where he got the fuel for all that activity—first screaming and then, later, running around all the time like a chicken with his head cut off. He used to go from toy to toy to toy with the speed of light and finish with them and be ready for something else in a matter of minutes. That was a headache, but we thought that it showed how bright he was."

Incessant activity, without any capacity for study or concentration on the matter at hand, can be one indication of an LD child. But another was to appear.

Tim's early physical development also had been erratic. His movements lacked control and coordination; to everyone else's laughter, Tim's howls and Betty's embarrassment, he had risen to the occasion of his first birthday party by jack-knifing into his cake. He never crawled; but just as Betty and Ed were beginning to worry, he pulled himself up by the side of his playpen, stood and walked. "Just like that!" says Betty. "We thought we had a real comer on our hands."

Almost immediately, Tim climbed, but fell off everything he climbed on—the piano, the table, the stairs. He ran—into everything. By the time Tim was two and a half, he had sent their best lamp crashing to the floor, burned the palm of his hand on the stove, turned over the coffee table, fallen out of his crib numerous times and given himself an inch-long lump on his head pitching over the back of his father's chair. Each incident brought on the old bloodcurdling scream, often out of all proportion to the cause. Once, a child his age gave him a tiny baby slap and Tim erupted as though he'd been kicked.

"The pediatrician saw nothing unusual in Tim's activity level," says Betty. "He said Tim would 'grow out of it'—how often I've heard *that* phrase!—though he made it pretty clear, particularly after a couple of fusses in his office, that he thought I should use more discipline. I tried, but I just couldn't seem to keep up with Tim."

At three, Tim was still a screamer and an occasional head-banger. He became sullen and elated by turns, shifting from one extreme to the other for no apparent reason. Betty gradually realized that Tim was still not consistently right- or left-handed, something that, she had learned from her reading, wasn't normal. The nursery school in which he was enrolled required he be toilet-trained, but she was finding that nearly impossible, so they had lied about it on their first application.

"I decided that maybe boys were more difficult," Betty says. "Luckily, a week before school opened, he managed to find his way to the bathroom and put his doings into the john. I guess I was so relieved I forgot how much trouble the whole thing had been."

On opening day at nursery school, Betty put Tim, howling at the top of his lungs, on the school bus. "The driver told me point-blank he knew how to handle this." But she decided to trail him to school in her car and arrived at the same time as the bus. To her amazement she saw Tim get off and run into the building, as if he couldn't wait to get there. "He seemed to have completely forgotten how unhappy he was," she says. The entire performance was repeated for the next two weeks. The bus driver told Betty that Tim would cry all the way to school only to emerge seemingly blissfully happy at being there. Then, a month later, Tim was kicked out of school for running around, snatching other kids' toys, ripping his paper, spilling his milk and behaving like a squalling tiger whenever restrained. For the rest of his third year, and in spite of all Betty's scolding, Tim repeated the same behavior at home. "I simply ran out of other children for him to play with," recalls Betty. "Even my own relatives stopped bringing their children when they came to call, which was less and less frequent."

Tim also added an almost incessant chatter to his repertoire, going over and over the same subjects, never seeming to stop. This was strange even to Betty because he had been slow to talk. "And his activity level," she says, "became incredible. He seemed to need to touch everything and was always dropping and breaking things as he went. I finally put most of the fragile things we had left into the cupboard."

"The pediatrician thought that all this was fine," Ed says.

"It showed Tim had an inquisitive mind. And as for the way Tim hustled around, frankly I thought that was great. I'd collected a couple of varsity letters myself and to me this indicated he was going to be a good athlete."

Betty put all this in the best possible light, and in lieu of nursery school she went out and bought Tim loads of educational toys. "We had mountains of them," she remembers ruefully. "He never spent any time with any of them but I thought he was learning from them. I also thought he was learning from television. He would sit and look at it for hours. That showed great powers of concentration, or so it seemed to me." Betty failed to realize that this was a sign of perseveration as identifiable as his constant chatter, perhaps because the TV watching was much less annoying.

Moreover, despite Tim's bratty ways with other kids—"which Ed concluded, along with our pediatrician, could be ironed out with a little more motherly discipline"—Tim had great charm with adults. "I *did* manage to teach him manners," she says, proudly. "And he always had this quick smile and hug for his grandparents and others when they visited, even though the next minute he seemed to have no idea they were there."

At four Tim was entered in an expensive private nursery school and, to Betty's relief, this time he stayed in. Betty needed some time to relax. Tim was still only sleeping a total of six hours a night, during which he had her up at least three times to get him a drink or put him back to bed. And during the day, there were always several crises—throwing tantrums when she tried to get him to dress himself, which he did poorly, or keeping him from pulling all his toys out of the closet and destroying them one by one. "I was worried about Tim's almost inane destructiveness, and the way he wouldn't mind," Betty says, "but I was more concerned about myself and what Ed thought. I got so tired I'd just let him do what he wanted. Lots of times I could get him off on the TV. He just loved it. All I could think was, Thank God for television! But Ed was really beginning to come down on me for being a 'softy.' 'Look,' he'd say, 'the kid needs discipline, that's all.' He thought I should really smack Tim around. But I couldn't bring myself to do it."

Both Betty and Ed were worried that Tim was such a lonely child. "When he was three he used to run up to other kids and beat their brains out or hug them to death before they knew what had happened," Betty says. "Now at four he'd just hang on my arm when they were around or hide behind me." Ed was particularly annoyed by the babyishness he saw in this, as well as Tim's continued tantrums. But Betty and Ed both decided that this was a phase like everything else. Tim would grow out of it.

"Of course," says Betty, "there were fewer problems with Tim because now we were accommodating our lives to him." Betty had begun giving Tim his meals whenever he demanded, allowing the TV to run through the supper she served Ed and herself, and they privately agreed not to leave the house after dinner because they didn't know what might happen with a babysitter. The one time they took Tim to a restaurant, he had refused to sit still and yelled when Betty and Ed tried to quiet him. Their meal uneaten, they left before they were asked to leave.

The only really uneasy note that year was when Mrs. Wheldon, the middle-aged head of Tim's nursery school, called Betty and Ed for a special conference. Betty went.

"Timothy," said Mrs. Wheldon, "seems to be having a grand time in school. He does not particularly enjoy playing with the other children, but he does enjoy building blocks and takes great pleasure in painting.''

"I wanted to ask her about Tim's painting," Betty says. "The only things I'd seen him do at home were kind of skewed and concentrated in the upper lefthand corner of the paper. But I let it pass. I guess I didn't really want to know."

"I would like to see him play with puzzles more," Mrs. Wheldon said, "and take more interest in reading readiness tasks." She paused and looked at Betty. "However, it is our policy to let our children advance at their own speed."

"I wanted to ask what she meant by 'their own speed.' Did that mean Tim was a slow developer or that he'd just grow out of it? But I was afraid to. I just didn't want to know."

Apparently Mrs. Wheldon sensed as much, because she brightened and went on. "We find Tim to be full of pep and energy, and all of us marvel at his wardrobe. You certainly dress him beautifully."

"I had a real twinge of conscience on that one," Betty recalls. "I couldn't understand how Tim could come home looking just as I left him when *I* couldn't get him to stay tidy more than half an hour. I didn't know until later—a lot later—that Tim's teacher put him back together a couple of times each day and always, right before he came home."

"We have spent a great deal of time this year," Mrs. Wheldon said, "teaching our three-year-olds and four-year-olds to button, tie and lace, and Tim does seem to have some difficulty in these tasks. But it's really nothing to be concerned about. We always have some children who don't acquire these skills right away and they often turn out to be our best ones by the end of the year. Timothy is such a darling boy and very apt."

"She seemed to stress all the positive, rewarding things about Tim," says Betty. She tried to dismiss her fears—not the least of which concerned the unusual occurrence of the interview itself and its bland results. "I guess she called the interview to bite the bullet and try to tell me her worries about Tim, but when she saw how defensive I looked, she must have changed her mind. And all the talks I had with her after that were just to tell me that Tim was doing just 'beautifully' or that he would certainly catch up. I guess she wanted to keep our business."

As the year progressed, Ed began to wonder why Tim never seemed to display at home all the new skills Mrs. Wheldon kept telling Betty he was learning at school. He had a hard time suppressing his irritation at Betty's constant talk about Tim "growing at his own speed." "What is he?" he only half joked as he noted Tim's continued inability to dress himself, "some kind of beanstalk?"

The next year produced even less progress for Tim. Mrs. Wheldon had at least tried to impart some skills to the boy. Tim learned to build a simple but shaky house of blocks, he could sing the alphabet song and usually recite the numbers from one to ten, that is, if anyone could keep his attention long enough. The early problems with social behavior had been solved by setting him to a task he liked—painting and building blocks—apart from the other children and letting him continue at it forever, it seemed.

But in the public kindergarten where Tim was entered at five—Betty and Ed had decided he was now ready and they could ill-afford to continue him at Mrs. Wheldon's expensive school—Tim was placed in a class run by a Miss Leary who believed in her own concept of an "open classroom." "This

41

meant," says Ed, "that her kids were allowed to do anything they wanted, when they wanted and how they wanted. I went once and it was unbelievable, sheer chaos."

That year, Tim did very little in school except to run around, and almost nothing at home except to watch television. He continued to throw tantrums when asked to do something—he would throw his silverware on the floor in a rage, for instance, when Betty complained about the way he shoveled his food—and he was still untidy. No one, including Ed, could get him to pick up a toy and put it away or keep his shorts buttoned, although Betty did manage to refine his manners, and his "yes, ma'ams" and "no, sirs" were quickly produced for most occasions.

Miss Leary expressed only slight concern with Tim. "It would be nice," she said, in one of her hasty five-minute conferences with Betty late in the spring, "if Tim would do a little better in writing and forming his letters. He also is having a difficult time with his alphabet—in recognizing the letters and in keeping them in the right order in the words he's learning. But I'm sure his work will improve in the next grade where everything will be more challenging." Miss Leary did not think that Tim's high activity level, his tendency to daydream or his inability to pay attention and remember instructions—all factors Betty had to deal with more than ever at home—were worth mentioning. Given her concept of a kindergarten class, Tim's behavior was not much worse than that displayed by most of the other kids. Mrs. Bell, the guidance counselor, agreed with her. She also told Betty that Tim might do better next year in a structured class—one where he would be sitting at a desk regularly and following a schedule. "I had my doubts," said Mrs. Bell, "about the good of all this romping around. The 'open classroom' idea was never meant to encourage kids to do just anything they pleased, with little or no supervision. It's actually a very sophisticated system which demands a lot of controls and consistency and effort from the teachers. But I only work here.''

Betty was mollified by what she heard. ''I'd completely bought the 'grow at your own speed' motto,'' she explains. ''And all I wanted to hear was that there was nothing wrong with Tim, particularly anything that would reflect on me.''

Ed, however, began to be truly concerned. He wasn't bothered that the work Tim was bringing home from school needed an expert to decipher. ''I'd decided that was Betty's department,'' he says. But he was annoyed that his son who had started out to be such a winner had, instead, turned into a whiner. And with all his early athletic promise—which Ed had deduced from his high degree of activity—Tim still couldn't seem to navigate around a playground or handle a simple game of catch. ''He'd even fall off the lower rungs of the jungle gym,'' Ed remembers. ''And then he'd cry like any baby.''

Ed decided to take Tim in hand the summer before he entered first grade. He took him to the playground and tried to teach him to play ball. ''It was no dice,'' Ed says. ''He was either looking the other way when I threw the ball or reaching for it long after it had passed by. I once got so angry that I threw it—it was a soft, big rubber ball—right at his head. I thought that might make him react. It didn't. And when it hit him, he started bawling and the next thing I knew I was yelling—the same way we had ended up so many times before.''

Taking his cue from Tim's joy in building blocks, Ed introduced Tim to the shop he had lovingly constructed for himself in the basement. There nothing worked either. "Tim would either decide to throw my tools around the room—he almost killed himself once when he threw a wrench into the power saw—or step into a bucket of paint or pick up the oil gun and start squirting it all over. One time I remember he dropped a hammer on his foot—just a small hammer that wouldn't hurt a flea. He really exploded and started pounding the hammer on the floor. And each time something happened, or when I punished him, he'd fly to Betty. Then I'd start on her and really let her know what I thought of the way she was babying him every time I spanked him or he got some little hurt."

Betty started producing a growing list of excuses for Tim. Either he was tired, or he hadn't eaten his breakfast, or this was too much for a five-year-old to handle ("which in some cases it was," Ed admits) or he needed more encouragement, even that Tim was a "sensitive" boy. "I never could stand the idea of anyone laying a hand on a child," Betty remarks. "I still have trouble with it. But I think I interpreted that into a policy of no discipline at all."

Ed too feels guilty in retrospect. "When I think of how I punished the kid—whacking him and sitting all over him with no understanding at all, just out of my anger with him—I feel like a real child-abuser. But some of it, I guess, did some good." Tim's tantrums stopped, at least when Ed was home, as well as some of his most annoying habits—throwing his silverware on the floor. All the punishment in the world, however, couldn't make him stop spilling his milk or obey when Ed wasn't around or when he was too tired or disinterested to make Tim toe the line.

By the end of a summer's fighting over Tim, the parents reached a truce. Betty would try to be a bit more forceful and

Ed was allowed to smack Tim if his behavior became too outrageous. This agreement lasted for two weeks until the morning of Tim's first day in first grade, when Ed woke up to find his son had just scribbled his new crayons all over the report he was to present to his company's president.

As Ed began to spank Tim—hard—Betty actually leaped on both of them. Ed left for work redfaced from shouting at her; and Betty, still shaking, put Tim on the school bus. The boy got on without a tear, as if nothing at all had happened.

At that point, Ed gave up. He began coming home long after Tim, and even Betty, were in bed, staying out working late or drinking later. He joined a poker club that met two nights each week and took up golf and tennis over the weekends.

"I wouldn't admit it to myself then," says Ed, "but I really was through with this screaming, whining, clumsy kid who didn't do anything right and whom nobody liked, including me. I hated him and I hated Betty. They were a real pair. They deserved each other."

Betty accepted this arrangement in silence. "It was like a vow, when I think of it now," Betty remarks. "If I really thought about what was happening, then I would have to admit the problem was Tim. So I just said to myself this kind of thing happened in all marriages and tried to forget the real issue, the same way I had managed to forget why Ed and I never went out any more."

It was at this point too that Betty and Ed took an even more complicated self-deception. Whatever they might feel privately about Tim—now buried under excuse after unconscious excuse—they both maintained a facade that their son was completely normal and even exceptional when he was on public view. They defended him against every complaint

45

from the outside. The more the complaints mounted, the tighter the defenses grew. "If we had only known what we were doing to ourselves, what we were doing to Tim!" Ed says. "Christ! Here we were at every turn saying the kid's fine, he's OK, why don't you just push him forward, when he couldn't even handle what he was doing, let alone face more. And we weren't helping him at all. I was never there and wouldn't listen when I was, and Betty wasn't doing anything either because she was all alone and didn't know what to do anyway."

To add to Betty and Ed's capacity for self-deception, Tim's behavior during his year in first grade *did* improve, though his skills were few and slow in coming and his attention span was short as ever. He couldn't get the hang of the two-wheeler they had bought him, even with training wheels, although most of the rest of the neighborhood six-year-olds were soon wobbling around without aids. Shoe-tying was a major effort, and getting him to keep his room neat was as impossible as ever. But he now followed some instructions, if only partially. "Put your toys away and get ready for bed" usually resulted in tucking away one or two toys—if not a move for bed. Tantrums were few and occurred only on those rare occasions when Betty mustered enough energy to try to make Tim do something he was dead set against. His activity level inside the house was reduced to distracted fiddling with toys or watching TV. Outside, he seemed to take out his energy in disappearing aimlessly, wandering farther and farther from home—something that frightened Betty but, since he invariably found his way back, could be interpreted as a sign of admirable independence.

"We didn't know," says Betty, "that this behavior was

also characteristic of an LD child—a child who doesn't know any better because he hasn't learned to be afraid." One day one of Ed's friends called to praise Tim's "guts"; he had been playing in a spooky wrecked car that "would have scared the wits out of most kids, but Timmy was cool as a cucumber when I found him."

Betty was uneasy about her increasing inability to reach Tim. "He started to be a real 'Where did you go?' 'Out.' 'What did you do?' 'Nothing.' child," she says. "Most of the time he just didn't answer at all. It was a little unnerving." But Ed, who had almost ceased to care, dismissed this as a healthy need for privacy, not realizing that such an incommunicado attitude was another tipoff to an LD child. Finally, for once Betty and Ed were getting no reports of bad behavior in school. Everything there, in fact, seemed to be going beautifully.

At her mid-term conference in the spring with Mrs. Wollman, Tim's formidable-looking but somehow kindly first-grade teacher, Betty listened intently as usual for any sign the teacher was disturbed by Tim.

"Yes, Tim," said Mrs. Wollman, with a far-off look, suggesting to Betty that she was trying to recall just which of her twenty-eight children he was. "Tim is a little slow in catching on to some of the skills we're trying to teach the children, but in others he's doing well. He's having difficulty learning left and right. He also seems to have difficulty with his writing and the alphabet, but he's shown progress there and perhaps you could help him by working on some of his letters at home. ("I remember wondering how I was going to do that," Betty says, "when I couldn't even get through to him, but I agreed.") In math," said the teacher, with enthusiasm, "Tim is doing quite well. He still tends to reverse his numbers the way he does his letters, but that's not uncommon with children at his age and his grasp of the numbers is more than satisfactory.

"I *do* wish he'd pay a little better attention and volunteer more," she continued. "And we'd like to see him be a little neater. All these things would help him do better in class. But I'm sure, with his mind, that all those things will work themselves out as Tim gets a little older."

Betty left, reassured but not much more enlightened. It was not an oversight; Mrs. Wollman had recalled Tim only too well, and as she watched Betty go she wished she had leveled with this quiet, nervous and probably overpermissive mother and told her her suspicions.

They had started with Tim's first day in her class, when he'd started howling at the top of his lungs after tripping on the stairs on his way to recess. "I always have a few cryers and snifflers the first day," Mrs. Wollman says now, two years later. "Everything is so strange and new. I just refuse to make any great fuss and put them right to work and that usually quiets them down. But Tim's was a full-fledged yell over a very small hurt. And when I went to help him up, he stopped immediately and then ran out to the playground without saying another word. That kind of instant recovery is very peculiar, particularly in a child his age. It was as if he was in another world."

Later Tim had thrown two tantrums in class. In both cases he was clearly frustrated with the task in front of him—one of them retying his shoes. Then he started asking to go to the bathroom every ten minutes. He constantly fidgeted at his desk and kept getting out of his seat. He would cry easily, particularly when the work made extra demands, such as copying from the chalkboard. "None of this," says Mrs.

Wollman, "was the behavior of an average first-grader, at least to this degree."

Mrs. Wollman quelled both of Tim's tantrums and prevented others by the tried-and-true method of making the punishment swift and telling. Without saying a word, she grabbed Tim by his ankles and upended him. His screams stopped in his throat. She handled everything else in the same quiet, forceful and consistent manner. When Tim asked to go to the bathroom, she asked an aide to accompany him the first time and then made him go on schedule with the other children. She patiently insisted he tie his shoes each time they came undone, even if it meant he missed out on something he wanted to do and brought on a scene. The same went for washing his hands. She seated him in the desk in front of hers, and whenever he started fidgeting or tried to get out, she'd command him to stop and get on with his work. When he cried, she pointed out that Judy or Johnny who had cried before had learned to stop and so could he. If he was honestly buffaloed by the assignment, she would prevent a scene by setting him to a simpler task that he knew and then later make another try at the first one.

Mrs. Wollman's rewards were equally consistent and geared to the needs of her children. Each child was allowed to paste a large red star under his name on a wall chart whenever he completed an exercise, and a gold one if he'd done it well. By the end of his first month Tim had acquired quite a number of stars, though mostly red ones and not nearly as many as the other children. He also had ceased being a major troublemaker and quite obviously loved his teacher. She, in turn, had found Tim's good qualities.

"Tim's manners were excellent," Mrs. Wollman notes, "and he was really charming. He wanted to please. The second week of school I asked him if he wanted to clean the board, he jumped up and thanked me, pleased as punch that he had been called on. The first few times, he kept dropping the eraser and left most of the dirt on the board, but gradually he got better and did it happily all year. Almost every day he would ask if he could help me. I was really put to it to think of things for him to do." Finally, Mrs. Wollman could find nothing wrong with Tim in the intellectual department. "His grasp of a problem, particularly one that could be done quickly and without too many ramifications, was better than most of the children in my class at the time."

Mrs. Wollman was less concerned that she couldn't control his many forms of immature behavior than that so many forms still existed in a child of six. Even more important was the realization that Tim, in spite of all her efforts, was learning little and retaining less. She had even gone so far as to discuss holding Tim back with Mrs. Bell and finally went to Mr. Lieberman. "I rarely take my problems outside my class," she says with some pride. "Normally I don't feel I have to." In this case, she could have saved her breath. Mrs. Bell commiserated but said there were too few specifics to go on; besides, she was too busy worrying about the many other kids under her care—some of whom were real behavior problems. The principal thought it ridiculous even to suggest retaining a child with Tim's background and mental abilities.

"What I wanted to tell Tim's mother, what I probably should have told them," says Mrs. Wollman, whose twenty-two years as an outstanding teacher certainly qualified her to give advice, "was not that she had an emotionally disturbed, hyperactive, brain-dysfunctioning child. I'm not sure I believe in all those modern labels even now and I certainly didn't then. As far as I'm concerned, the causes are immaterial. What I saw in Tim was an old-fashioned 'problem child.' He needed extra help. And he needed a lot of attentive, firm, consistent management if he was going to make any progress at all. There was no way he was going to get either in this school if he continued on. The classes were too large, and most of the teachers were so into progressive, liberal, unstructured education that they couldn't manage a child. Besides, they weren't allowed to—my little tantrum trick is something the PTA would frown on, I'm sure. And I didn't see where Tim was getting this kind of thing at home.''

What prevented Mrs. Wollman from telling Betty her thoughts? First: ''Probably they never would have believed me.'' But, second: her same twenty-two years of experience had given her ample time to learn the code of silence that exists in almost every public school system—a code designed to protect the system from parental, and taxpayer, wrath at the suggestion that something is wrong with their child. Better have proof positive, it says, better show a real, specific problem or hold your tongue. And so, on schedule, the next fall Tim entered second grade.

Not, however, before the school allowed the first shoe to drop, though Betty and Ed hardly recognized it as such. After standard tests of reading and reading readiness, Tim was placed in a slow-average class, the third rated in four levels of ability.

''I was furious,'' says Ed, ''but we got nowhere.'' A consultation with Mrs. Wollman only reinforced the opinion that Tim, as shown by his tests, was not working up to his potential. Mrs. Bell agreed that Tim would do better and have more satisfying experiences at the top of a slower class than in the middle of a faster one. "I was disgusted with the school," Ed says. "First, the mess in Leary's class and now this. I was convinced that Mrs. Wollman was one of these old biddies who couldn't appreciate Tim's abilities. If only I had known, I would have gotten down on my knees to her."

Because Miss Peabody, Tim's second-grade teacher, *was* an old biddy, and her choice as Tim's teacher privately dismayed Mrs. Wollman. "I guess all they heard up there in the office was that Tim was a behavior problem. Peabody usually ended up with those because no one else wanted them; and when she was done they were usually worse than ever. She was only a couple of years from retirement and, with tenure, they couldn't fire her. But she was known throughout the school as a real tyrant who couldn't take the least disturbance."

As Peabody's aide related it, within a week of the start of school Tim was dragged screaming to the back of the classroom and planted at the "cooling off" table for squirming in his seat five minutes after Peabody had barked at him to sit still. On numerous other occasions he landed there for toying with a wire coil he'd found on the playground, daydreaming, answering out of turn, getting out of his seat without permission, fooling with pencils, taking someone else's pencil and then denying he stole it, humming to himself and bothering the child sitting next to him.

No one can say for sure, but considering Tim's condition, none of these actions, initially, was probably intended or aimed at Peabody. She, however, interpreted them as a scheme to derail her class. Scene followed scene, to the accompaniment of approving titters from his classmates. Miss Peabody wasn't allowed to hit Tim the way his father could, but she could send him to the back of the room. Tim wasn't alone in his trips that year—at one point or another most of Miss Peabody's class made the journey—he just proudly became the most frequent visitor. But not until he learned the futility of any more constructive method of winning Miss Peabody's attention and approval; Tim learned early that that was impossible. His offer to provide his talents as a chalkboard cleaner brought a rebuke for speaking out without first raising his hand.

Eavesdropping on the playground added another skill to his repertoire. It was here that Tim began to add "fuck you" and "shit" and "up yours" to his dancing-eyed "no, ma'am's" and "thank you, ma'am's," eliciting even more amused support from the class. When they started easy second-grade reading, Tim got another booster shot of giggles from his cohorts as he took his turn and read out loud. The words either weren't on that page, were the wrong words, or they were jumbled in order. After a few sharp hassles, Miss Peabody stopped calling on Tim to read. She also quickly gave up getting him to correct his sloppy writing—with its persistent reversals in "b"s and "d"s, numbers and words—while it rollercoastered all over the lines on the paper. Finally she stopped calling on him at all, even in math where he showed promise, and told him to keep quiet when he persistently raised his hand. Needless to say, Tim's academic progress that year was zero.

His progress in the complaint department, however, was astounding. Miss Peabody and Mrs. Bell, now alert to Tim, took turns dishing them out to his defensive parents. "It seemed as if we were getting another complaint every day," Betty said. "They made Ed so angry that I stopped telling him about the problems Tim was having with his teacher, just as I had shut up about most of mine. And it seemed to me that Tim *was* bored. Why shouldn't he be? With that hag of a teacher, no child could do anything right.''

Betty *did* think it strange that Tim still had made no friends in school, none that he brought home to play. ''What I didn't know was that he'd turned into the class bully,'' she says, ''starting fights with other boys—usually younger ones—and even beating on the girls—all for no apparent reason. I guess this was the only way he could get close to any of them or back at them. He couldn't play the games they played so they kept him out.''

At home that year, Tim reverted to his old ways and then some. Screams were accompanied by a stream of abuse at any setback or change in routine or attempt to get him to do the chores he'd finally learned, such as straightening his room. Betty was shocked at the foul language and punished him, severely, hoping to stop it at home. ''But I certainly didn't think that was any sign of an emotional or learning problem. It was just boys will be boys.'' And when the school psychologist gave Tim what Ed interpreted as a good report, Ed was convinced Bell was one of these new fogies who didn't know what she was talking about.

Nancy Johnson had seemed like the answer to all Betty's and Ed's school problems. ''She was so young and fresh and energetic, so full of ideas,'' Betty says. ''I guess we were grasping at straws, even then.'' But to her credit, Tim's third-grade teacher *had* tried to make good on the promise she saw in him.

''I really thought that I could change him,'' Nancy Johnson says. ''I'd heard all about Peabody, and Mrs. Bell didn't seem very convinced that there was anything basically wrong with Tim that couldn't be handled with a little effort. It seemed like it would be easy to get Tim to come around. What a dope I was!''

Nancy had started Tim the first day of school with the most stimulating materials she could find for his grade level. When none of them seemed to hold his attention, she spent extra time trying to help him. But she couldn't seem to reach beyond his squirming, monosyllabic evasion of her questions or a set stock of equally evasive and flippant remarks, along with a charming smile she'd come to hate. She even permitted him to wander around the room, hoping he was absorbing some of what she was teaching—a privilege that ended abruptly one morning with a surprise visit from the principal and a reprimand to keep her class in order.

Nancy then put Tim in the last seat on the outside aisle near the window. There he would be least likely to distract the other children. She kept him there by alternating threats to tell the principal if he got up or bribes not to report him if he kept reasonably quiet. This worked, for about a week. Then he started using Joe beside him and Tommy in front of him as punching bags. When Nancy scolded him, he answered her in the worst language she had ever heard. Finally she reported his behavior to the principal and to Mrs. Bell, who filtered it back to Betty. It was then that Bell and Lieberman decided to send Tim back to the school psychologist.

This time, the psychologist, taking his cue from Lieberman's obvious desire to get rid of Tim, came back with a definitive report. "Tim has serious emotional problems," he wrote, "as shown in my analysis and by his past school record, and they have developed to the point where he no longer can be handled in school." The jig was almost up, but Nancy asked for one more try.

A week later, however, and the day Tim was finally sent home, Nancy finally had to admit she had failed. The scene that precipitated it had begun quietly enough—during an ordinary reading lesson.

John, one of the slow readers in Tim's group, was reading haltingly, "The . . . big dog ran . . . after . . . the . . . cat," when Nancy noticed that Tim had wandered over to the fish tank and was swirling his hand around inside.

"Tim," she had cut in on the sentence, "please come away from the window and get back in your seat." Acting as if he'd never heard, Tim moved to the washbasin and turned on the water.

"I said, get back in your seat," Nancy said firmly, hoping her nervousness didn't show. Tim had thrown her an impish grin and scrambled back to his seat.

Nancy turned to John, and as he read the sentence, Tim squirmed in his chair and began fiddling with his pencils. Nancy then called on Henry, a small black child who was making good progress in her class and who gave a quick rendition of the next sentence: "Jane saw the big dog run after the cat." Tim started tapping a pencil louder on his desk. Nancy ignored him. Tim poked Joe in front of him who scowled back.

"Tim," said Nancy sharply, "stop bothering Joe. I'm telling you this for the last time."

"Yes, ma'am," said Tim, angelic and the perfect gentleman, giving Nancy that manufactured smile. The class started to giggle. Nancy went on, calling on Janet, a tiny freckled-faced, blue-eyed child, who negotiated "Jane called the dog" with some difficulty. Nancy made a mental note to talk to Janet's parents about her health. She always seemed to have some kind of sniffle—perhaps an allergy—and Nancy thought this might be holding up her progress in school. Again Tim poked Joe, a fairly phlegmatic, obese boy with glasses. Joe edged away.

Nancy was about to call on Carol for the next sentence, but something inside her had boiled up and instead she turned to Tim. She was sure he himself hadn't done that lesson—the class homework—because his paper was too neat. Maybe this would teach him once and for all.

"OK, Tim," she said, "read the fourth sentence."

Tim went back to tapping pencils.

"Look at me and pay attention," Nancy snapped. "Now read the fourth sentence."

"What sentence, teach?" Tim answered back, grinning and nudging Joe again. Giggles rose from the class.

"The fourth one," said Nancy. "Number four. Look in your book and read it. And my name is Miss Johnson, not teach."

Tim glanced down at his book for the first time and then looked around grinning. This time no one responded. His grin faded and he looked back at the book. Good, Nancy thought, now I've got him. Maybe I can make him work. She bore down.

"Read it, Tim," she ordered.

Silence from Tim. The class started to laugh again softly.

"I'm waiting," Nancy said balefully.

The giggles started rising, but now they were directed at Tim. There were few kids who hadn't suffered from Tim's bullying or who didn't resent the special treatment he'd been getting.

Nancy waxed sarcastic. "What's the matter, Tim, can't

57

you read? Your parents tell me how bright you are—a regular little Einstein. Now's your chance to show me and the rest of us that you're not really stupid. Go on. Read.''

Tim looked at the page:

> The dig bog ranafte thecat.
> Jane was the digbog ran after thecat.
> Jane caleb the bog.
> The dig dog to ran Jane.

''Why don't you shut your mouth, you bitch,'' he said under his breath.

''What's that you said, Tim?'' Nancy said sharply.

''Nothing, ma'am,'' Tim replied in a whisper, his head still bowed.

But Nancy's anger had gotten the better of her. ''Speak up, Tim,'' she said. ''Or maybe that's your problem—you just can't talk. I thought it was just because you're stupid.''

''You fucking bitch,'' Tim shouted. He whipped around and started off for the door at a run only to plunge into Joe, who had braced himself and toppled Tim to the floor. Tim got up screaming and hit back, cracking Joe's glasses.

''You little brat!'' Nancy had yelled in full rage, as she grabbed Tim and shook him while he kicked at her. ''You spoiled baby brat!'' With that she had dragged him off to Siberia in the back of the room, and leaving an aide to watch over him, stormed into the principal's office with the humiliating news that she had a problem she couldn't handle in her class. She still didn't know what it was.

None of this information—mainly because it was unknown, glossed over or misinterpreted as it typically is with most LD children—helped Betty and Ed as they drove home in stunned silence with an equally silent Tim in the back seat. All they knew was that, for reasons they were still trying to comprehend, their son had been fired. It seemed like the worst humiliation in the world. "You hear about dumb kids, rotten kids, vicious kids being kicked out of school," says Ed. "But not your kid."

But this was only the beginning. They were soon to embark on the long, heartbreaking odyssey, encountered by all too many parents of learning-disabled children, traipsing from doctor to doctor, searching for answers where there are no answers, encountering diagnosis after conflicting diagnosis—no cures, no certainty of finding one—while expense piled on expense.

First they tried a psychologist, who seemed to be getting somewhere, probably because he was spending as much time with Betty and Ed on their management of Tim as he was with Tim himself. With no school, Tim was under no real pressure; his behavior improved. But after two months of the "home study" program—which Ed described to their friends as a special experiment the school was working on for gifted kids—Tim was still making no progress academically, and in fact was falling behind. "All he did was play around and chatter with the teacher they sent twice a week," says Betty, "and she seemed to have no real interest in teaching him anyway."

Betty found it difficult to follow the psychologist's instructions and be consistent and firm with Tim, after so many years of giving in. "I guess I got tired," she says, "and slacked off. Without a schedule, I began allowing him to go to bed when he pleased again and letting go on lots of little things."

The psychologist also found little sign of a specific emotional malady. "He was as vague as Tim's teachers had been," Betty explains. "And he kept blaming everything on us. Ed and I felt guilty enough. For all we knew, it *was* our fault. We were faced with the frightening prospect of sending him to a school for crazies. We weren't prepared, certainly then, to take it all on the chin, particularly when he couldn't seem to point to anything specific."

Ed and Betty hired a private tutor to beef up Tim's school work. Within two weeks the tutor, a former first-grade teacher taken out of the ranks by marriage, was gone—fed up with Tim's screams, abuse, and finally, his flailing, biting, kicking attack on her every time she made a demand, or just trying to find him where he was hiding whenever she arrived. Tim reverted to his old ways and Betty and Ed were back at square one with three months of expenses down the drain.

Now the trek really began. They fired the psychologist and took Tim to a highly recommended child psychiatrist thirty-five miles away in the city. The psychiatrist prescribed three sessions a week (the psychologist had required only one)—at fifty dollars a session. He also prescribed a drug—Thorazine—to help calm Tim down. When the initial dose failed to have the desired effect, he began prescribing more, then more. Betty and Ed followed the routine religiously, Betty driving an increasingly doped-up Tim to the psychiatrist's office and giving him the drug daily, trying not to notice how it affected him. Finally neither Ed nor Betty could take it any longer. "His activity level dropped all right," Ed says. "It sure did. He was like a zombie. And he wasn't doing anything, let alone any kind of brainwork. I couldn't help wondering what this guy was doing to my kid, was he experimenting or something? I figured that wasn't the kind of help we needed." Betty and Ed dropped the psychiatrist and the drugs. Tim was back to his old self—nowhere. "But at least we could recognize him," Betty comments.

Something, however, had to be done. "Tim just couldn't stay this way forever," Betty says, "though I began to have nightmares about it. So did Ed, I'm sure, even though we weren't talking much then. We'd gone back to our rule of silence. I began to envision having this child, full-grown, maybe thirty or forty, dependent on us for the rest of our lives, you know, like a retarded child. Either that or stuck in an institution, never right, never normal—just sick, sick forever. I know it sounds paranoid now but it was very real then. It still worries me once in a while. I've developed this real sympathy for parents with permanently handicapped children. What do they do? How do they live with it? I certainly don't think I could after what we went through. It's bad enough the way it was."

Moreover, the school was pressing Betty and Ed on the very decision they had gone to all this trouble and expense to avoid—the school for emotionally disturbed children. The guidance counselor had called several times already, inquiring politely but firmly about when they could make an appointment for all three of them to have Tim evaluated. Each time Betty and Ed had evaded the issue. They insisted that both the psychologist and then the psychiatrist were making progress with Tim, that neither had found any severe emotional disturbance or psychosis in his behavior (which was true), that they had hired a tutor who clearly expected to have Tim in shape for regular school shortly (which was not), even that Tim's behavior had improved markedly under the drugs. "We wanted to believe that it was all true," Betty explained. But at this point, with no psychiatrist, no tutor, no drugs and a "home study" teacher who was surely reporting no progress, there was nothing they could fall back on except—where? what?—something new.

Betty came across it in a magazine article on dyslexia, believed, the writer said, to be a slight neurological disorder. "Maybe that was what was wrong with Tim," she remembers thinking. But she decided to act herself and not tell Ed. "I was willing to try *anything,*" she admits. "I couldn't just do nothing."

Betty called Dr. Shaw, their pediatrician.

"Dyslexia?" Shaw said incredulously. "Come on, Betty, what kind of nonsense is that?"

For once Betty stuck to her guns and got Shaw to make an appointment for Tim with a pediatric neurologist.

Betty got her first jolt when she walked into Dr. Putnam's waiting room. Two children about Tim's age sat there with their mothers. One was spastic, with a constant drool and a lolling head. The other stared straight ahead blankly, rigid and numb. She watched them covertly, while Tim kept moving around and around the room, bothering Putnam's nurse and, once she'd got him to sit down, zipping badly mangled paper airplanes—made from ripped magazine pages—at the wall. "I was too upset," she says, "to try to make Tim mind. All I could think of were those children. Was Tim going to be like them? Did he really have an incurable disease or injury? I wished I hadn't come."

Just at the point where Betty was about to grab Tim and run, the nurse called them inside, gave Betty a four-page questionnaire and the doctor took Tim, yelling at the top of his lungs, for forty-five minutes of testing. The questionnaire, as had the psychiatrist's, asked for extensive information on Tim's childhood, illnesses, birth problems and behavior. Some of the questions were difficult, if not impossible, to answer even now; besides, after what she had seen she was inclined to play down Tim's difficulties. When she got to the question about Tim's activity level she finally answered "very active," even though the psychiatrist had already diagnosed him as hyperactive due to "emotional problems." She herself had no gauge to determine how active "active" was. Once finished she returned to the waiting room—now occupied by two more children as obviously disjointed as the first.

Dr. Putnam went over the questionnaire with Betty carefully, drawing out more and more background. Any unusual childhood illnesses? Any unexplained high fevers? This took half an hour. Then he gave Betty his diagnosis in just a few words. He didn't believe in too many preliminaries with parents.

"Your son," he said, "is, in my opinion, a hyperactive child. He also probably is minimally brain-damaged, something we call a minimal brain dysfunction, though nothing shows up organically on the electro-encephalogram. I'm prescribing five milligrams of Dexedrine per day to be given first thing in the morning and at lunchtime. I also believe he will need a special school and I'll be glad to put this in writing for you. And please make an appointment for him next week with my secretary." The neurologist, a busy man, smiled at Betty and ushered her out.

Ed was as numb as Betty when he heard the news. "All I could think was, 'My God, my child is brain-injured. He can't help himself. He's incurable.' The neurologist had mentioned a school but he'd said nothing to Betty about possible cures or any real help except more drugs. I felt guilty thinking how I had pushed him around and beat on him."

But Ed felt more than guilt: "Frankly, at that moment," he says in a whisper, "I wished he were dead, that he'd never been born."

Tim began taking the amphetamine. When his activity level didn't respond to the dose within a week, the neurologist increased it, as had the psychiatrist. His activity level became almost normal, but he began to sleep less, eat less and became pale and thin. After two weeks, the doctor switched to Ritalin, assuring the parents that since it was an amphetamine substitute, it wouldn't have the undesirable side effects. Again, when the first dose didn't work, the doctor increased it. And again, as with the psychiatrist, Tim turned into a zombie, nodding away his days. "He didn't look much different from that child I saw blankly staring in Putnam's office," Betty says. And still no progress in getting Tim back to normal school.

It only took a month of this before Ed did another turnaround and pulled Tim out from the neurologist's care and the drugs he prescribed. "I began to feel these doctors were playing poker with my kid's head. They were turning him into a pill-head, and for what?"

But there was still the school. In desperation, they took Tim's new diagnosis back to his regular school, hoping it would keep him out of the class for the emotionally disturbed. It did and, luckily, more.

Mr. Lieberman, the principal, explained that the system had no facilities for children with mbd—something he privately didn't believe in—and was about to leave it at that, except for urging them to come "for an evaluation of emotional disturbance."

"But Mrs. Bell," says Betty, "who was more kindhearted

than we ever thought, perked up. She must have sensed what hell we were going through."

She took Betty and Ed back to her office. "She had heard of a doctor in the area," says Betty, "who'd had a lot of success with such children. She fished out his name for us. She said he was working in a new field called perceptual training."

"Perceptual training!" Ed remarked when they left. "That woman is a bigger fool than I thought!"

"But there wasn't anywhere else to go," Betty says. "We'd been everywhere."

A week later, Tim's parents called and made an appointment at my office.

5

I looked at the tense couple sitting in front of me in my office that spring afternoon. Betty's hands were clenched in her lap so tightly that the knuckles were white; Ed was glaring at me, hostile, skeptical.

Betty did most of the talking, answering my questions about Tim's background—much the same as those of the doctors they'd already seen—and recounting all their earlier steps. They had been to this doctor and that doctor for this evaluation and that. Tim wasn't in school, she reported, and they didn't know where he was going to go to school. (Tim, in fact, at that moment was giving my assistant a whale of a time in my outer office.) Yes, Betty said, Tim was active. Yes, the psychologist to whom they had taken Tim initially— quite a good therapist for Tim, as it later turned out—had mentioned their son probably had some perceptual problems. (Betty's vague look indicated she had no idea what a perceptual problem might be, let alone what to do about it.) The psychiatrist said—Betty's voice dropped—that Tim was emotionally disturbed and the neurologist said—now her voice was barely audible—that he had a brain dysfunction and had prescribed drug therapy.

I had heard this tale a hundred times before but it was no less heartbreaking. All these professionals—doctors, educators, therapists—evaluating away and few of them able to do much more for this kid than apply a label to him and perhaps prescribe a dose of drugs. And there is a growing tendency automatically to prescribe drugs (often in large doses) for every child who exhibits a learning or behavior problem in school. It is true that amphetamines like Dexedrine and Ritalin, an amphetamine substitute, have a paradoxical effect on many mbd children and tend to calm them down rather than rev them up. Many types of tranquilizers work also, usually with kids whose problems are more emotional than organic. And it is true that the suspected chemically based hyperactive child seems to respond to these drugs and may need them initially to enable us to hold his attention.

But it seems extremely risky to play with any child's head by dosing him with drugs. A kid may turn into a walking zombie, and there are often unpleasant side effects, such as poor appetite, sleeplessness and, in some cases, hallucinations. In addition, no one knows the long-term effects of these drugs. I'm happy to say that only ten to fifteen percent of our students is ever on medications.

Medication, it seems to me, is the quick way to reach a very short-sighted goal—a nice quiet kid. Here is a kid who was bombing around and creating a continual disturbance now sitting quietly nodding in his seat. The teacher's problem has been solved. But what is the kid learning? Forget reading and writing—is he learning to control himself and sit still and pay attention, a prerequisite for any kind of learn-

67

ing? The drugs won't teach him any of that and they may well mask the real reason he was a problem in the first place. Well, the Wilsons had come to me to get some answers, not cover up the problems. But first, with their permission, I was going to put Tim through another test, in fact, a whole battery of them, but tests that would, hopefully, point to a solution. I also suggested they see another doctor, a neurologist I knew who had what I felt was a very level-headed approach to the use of drugs.

Ed was immediately suspicious. "Are you saying that Tim really is brain-injured?"

"I don't know for sure," I said. "It's not my bailiwick to decide that. But from preliminary observations it does seem that he shows many of the symptoms we see in our kids who are diagnosed as minimal brain dysfunctioning. And that, by the way, is not considered a true brain injury."

"Then there's no cure," Ed said, barely able to hide his disgust. "Tim's going to be like this forever."

"That's right," I answered, "there's no cure that we know of. But there is help and there are schools—mine is one of them—where mbd kids are being taught and quite successfully. And quite a few of these kids have been able to reenter regular school in two or three years and lead normal lives."

"Are those the special schools for children who are—you know, not quite right in their heads?" Betty asked, with a nervous little titter.

"Come visit us and see," I said.

The next week Betty and Ed turned up with Tim, but this time they met me at school. They had completed a questionnaire on Tim and brought a report from the neurologist who had examined Tim thoroughly. The physician had reevaluated Tim, diagnosed him mbd as had the earlier neurolo-

68

gist, and put him on a small quantity of Meleril, a mild tranquilizer. Tim had been taking it ever since and Betty reported it seemed to be working fairly well and was apparently causing no bad side effects. The neurologist had also recommended that Tim be placed in a special school.

Both parents looked more relaxed, but they still were uneasy. Sensing what was on their minds, I took them on a tour of the building and, more important, the classes. When they saw for themselves that none of my kids had two heads or was babbling away in a strait jacket, their relief was palpable. Flashing a big grin, Ed put his arm around Tim; you could see they had hopes of some light at the end of a long black tunnel. Back at my office, I scheduled the first perceptual and visual tests that would give us a much clearer picture of Tim and his problems.

The initial tests I gave Tim were purely concerned with the physiological functions of the eye, something that I never ignore. The first was a standard refraction. As expected Tim had perfect sight in each eye—he was not nearsighted, farsighted or astigmatic. However, as we progressed to the finer workings of the eye—Tim's ability to team his eyes, converge them properly, and focus and shift focus—some faults typical of mbd children who are hyperkinetic began to show up. He overconverged his eyes, particularly when trying to sight at near, the point most necessary for coping with schoolwork. Betty had told me he had often come home red-eyed from school. This told me why.

Many normal kids develop overconvergence patterns, but that was just the beginning of Tim's visual problems. Next I found that Tim had trouble focusing and shifting focus and in teaming his eyes. Unlike most of the other kids in school, this meant Tim had difficulty shifting focus from his book to the chalkboard and back again to the page—or shifting across that same page in reading. After a while, the words on chalkboard and page would begin to blur.

In addition, Tim's tracking abilities were only minimally developed. There are several kinds of tracking movements. One is called a "pursuit" movement—a broad, generalized sweeping eye motion used in scanning the environment. The second is a "saccadic" movement—short, rapid, precise movements used in reading. Another movement used almost exclusively in reading is what we call a "Z" motion, the ability of the eyes to track in Z-like fashion from the end of one line of words to the beginning of the next line and start tracking again. Kids (and adults) who haven't mastered these more complicated eye tracking maneuvers will read erratically, if at all, skipping words, phrases and whole lines at a time and losing more and more sense as they go down the page.

Tim could hardly keep up with the grossest pursuit movements, let alone the more complicated saccadic and Z-motions essential to reading. In addition, he showed a slight mid-line jump in tracking—a kind of hippity-hop motion as the line of sight he was following was blocked by his nose, and the other eye hesitated before picking it up as quickly as it should. With all these ocular motor problems, Tim, like many of our kids, had just given up; instead of just following with his eyes, he compensated by turning his head and whole body, which led to swiveling around and looking at things—and contributing to his hyperactive appearance.

In Tim's case, the mid-line jump pointed to a more basic problem: his inability to integrate his two sides and fully process information from all directions. And lest anyone think that this is peculiar only to left-right orientation of English reading, some of these kids display the very same difficulties when reading Hebrew, which tracks from right to left.

I had already noticed that Tim waddle-walked, unable to use his diagonal arms and legs efficiently in a reciprocal fashion. This was another indication of the same problem. To further explore these important perceptual skills—skills we put under the headings of "directionality" and "bilaterality"—I put Tim through a series of tests on the basic motor level.

One of the first involved the chalkboard. I gave him some chalk and asked him to draw circles with both hands simultaneously—first clockwise and then counterclockwise. Moving both hands in the same direction at the same time requires the brain to ignore the natural mid-line separation of the body, and this enables us to see whether the child can coordinate both sides of his body in a balanced fashion. A child who cannot—and this is typical of very young children—may completely stop making circles with one hand or make a straight line while continuing to make circles with the other, or make one circle elongated and larger than the other. A somewhat older child—five or six years of age, say—unconsciously will choose a less complex bilateral pattern and reverse one hand so he's going clockwise and counterclockwise at the same time. With some—those with a problem in bilaterality—one circle becomes much smaller than the other. Tim's approach was to reverse his circles and make the one on his right much smaller than the one on his left.

Asked to crawl on the floor, another test in this area, Tim could only move very awkwardly. He had skipped the crawling stage completely, as many LD kids do, but he'd also never developed the "two-sided" skills needed to walk properly. When asked to walk a two-by-four rail placed on the floor, he was similarly buffaloed, falling off after two steps. The next test I tried is based on the old game of Angels in the Snow. I asked Tim to lie down on a mat and swing his arms and legs together—flapping up and out, down and in—first to the left, then to the right. But Tim sent his left arm flapping when his right was asked for, and was totally confused when called on to move his diagonal arms and legs together.

Throughout he showed a definite, abnormal orientation to his left. Though he wasn't as "one-sided" as some of my kids (some will run all the way around the monkey bar to enter it from the right when the entrance is immediately to their left), this distortion went far toward explaining the left-ward skew of Tim's drawings and the fact that much of his paperwork was confined to that area. Little on his right side was imparting any meaning. After a few more tests, I con-cluded my evaluation of Tim's left-right directional abilities at the gross motor level. They were lousy, averaging out to those of a five-year old.

The next session began with a simple series of tests—hopping, first on one foot and then the other; jumping; stand-ing up, sitting down; and then a series of these exercises on command. Most of these tests are designed to determine a child's ability to deal with gravity and his basic sense of up and down, but they also test his ability to order and organize himself quickly and efficiently, especially in sequential ex-ecution. Tim's anti-gravity control seemed well-developed, and he showed no fear (some kids I have to lift off the floor), but when it came to organizing himself and following com-mands to hop, skip, then jump, stand up, sit down, etc., he again tested as a normal five-year-old. More tests—tapping one knee, now the other, now your forehead, now your hand—only confirmed Tim's organizational immaturity.

After this, I tested Tim's manual skills, the fine motor skills that govern the way he grasps and manipulates objects, like a pencil. I had Tim pick up pegs and put them in a hole, thread screws in bolts and pick up coins from a flat table surface. Again he scored about three years below his age—one good reason for not only his sloppy schoolwork but his clumsiness and refusal to tie his shoes and button his shirt.

Next we measured what professionals call object constancy, the notion that tells a small baby that his bottle is always a bottle, that it doesn't change shape or character when it is moved to another angle. Though this percept is readily noticeable in a child two or three months old, we have kids Tim's age and older who haven't really grasped it. So how can they be expected to make or remember the distinction between a circle and a square, let alone an "A" or "B," if it's constantly changing when viewed from one angle or another?

Here I used my own tests with three-dimensional objects—identical cubes and toys—placed in various perspectives. Tim was asked to match the right ones, and did quite well.

He also performed adequately on the size constancy test. Many LD kids can't grasp the notion that an object moving away—a car disappearing down the road—may look smaller but doesn't actually *become* smaller. To test this, we use a device called a vectograph, which reverses a law of nature and makes an object look larger instead of smaller as it recedes. But Tim stuck to his guns and said it remained the same size, even though it looked larger.

From here we measured Tim's visual motor skills. One of the key tests is a circus puzzle—a simple puzzle with a slot for each animal, and the child is asked to put each animal in the appropriate spot. The test is one measurement of eye-hand coordination—by observing whether the child can place a piece near its proper slot without excessive shuffling, a tipoff that he is relying on his sense of touch instead of his eyes. It also provides another reading on bilateral skills: does the youngster use just one hand to position the animal or two—a highly mature operation. But, most important, this is our first real test of his figure-ground abilities which, along with directional skills, are our kids' greatest weakness.

Figure-ground perception involves selectivity, the ability to pick out the significant object (the figure) and block out insignificant elements (the ground). Literally the ability to see the trees for the forest. This enables a tennis player to sight the ball and hit it accurately; for that instant he must ignore such distractions in his visual scope as the linesman, the fence, the audience, while he concentrates on that little spheroid coming at him. Highly developed figure-ground abilities can usually be found in great athletes.

But well-developed figure-ground abilities are needed for any kind of schoolwork. If you can't spot the different letters in a word as figures among ground, it's not likely you're going to excel in spelling. On the other hand, if you can't see the whole word—making the ground the figure—or, worse still, can't pick out a word from all the others on the page, reading is virtually out of the question. Many of our kids, particularly the highly hyperkinetic ones, can't even begin to block out these differences. Stimuli come at them like pellets from a shotgun, and they give equal attention to everything they see, whether it's the word on the page or a scratch on the desk.

In the circus puzzle, Tim did too much rotating, twisting and pressuring the piece into the wrong slot, indicating trial and error and showing he wasn't being as visually selective as he should be.

As a matter of fact, Tim did poorly on all counts in this preliminary evaluation of his figure-ground abilities, netting out to about age six. Later on, the Frostig booklet test—one often used in conventional schools for perceptual evaluation—showed him unable to solve figure-ground problems at his own age level. He also had difficulty matching and differentiating between various imaginary animal-like figures which could be told apart by picking out distinctive squiggles, tails and spots. A final rating of Tim's figure-ground abilities put him closer to five and a half.

In later tests, he also did poorly on visual closure, a skill closely related to figure-ground. Visual closure enables a person to judge an object when only part of it is showing. Given the picture on the following page, many of our kids see only some kind of weird tree with arms and legs.

The inability to perform this visual closure task leads not only to obvious problems in comprehension—very little in the world is exposed in full and, on a higher cognitive level, one must often solve problems based only on partial information—but also to such common errors as writing an "A" without one tail so that it comes out looking like a funny "P."

And when shown a picture of fish partially obscured by rocks and weeds, and a room with shoes partly hidden in clutter, Tim's performance put him around age four.

Next we went to several pegboard tests, which measure many of the same things as the circus puzzle, but evaluate organizational abilities as well. On one board Tim was given three pegs and asked to copy existing designs by placing

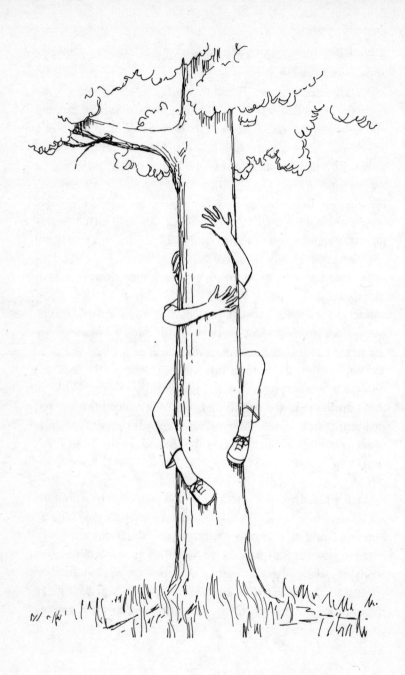

them, first, in a vertical sequence, then horizontally, and then on a diagonal. He was to start at the top or from either side. After much trouble manipulating the pegs, he managed to get the vertical sequence right, but began not at the top but in the middle. The horizontal one gave him much more difficulty; he started from the left—not the right as asked—and left a space between the pegs that wasn't indicated on the board. Even after several tries the diagonal design—something the normal child of seven can reproduce—came out every which way, showing total confusion. (The results of Tim's peg-board tests appear on the following page.)

These tests, as well as the three-dimensional cube tests, took about two hours. We prefer these tests to the booklet tests, relied on almost exclusively by conventional schools to detect perceptual problems, because the child is not required to use a pencil, a skill in itself he may not have mastered. Besides, I find it is hard to measure a child's sense of spatial relations from the two-dimensional limitations of a page in a book; the all-important element of depth is left out. Nevertheless, I always save an hour to administer these booklet tests, using them in conjunction with my earlier findings to get a better reading.

I gave Tim the Winterhaven Copy Forms test, which required him to copy seven simple designs—a circle, a square, a triangle, etc. This not only measures a child's sense of shape constancy—a circle is always a circle and never a square—but lets us see how he makes them. Skewing them to the left or right indicates a directional problem, while making their forms larger or smaller than those on the sample page suggests a problem with what we call size constancy—the child isn't perceiving the true dimensions of what he sees. Beyond this, the Winterhaven also provides a subtle measure

CORRECT | INCORRECT

Horizontal

Diagonal

of the child's sense of structure and order. Though no specific instructions are given, he is first shown all seven forms in sequence in a horizontal line across one page. Most normal children of Tim's age pick up this cue and draw their own forms in sequence left to right across the page. Tim put his forms all over the page instead. He also gave them a decided leftward tilt and was completely stymied by the diamond shape. His sense of shape and size constancy, however, was quite good, which was borne out in the Beery-Buktenica Test of Visual-Motor Integration, a test which uses twenty-five forms of progressive difficulty, such as overlapping triangles and squares.

On his overall ability, and I gave Tim several more tests just to make sure, Tim averaged a little better than he had earlier—rating at about the level of a six-and-a-half-year old. However, once we got to visual memory, largely determined by the Memory for Designs test that asks the child to reconstruct a shape from recall, he dropped down to about a four-year-old level. His retention was almost nil.

Finally I put Tim through one of my favorite series of tests—the Illinois Test of Psycholinguistic Abilities. Like the others, it tests visual reception and differentiating abilities— "Look at this picture (of an apple), find one *just* like it (an idéntial apple among oranges and pears)." But it also goes into several other highly important visual skills. One is association—"Look at this picture (of a garbage can) and find one most like it (a pail)."—a skill that is important in reading and other learning techniques. If a child learns a word in print, can he recognize it in longhand? On the aural/oral language level, ITPA also measures auditory reception with a series of questions requiring Yes and No answers. "Do bricks float? Do airplanes fly?" Others, measuring association through hearing, require the child to complete the statement: "If a mountain is high, then a valley is ———." In the area of visual sequencing and, *more important*, the child's ability to *remember* things he sees in their proper sequence, the series provides progressively longer and more difficult arrangements. He is then asked to repeat in order a series of numbers—"1,3,5,7"—or words he heard.

Sequencing is an important perceptual skill, essential not only to any kind of cognitive learning, with its high demand for systemizing, planning and reaching a solution step by step, but also to solving a simple problem like getting out of bed in the morning without falling on your head through a process of trial and error. That requires the knowledge that things follow in sequence in any physical operation. "Thirty days hath September" is a fine mental crutch to remember irregularities in each month, but it's not much use if you can't picture that each month is made up of days that follow each other in regular order. Along with this faulty sense of physical sequencing, these kids invariably lack any sense of time. An hour is the same as a minute, yesterday might as well be tomorrow, and everything promised in the future or remembered from the past happens right now.

Tim performed in all the ITPA tests much as he had on earlier tests. His basic matching abilities on a visual level were so-so. He associated on a visual basis well below his age level, though he associated on an auditory basis about a year higher, which was still inadequate. The same held true for his sequential memory. Like many learning-disabled children, Tim scored lowest of all on his visual sequential memory, upping his score substantially when he could hear the sequence.

We spent the last of Tim's five sessions testing his hearing and giving him the best test available for auditory discrimination, differentiating one sound from another. Much less is known about this area than that of visual perception but it presents its own problems to many LD children all the same. Some of our kids can't seem to understand what is said to them, even though their basic hearing acuity is fine. Though their hearing tests perfectly normal on the decibel scale, they can't discriminate between sounds—"B" and "D," both very similar; a soft sound or a loud sound; whether the sound is coming from left or right, in back or in front of them. They don't have the "sense" to get out of the way of a car rushing up behind them. Not only does this make it difficult to absorb what they take in, words spoken to them, but it wreaks havoc with what they put out, the words they speak. They have difficulty not so much in the physical articulation of words—the way a stutterer might—but in the way they say words and form sentences, which is usually in a baby-talk manner, with jumbled syntax, missing elements and mix-ups in terminology. "I home going" is not an unusual sentence for one of these youngsters, nor is it uncommon to hear them call a caterpillar a pillowcase.

Again Tim followed the common LD pattern. His auditory abilities were much better developed than his visual ones, though still under par for his age. Obviously, the best way to teach Tim at this point would be through an auditory learning program, reinforced by visual and auditory perceptual training.

All through the perceptual testing, however, I had been discreetly testing for something else. Could we reach Tim? Was he psychologically still receptive enough to tolerate the dull, repetitive and seemingly endless programming he needed to put him ahead? I decided we had a good chance.

Though he became distracted easily and showed his frustrations, constantly whining at every turn throughout the rigorous testing periods, spaced out over many sessions, all it took was a little teasing and a real show of interest and firmness to send him back to finishing what he had to do. We even had several good laughs over his clutzy behavior and his odd test results. This kid was not so far gone that he couldn't be taught, but he would need a lot of work. Finally, after the last test, I took Tim back to my office, where Betty and Ed were now waiting, and told them my findings: though Tim was better at some things than others and seemed teachable, their eight-year-old son netted out perceptually as a five-year-old child.

I didn't expect either Betty or Ed to be exactly overjoyed with this news. They weren't, and questioned some of my results. But they'd done enough doctor-hopping, without prospect of any improvement in Tim, not to be willing to give it a try. They then faced the question of school.

"Would there be room in yours?" Ed asked.

I said that Tim's perceptual profile was much the same as many of our kids', and his deficits were those our setup was specifically designed to remediate. His psychological evaluation—as well as my own observations during testing—indicated he should fit in with our normal class of ten or twelve kids. At least once we worked with him and got him adjusted. But it was now April and we were well into the term. It was our policy not to introduce new kids—with all the initial disruptions one could expect—at this late date when the kids were knitted together and classes going strong. Their control base still was necessarily fragile, and it seemed unfair to risk a possible setback. I told Betty and Ed that Tim would have to wait till September, and why. Then, following my normal

82

policy, I suggested they look at several other schools before making a final decision. And I also suggested they put Tim and themselves back in therapy to keep him on an even keel.

Betty and Ed were disappointed at the wait. Like any parents who have gone through this ordeal, they wanted to start Tim on his schooling right away. But they agreed to take Tim back to the psychologist to deal with any emotional problems, and in the meanwhile visited two other schools.

A week later Betty called to say she and Ed had decided on our school, and brought in Tim for the four reading and math tests we give to all entering students. Like many LD kids, Tim was much better at math than at reading—perhaps because reading requires much more sophisticated visual skills. He was only about a year behind his age in arithmetic, but was reading at a five-year-old primer level—essentially a non-reader. I informed Betty of the scores and outlined the prescriptive teaching program we would probably use—one relying heavily on auditory teaching but also geared more to sight and touch, as well as at least one standard sight-recognition course corresponding to a regular school program. All this, of course, reinforced by the perceptual and visual training program. When I told her I thought Tim's problems could be remediated within three to four years, after which he would be ready to return to normal schooling, I thought I'd never see a happier woman. That was something to take home to a still skeptical Ed. And once Tim began to come to my office once a week for perceptual training, Ed too became convinced. By the time Tim entered school that September, his perceptual abilities had advanced to those of a six-year-old and he was playing ball with his father. Best of all, he was beginning to look a lot happier. But we still had a long way to go.

6

The room is pitch-black. The only sounds are those of a pop group singing "The Age of Aquarius." The kids lying around on the floor have all been given flashlights, but they are paying more attention to the song than to its source—a toy phosphorescent spaceship revolving somewhere around the ceiling. Suddenly a ghostly (tape-recorded) voice cuts in over the music:

"Mr. Spock is watching you. Watch *us* or we'll zap you!"

A dozen flashlights snap on, pinpointing the circling spaceship. Then, after a while, the beams falter as the kids begin to lose track of its whereabouts.

"Mark!" says the spooky voice (mine). "You're not watching. If you don't keep following this starship with your flashlight, it will go into Warp One, and you'll be stuck in another galaxy."

Mark nails the spaceship with his light. Bullseye!

"Good. Peggy—pay attention. Captain Kirk tells me you got an A in math yesterday, right? You want another A today? Then catch up with your flashlight."

These kids aren't studying to be astronauts or TV stars (although they *are* all honorary "Trekkies," *Star Trek* fanatics)—they're going through one phase of our perceptual training program, which is compulsory for every student in school.

In spite of the dark room and flashing lights, there's nothing mystical about perceptual training. It's based on our findings of the way normal children develop. As they progress from infancy to school age, they learn the perceptual skills that enable them to succeed—to read and write and get along with their classmates. Our kids have developed their perceptions by this time, too—but imperfectly. Whatever these other children learned, ours *didn't*. So perceptual training exercises are designed to put our kids through the process again. In terms of perceptual growth, they are repeating the learning experiences of those crucial six or seven years—with us standing by this time to make sure everything goes right. And we can do this because perception is not a gift, it's a skill.

Back in the late '20s, it was our old friend, the optometrist A. M. Skeffington, in taking the quantum leap from vision training into the still controversial field of visual perception, who concluded that perceptions are not automatic but *learned*. To truly "see" or perceive something, he found, an image not only had to reach the brain through the retina of the eye but be correctly interpreted by it. Only by experience does a child *see* that a flame is hot without having to touch it with his hand, or learn that a table remains the same height whether he is below or above it.

Skeffington's findings were bolstered years later by the research of the noted Swiss psychologist Jean Piaget. All of us, maintained Piaget, are essentially "perceptual" beings up to the age of six or seven, devoting most of our energy to the job of figuring out our immediate surroundings—colors, shapes, near, far, that Mommies are big, and babies are small. Even though children display measurable intelligence by the age of twelve to fifteen months, it is only after we have internalized these perceptions of the concrete world that our intelligence is free to launch into more abstract learning, such as ideas.

Piaget thus acknowledges that such concepts as object, shape and size constancy must be learned, and his years of research also support the developmental nature of figure-ground abilities and directional skills. But most optometrists dealing with perception have gone even further. They believe virtually *no* perceptions—particularly the visual and aural, man's highest orders of perception—are innate. To perceive something—to assign it proper meaning, as a child does when he perceives the fire is hot—you must first have experience with it, or at least with something somewhat similar. Unlike many other animals who are frisking around hours after birth (and whose perceptions develop at the same rapid rate), a human infant comes into this world with no prior experience beyond his limited, muffled life in the womb. Not only is he feeble (as compared to his animal counterpart), he cares only about his visceral perceptions, those that affect his physical comfort. He couldn't care less about anything so remote as that chair across the room or even his bottle; right now, all he perceives is the immediate fact that he has a wet bottom.

If an infant's needs are primitive and self-centered, then his perceptions—especially his visual and auditory ones—are even more so. They will all have to grow before this human organism has refined himself into the sophisticated perceptual mechanism known as a school-ready, reading-ready child.

How does he reach this level of perception? He learns. And he learns according to a clear, well-defined pattern of development common to all children, whether normal or abnormal. All basic perceptual learning proceeds as follows: it starts on the motor level—his senses of touch, taste, smell and movement. Next the child begins to make preliminary visual and auditory associations with an object he has experienced, or a motion he has performed. Slowly he firms up those associations, advancing into the visual-motor stage, where those associations become the main factor in his identifications, with reinforcement from his motor base. Finally he reaches the visual stage, where he not only "sees" but perceives and identifies objects without having to refer to his motor base to give them proper meaning.

To illustrate, here is how we believe a baby learns basic figure and ground in terms of, say, his bottle.

At first he only knows his bottle *is* his bottle when he's holding it and sucking on it.

Next he begins to watch his bottle while he is feeding from it. He associates the shape and feel of the bottle with the satisfaction he always gets from it, but once the bottle is removed he's not really sure what to yell for. He may grab his rattle instead and put that in his mouth. Visual associations are being made, but they're still random and unreliable.

As he begins to make more associations, however, he will be able to spot his bottle on a table nearby and cry for it—but he'll keep crying until it's actually in his mouth. He still needs the reinforcing motor experience to be sure he's got it right.

Finally, in the last stage of development, the child sees the bottle and starts to cry and reach out. But now he stops fussing as soon as he sees it coming his way because he knows for certain, *on a visual level,* just what the bottle means.

Along with climbing the ladder from motor to visual perception, the infant is learning other fundamentals as well. He is constantly exploring his body, finding out how it moves so he can control it, and building the foundation for a self-image. He is also acquiring his first sense of order and sequence. He learns that to crawl, for example, one hand and one leg have to move before the other hand and leg. They can't all go together; certain actions must precede others if he expects to achieve any kind of success.

Perhaps more important, the child is reinforcing a process he's been practicing since birth: he has solved a problem. And until he has solved enough problems, until he has achieved perceptual proficiency at the relatively simple motor base, he can't progress smoothly into becoming a visual and auditory perceiver. Most LD kids *don't* achieve this motor proficiency—but they move along the developmental path anyway. They may skip steps (as Tim skipped crawling), or move into a higher stage of development before they've really mastered the previous one. By the time other children are functioning primarily as visual perceivers, our kids are operating on all levels at once, compensating for their deficits as best they can. This is why, regardless of their particular deficits or levels of skill, we start out all our kids at school on the motor level—crawling, hopping, walking rails and touching every object and texture we can lay their hands on. Not until they are competent on that foundational level do we move them up the developmental ladder, retracing their earlier progress, but this time doing it right.

Sometimes, if the kid is loaded with visual-motor perceptual problems, that first step may take up to a year. Others breeze through the basic physical exercises in a month or two. But each kid, no matter how proficient he may be, starts at the bottom, working on his base motor skills, and is allowed to progress to the next perceptual level only after he's shown he can perform satisfactorily.

This doesn't mean we're interested in teaching eight-year-olds to crawl. But we find that teaching them to crawl has surprising and solid results. In these sessions we never tackle specific problems like the difference between "b" and "d." Yet after they've been put through the entire spectrum of motor exercises, an exciting thing often happens. A kid's persistent reversals will cease and he will begin to catch on in class. When this happens, all our systems flash "go." But we do not stop there. We continue with physical exercises (since reversals are often a symptom of many motor deficiencies), but we also start working above the motor level, putting him through the more complex perceptual exercises that will eventually make him much more capable of logical thinking and efficient conceptualization.

As far as I'm concerned, perceptual training has another purpose. After I've put a kid through his perceptual paces from "A" to "Z"—from gross motor skills to the finest visual distinctions, some forty areas in all—I can look forward to seeing a much more rounded child, one who not only can play a game but can more fully appreciate the objects, people and space around him. Our perceptual training is designed to open up the world for our locked-in, one-way kids, and that, in the long run, may be just as important for them to learn as the art of reading.

One of the first perceptual routines I teach my kids deals with simple left-right sequencing. Since it is done on command, it also gives a child a basic lesson in listening.

The child is seated in a chair, feet flat on the floor, one

hand on each knee. He is asked to tap each knee twice on commands given to the count of a metronome—right, right and then left, left.

Once the child gets the hang of this (we often spend the first sessions indicating which hand he is supposed to use), the metronome is speeded up. Then, if he can, we ask him to recite the alphabet to the same metronome beat while he is tapping. Lots of kids know the alphabet song by heart, yet can't recognize the letters or recite them in sequence without singing them. What we want is to separate the auditory-motor act of recitation from the conceptual act of thinking about the alphabet. Making the kid recite to the beat of the metronome—"A" click, "B" click, etc.—helps break the rote memory pattern of the song and forces him to *think* about the alphabet.

After this, we ask the child to cross-pattern—tapping his right knee with his left hand and vice versa. We extend this to touching his feet alternately, then ask him to bounce a ball on the floor, first with one hand and then the other.

Next, we test our child on gravity, balance, and up and down motions. He is asked to jump, then hop. He is asked to hop on foot and then the other—back and forth, again in sequence. We get him to follow simple orders on command and in sequence—stand up, sit down, stand up again, repeat what you just did—and then add hopping, turning around and other physical movements to make the sequence more complex.

At this level we also use a very simple kind of Simon Says game to build up sequencing and listening abilities. Simon says: "Touch your head, touch your knee, touch your stomach." If the kid can't do all three in order, then back we go and give each instruction separately and slowly in the same sequence until he gets it all together.

We also start quite early tying in the visual element. One of us demonstrates three separate motions and tells the kids to repeat them in the same order. With kids who are still confused even at this basic level, our teachers play a game. Before dismissing their class they will place some objects on a shelf; the next morning, before the kids arrive, they will move one object out of the original order. The kids are asked to correct it, and get a big kick out of doing it right.

Our exercises at the pure motor level bear on other areas as well. All the body touching helps develop body image, a knowledge of each part of the body and its function. This is essential, I believe, to any kind of movement control and in manipulative tasks, like writing. It's also basic to the development of a self-image. Both of these areas—body image and sense of self—tend to be weak spots for most of our kids.

Jean Piaget, among others, has observed that the newborn infant is a kind of "global narcissist"—not intentionally but because he hasn't any idea he is different from anything around him. Later, as a toddler, he has learned this difference, but still sees himself as the focus of the universe. He understands the sun and moon, but believes the former follows him around all day and the latter disappears when he goes to sleep. Only around the age of six or seven does a child begin to perceive that there are others he must interest and cooperate with; that there are moral values existing independent of himself; that there is another point of view besides his own.

We believe the young child's intense self-absorption may

be dictated by his driving need to make sense out of the crazy, muddled, mammoth world he was born into—and the easiest way to order the world is to view it in terms of himself. If the child is ever to truly learn, he has to pass through this self-centered phase and see the world in other, larger terms. That's why it's so important for us to help our kids define their egos—so they can understand where *they* leave off and the world begins.

How do you teach a kid who has never had any real sense of identity how he specifically differs from all those around him—who he really is?

We begin with some "dumb" questions.

"How many heads do you have?" I'll ask.

"One, dummy," says the kid, snickering.

No snickering allowed. "How do you know you have only one head?" I'll continue.

"Because everyone has only one head," he pipes up intelligently.

Not good enough. The object is to make him pinpoint *himself*.

"What kind of dumb answer is that?" I'll say. "Isn't there any other way you know you have one head? Or do you really know?"

Finally, after much probing, we get the kid to realize he can feel his head or look in the mirror and say: "I know I have one head because I can feel only one. I can look in the mirror and see I have only one. My friends can look at me and see that I only have one head."

We go through the kid's other body parts in the same manner—yes, he has two feet, two hands, one nose—and use materials like dolls, puppets, cut-outs and even other kids to reinforce his body image. After that, we progress to individual functions—looking with his eyes, sniffing with his nose, etc. One of the most enjoyable ways we find to do this is to get the kid play-acting and pantomiming.

From here we really start working on self-image, playing the What Makes Me Me game and What Makes Me Different from Johnny or Tommy—again using body parts. However, now the emphasis is on discriminating differences between oneself and another person—first on a physical basis (I'm me because I have blue eyes and you don't . . . my hair is blond and yours is brown'') and then on a more sophisticated psychological basis (''I'm shy''; ''I'm loud''). The child has to verbalize each difference until he gradually begins to feel like a distinct and unique entity.

One way we help him achieve this goal is to tape record a kid's description of himself, muffling the microphone with a tissue so his voice can't be recognized. A few days later, the teacher plays back the tape and the kids try to guess who is being described.

Though we may spend months, particularly with very hyperactive kids, on basic sequencing and body awareness activities, most of our kids move on very quickly to more complex training. These exercises are designed to develop balance, a sense of two-sidedness, and a sense of direction, but they also increase the kid's consciousness of how his body works.

One such exercise is the soldier walk. To the accompaniment of music or the metronome, the kids are asked to walk in the exaggerated jerky manner of a robot, emphasizing the alternative reciprocal motion of their arms and legs. Any obvious errors are greeted by the rebuke from TV's *Lost in Space* robot: ''Does not compute.''

Another that the kids enjoy is the Bust the Balloon walk.

93

Balloons are blown up and taped to the floor in two parallel lines. The kids must take off their shoes and, walking down the line, break the balloons in time to the metronome. If a kid misses a beat or fails to break a balloon, he loses a point. The champion balloon-buster of the day wins a reward.

At this point we get into creeping and crawling. Normal kids begin to crawl in a homolateral fashion—using the left leg and left hand together—and it may take them a good while to discover it's much more efficient to locomote in bilateral fashion—using the diagonal limbs together in a cross pattern. When they start to walk, they again drop back to this homolateral pattern, displaying a waddling, penguin-like gait, then quickly move into the better balanced, more efficient cross pattern.

In perceptual training, we first ask the kid to creep and then crawl in the basic homolateral pattern, which he should be able to do even if he walks badly or has never crawled. Then we start the cross pattern. Next, we give him a target to crawl toward. Then we move the target, usually a ball on a string, swinging it from left to right in his line of vision, and we tell him to keep his eye on the ball without changing his body direction. He's told to lead with his eyes, and to keep his head and body from swaying with the ball. Many of our kids can't do this initially because they haven't learned that they can move their eyes without moving their heads. This refined scanning skill gives humans a degree of visual freedom unknown to lower animals, most of whom must turn their heads to bring things into their line of vision.

"My God," I'll say to the kid, "what do you think you are—an elephant? Only elephants sway like that. Stop moving your head."

"I'm not moving my head."

"Yes you are," I'll insist. "Try just using your eyes."

94

After a lot of wails and "I can't"'s, we usually get the kid to do the exercise and he has solved one more problem he couldn't handle before.

If the target has been placed over to one side, we will ask the kid in which direction he is going and which hand and foot he plans to use first to get there. We also have him crawling around big letters taped to the floor so that he begins to realize that letters have direction too. The "A" goes up and then turns a corner and comes down. The "O" keeps going round and round. In addition, we ask him to judge distance—how many crawl steps does he think it will take to get to the end of the room?

Next we move to the walking rail—an eight-foot-long, two-by-four board laid on the floor. This requires much more balance than crawling. The kid must have a well-developed cross-pattern in his walk in order to keep his balance.

Once the kid has learned to walk the rail backwards and sideways and to the end—a task that can take months—we tell him to look at a target and then a swinging ball, while maintaining his balance on the rail. Generally, the first thing he does is fall off. Once he's mastered that, we give him a bat and ask him to swing at the ball while staying on the rail. This usually is too difficult at first and he may start to cry, but we keep at it until he has accomplished the task—which makes him proud of himself.

At the same time that we are doing these exercises—we repeat the series on a balance board and a jumping board—we also are working on some specifically visually related tasks. We will have the kid doing chalkboard circles with both hands, first counterclockwise and then clockwise. In addition, we'll have kids make a star by drawing lines in and out from a chalked "X".

But teaching the elusive concepts of left and right and

judging distance is not just confined to perceptual training periods. One of our favorite locales is the gravity-free environment of a swimming pool. There is nothing better than splashing around in a pool to get the feel of arms, and legs, and sides, and most of our kids love to swim. They may be waddle-walkers and elephant-crawlers on the ground, but in the water they swim like demons.

The early motor training discussed so far deals mainly with balance, two-sidedness and direction, and spatial relations. The exercises are designed to eliminate left-right reversals, to teach letter recognition and to give the kids a sense of form. But very early we also use a purely tactual approach to this problem of form recognition.

One of our most useful basic training aids is the grab bag. Each morning we ask the kids to identify as many objects inside the bag as they can, and those who make a perfect score receive a token award. We make it increasingly difficult to differentiate among the objects until we have the kids identifying letters of the alphabet, numbers, geometric shapes.

We also use blindfolds and ask a child to match similar objects on the basis of touch alone. He is asked to verbalize what is different or alike about the objects he's touching. Then, on a motor-visual level, we ask him to investigate certain objects in the room, again using only his sense of touch, and tell us what each one feels like. Then we take off the blindfold and let him view the objects from different angles—standing up, lying down, upside down—and ask if they have acquired different characteristics from the new perspectives.

At this motor-visual level we also work with templates, which are paper or plastic stencils the kids can use to trace the outlines of objects or letters. Unlike many teachers who use templates, we don't care if the kid reproduces the outline perfectly—that will come later; as long as he seems to be getting the "feel" of the arm motion required, we're satisfied.

Obviously, not all our kids need to spend the same time on this basic training in the motor and motor-visual areas. Usually the period lasts about six months for our younger children, three months for our eight- to seventeen-year-olds. Some few of my kids never make it, and then I find I must search around for splinter skills—skills learned under pressure which haven't been generalized. If a kid has learned to ride a bicycle, yet still can't balance well enough to walk a two-by-four rail lying on the floor, I latch on to his splinter skill—bike-riding—and try to use it to improve his balance all around. But until they show me they can solve most of the basic motor problems, I feel it's useless to push their reading and classwork. They need this basic knowledge to proceed to more precise visual and auditory work, and need the confidence instilled by doing these perceptual exercises right. Premature pressure on reading—something they haven't been able to cope with before—would only tend to shatter that fragile self-confidence.

This is not to say that we ignore a kid's reading and writing and arithmetic at this juncture; we just don't insist he meet what we consider unreasonable academic demands at that stage. Though we point out his errors, we don't make a big deal about his reversals, his sloppy paperwork, his inability to spell or recognize words by sight or any of the other areas where he's weak. These first months consist of a sort of vacation from the kind of academic pressure he's left behind—though the pressure on him to control his behavior in class will be unremitting from the beginning.

97

As soon as we reach the more sophisticated levels of motor-visual exercises—after the child has mastered rail-walking and begun batting a ball—we begin to push harder on classwork. And it's now that I begin to concentrate on pure vision training, teaching the eyes the movements they must use to cope efficiently with reading.

Because the eyes are such an important tool for the highly visually oriented human being and because they are so complex, we find the normal infant spending much of his time just "looking" and exercising his eyes, trying to master their difficult function. My kids haven't even learned to handle their own gross motor functions, so it's not surprising that many of them have trouble controlling so fine a mechanism as their eyes. That's why I wait until after motor training to begin visual training.

But there is another reason for making eye training the second step rather than the first. That same normal infant, while learning to control his eyes, is also integrating them with his motor actions. He tries to teach himself balance, for example, by sighting on an object with his eyes and grabbing for it with two hands, which involves control over the midline of his body. The newborn infant also spends a lot of time sighting with one eye on his outstretched fist, opening and closing it, a preliminary to eye-hand coordination. As he develops body control, he learns to coordinate his eyes with his body movements. For example, I have seen more than one child with a wall-eyed tilt to his eyes, suddenly converge them perfectly at the peak of a jump on the board or trampoline in sheer desperation to keep his balance. Just as the exercises requiring balance help a child learn to converge his eyes properly, so the left, right, alternating tapping, hopping and ball-bouncing exercises, and tracking a target swinging from side to side, help him learn to scan a written page without turning his head and ease that mid-line jump when he's reading from side to side.

In tracking, we start with the grosser pursuit movements. We place a phosphorescent ball on a string and swing it slowly and then faster and faster around a dark room. The kid must follow it with his eyes. To make sure he does, we give him a flashlight and tell him to keep it trained on the ball.

Our phosphorescent spaceship is one variation of this; shooting at moving targets with a water pistol is another. Sometimes our tracking exercises take us to the race track, a long curving path marked out on the floor with a double line of chalk. The kid runs down the track as fast as he can without hitting the sides. To do this he has to keep his eye on the chalk, and the kid who manages to reach the end fastest without going off the track gets a token prize.

The point of these exercises is not just to have the kid *think* he's following an object—a ball, his hand, a moving spaceship—but to *know* whether he is or he isn't. That's why we make him aim a flashlight or a gun at it. By the time we reach racetrack stage, we are building in eye-hand coordination. (With a kid who shows problems in this area we resort to simpler exercises, such as studying the movement of his hand as he picks up rings with a stick and places them on pegs on a board.)

Once we've built pretty fluid pursuit movements, we start on the saccadic movements. We ask the kid to look at my hand. Only the pinky and thumb are extended, and we ask him to switch his eyes from one to the other to the count of the metronome. If the kid can't do this, we let him touch my pinky and then my thumb. We also use pictures that light up in different parts of the room and viewers that quickly flash pictures at regular intervals—on the left, on the right, up, down.

We will draw pictures on the board and give a kid a pointer and tell him to touch the cat, touch the dog, touch the man—all in staccato sequence to a fast metronome count. This too is an exercise for eye-hand coordination as well as eye movement.

By now, in the final phase of our motor training and eye training, we should have a more controlled and coordinated kid who *can* pay attention because he has gained control over his eyes and body; a less distractable kid because he has learned to perceive his environment better; and a happier kid because he has solved a number of problems. He's about ready to read and do puzzles and learn. And now we not only expect to see him perform better academically—drawing, coloring within the lines, making his letters and numbers correctly—but we demand it, usually over his emotional resistance. At this point our kids, when asked to make a string of "O"s, can no longer get away with scrawling all over the page without having their teacher come down on them: "Make those 'O's or you're not getting any lunch!" (They make those "O"s perfectly.)

It's ticklish to judge just when a kid is ready to perform academically, when his "I can't" is real or just caused by his fear of habitual failure in school. But at some point the school honeymoon has to end; and while the perceptual training continues, now it's more desk- and classroom-oriented. It's also more visually oriented. Now that we have built up his directional skills and tactual selectivity, we're mainly concerned with skills basic to reading.

Reading begins with matching—identifying a letter on the page and knowing what it's called and how it sounds. We subject the kids to a barrage of template drawings, parquetry designs, pegboard work; we ask them to match objects by shape, color and size, and actual measurements, and we constantly reinforce it all with motor and auditory cues. We also don't forget our old sense of direction and feel. When the kids did templates—tracing around a stencil of the letter "A"—they were asked which direction they were going in; we still ask them, but now tell them to pay attention to the quality of their work and try to improve it. We set up parquetry blocks vertically on the parquetry board and ask them to reproduce the pattern on the horizontal plane of their desks. We give them pictures of blocks arranged in more complicated perspective, and ask them to arrange their own blocks in the same perspective on their desks. We ask a kid to describe the attributes of objects—is it soft, hard, oblong, square?—and then let him handle them to see if he's answered correctly. We ask him to mark off on a length of string how wide he estimates a chair on the opposite side of the room to be—and then measure the string against the chair to see if he was right. We try to get as much action and motor reinforcement as possible.

Reading entire words involves not only matching disparate symbols but keeping letters in proper sequence so that "cat" does not come out "tac" or "act." To develop sequencing, we play games like How Many Things Can You Remember? A kid will call out three things—"cat, dog, fish"—and then be asked to repeat them in order. I'll add "curtain" for the next round and "horse" for the next. The kid who gets most things right and in order wins.

In addition to those objects the teacher has mixed up on the shelf, we also use something called motor expressive cards— cards that illustrate in sequence a familiar action, like putting

101

on shoes and socks. One card will show the sock next to the foot. The next card will show the sock on the foot. The next will show the shoe next to the socked foot, then the shoe on the foot, and then the shoe on the foot with the laces tied. We shuffle the cards and ask the kids to put them in the right order.

As we begin to work with our kids on this increasingly visual level, I like to get after reading and word-recognition by the tachistoscopic form method, illustrated below. We begin by drawing each kid's name in the configuration it makes and then showing him the form without the letters. (This, by the way, is one of the best ways to teach elementary letter and word recognition.)

The kids quickly latch on to the configuration of their name. As they do, we begin to add longer and more complicated words. We also begin to reinforce shape and form concepts by the use of other tachistoscopic techniques.

One of the games we play at this level of form matching and recognition is something I call tachistoscopic baseball. A kid stands at the chalkboard and a form is flashed on for a second. The kid is asked to draw it in the same place on the board, the same size. Every correct form—verified when flashed back—is a hit, every incorrect form an out. The kids choose up teams and really compete to win.

It's at this phase that we pour on the language training. We have them listening to sounds and trying to describe them (soft, loud, fast, slow). They listen to musical instruments and try to play them. We try to build rhythm into their speech and listening—often a kid who speaks choppily will also listen choppily and read choppily. For those kids with more noticeable problems, our language teacher will go over the separate sounds made by each letter and phonic unit.

Somewhere around now I'm beginning to get a kid who can work almost totally on the visual level, with auditory cues. Here's where I start giving him a steady diet of purely visually oriented tasks. One of them is shown on the following page. It tests figure-ground and matching abilities. Can you do it?

I also have a kid who can generalize from all his past experience on the many levels he's passed through and become an efficient learner. Finally we get to his conceptual processes and his ability to deal in the abstract. One of the games we use here is something I call Copy Cats. It utilizes a chalkboard, a piece of paper, a pencil, a group of witnesses and a willing, though confused, kid. The kid is asked to draw on a piece of paper a simple form which he will then tell me how to draw on the board. But there's one catch. He can't call it by name. Let's say he draws a square. He can't tell me to "draw a square," he has to tell me *how* to draw it. Also he has to turn his back so he can't see what I am doing. The tape recorder and the witnesses are there since we may not all agree on how well I followed directions.

The kid, holding the drawing of a square in front of him, says: "Draw a line on the board."

I do, at the same time saying: "I draw the line in any direction, straight or curved, any place on the board."

The kid is concentrating on his work. "Now draw another line connecting it to the top."

"With that information, I draw any type of line any length as long as it connects to the top."

By this time, the class is laughing and the kid is getting worried.

"Are you doing what I say?" he demands.

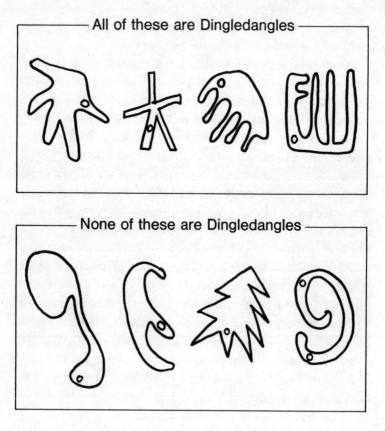

All of these are Dingledangles

None of these are Dingledangles

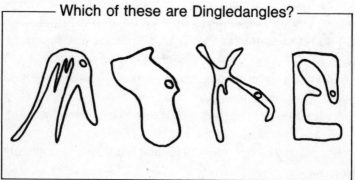

Which of these are Dingledangles?

"Yes," I say, "and we can check it with the tape recorder later."

"Draw another line connecting to the bottom," the kid will say. When that is done, he'll say, "Join the two lines." He then turns around and comes racing up, beaming, to see what I have done. This is what he sees:

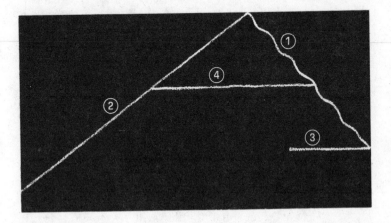

At this point, my confused kid will accuse me of cheating and making a fool of him. But he quickly quiets down when I call on some other confused kid to explain why my form doesn't look like his square and he proves to be just as bewildered. Then we turn on the tape and discuss the directions and my answers to them.

After a series of practice sessions, you'd be surprised how quickly a child, even at the age of seven, learns how to give explicit directions for drawing a square. They may sound like this:

"Place your chalk on the board and draw a line to the window (or right or left) about as long as a cigarette. Keep the line straight, not wiggly. Stop. Do not remove the chalk from the board. Now make another straight line straight down in the direction of the floor about the same length as the line you made before. Etc.'' This kid should be able to give anyone directions. Best of all, he's learning how to handle abstract concepts.

Once I have a kid at this level, he has pretty well taken the course. But until he leaves us he will be given increasingly more sophisticated games and problems to solve in perceptual areas. He will have to complete more and more complicated shapes in tachistoscopic baseball. He will have to keep working on that old self-image. He will play as many games and compete in as many perceptual activities as I can devise and make interesting.

Because, in spite of all his improvement, this kid still is learning-disabled. And much as any kid needs constant redundancy to learn, this kid needs it more. And if he wants to keep up once he gets back to regular school, he'll need a lead on the other kids. Perceptual training will give him that lead.

7

Perceptual training provides our basic academic framework, but it's not the whole answer. Perceptual training by itself is never going to teach a kid to read and write and do arithmetic; it just gives him the basic tools to make those tasks a lot easier.

So along with perceptual training we have a regular academic program. And though we use different combinations of programs for different problems, a typical reading schedule for a typical kid—one entering with visual rather than auditory perceptual problems, a third (or even fourth) grader who nonetheless is reading not at all, or on the first-grade level—probably would be drawn from as many as four separate programs.

The first would be the Bannantynne reading program, which emphasizes the auditory aspects of language and reading word comprehension. Bannantynne relies largely on phonics, sounding out words and parts of words and letters, and on teacher/student exchange. A teacher will read the kids a story and then ask them questions. It tends to be noisy and that's why we favor it as the foundation for our kids, who usually respond best to aural instruction.

Bannantynne also provides highly stimulating visual reinforcement. At the outset words are identified by color code (red apple). In addition, the child is required to do a great deal of coloring himself. He must color his letters, color pictures of a cat or dog with the word alongside it. Moreover, it involves many language arts games such as a treasure hunt to find a given word on the page. It is aimed at developing receptive, associative and expressive skills.

The second program we would probably use is the Michigan Language Program. This employs tapes and scripts for improving listening skills by developing auditory discrimination. A child will listen to three words—car, cat, car—and be asked whether they are the same or different. The series get progressively harder ("shoe, shoe, shoes" . . . "threw, throw, threw").

But the Michigan program, while containing auditory material, is primarily visual in nature. Its main object is to orient the child spatially and directionally, particularly in terms of left and right, and to develop figure-ground abilities and tracking and eye-hand coordination. To teach tracking, the child will be shown a paragraph of nonsense words and asked to pick out the first "A" he sees, the first "B," the first "C," going from left to right.

In other Michigan Language exercises, the child must connect dots on a page to form a line identical in shape and length to one printed on the page. This exercise improves his figure-ground abilities on several levels. First, he must distinguish the dots from the rest of the page, an elementary figure-ground discrimination. Next, he can't begin to connect the dots until he visualizes how the printed line—a separate figure on ground—can be reproduced in a different environment (the dots). The simple dot drawings—straight, curved and oblique lines—sharpen the kid's figure-ground perceptions, and he is eventually able to go on to more complex letter configurations and then parts of words. As he gets more experience with the dots and lines, they gradually cease to be a jumble and start to serve as guidelines, helping him fathom spatial relations. These exercises help teach him the directions of letters; help train him to write on the line, instead of below or off it; and keep him aware of the proper size of each letter relative to the next. This part of the Michigan Language program, we feel, is one of the best ways to teach our kids to write.

The next program we would add to our child's schedule is the Lippincott Beginning to Read, Write and Listen Series. This is a highly creative and innovative intersensory program built along *Sesame Street* lines. The children learn each letter of the alphabet in a separate letter booklet—twenty-six booklets in all. Scratch some of the pictures illustrating each letter and they give off an identifying aroma (orange for "O," a pickle smell for "P," a rose smell for "R"). Within each booklet the letter is introduced in other ways. They may be beaded or sandpapered. They may form part of a chord—"C" will be "C" on the piano, "A" = "E," "T" = "G"; you divide up the class into three groups, ask each to sing their letters—and the word "cat" becomes a C-major chord. There are many songs about each letter, and if the child finishes coloring his alphabet booklet, he'll end up with his own comic book.

Along with the letter books is something called My Book Book, which features tapes and two great characters—one a kid named Mooney who, like themselves, doesn't want to read, just watch TV; and an adult named Henry Friendly who tries to convince him that reading is fun. The only problem with the Lippincott series is that it's so stimulating we could spend a whole year teaching just the alphabet. Consequently, we use it as just one of our reinforcing programs.

The fourth program for all our kids, regardless of deficit, is a basic word-sight recognition course used in many public schools. While it is nowhere as stimulating or instructive as the others, we feel it is necessary to keep him aware of normal reading modes in the schools to which we are hoping to return him.

Math will present problems for our typical kid, but probably less than reading, because it can be learned by rote and is less complicated visually. Our kid usually will do rather well in computation. His math will start to fall apart when he has to begin problem solving—usually at the third-grade level. Ironically, he will find his main difficulty is reading the problems.

As with reading, our base program in math is aural. Instructions are read aloud; we teach computation by rote and theory. We have found that our child responds well to the real-object approach: he'll spend the day happily counting real toys and beads and working with real number lines, which gives him a much clearer concept of "oneness" or "twoness" than he ever got from abstract numbers printed on a page.

Problems in spatial orientation and direction show up in number work as well as letters. "What comes after 199?" we'll ask. Our kid will start out by saying, "Two . . ." pause, and then shout: "299, Doc, right?" Here is where real-object counting makes a big difference.

Our spatially disoriented kid often will have trouble setting up a math problem properly. He may do it like this (and sometimes he even manages to solve it!):

$$643$$
$$76$$
$$112$$
$$69$$

One method we have devised to help these swaggering column producers is to place templates on their page and ask them to write one number in each slot. These template devices are not only useful for math but they help him stay on the line and not lose his place when reading. We even have reproduced many stories in braille-like fashion so the kids can use their fingers to feel the words as they look at them.

In math too we try not to stray too far from the public school. Instructions for problems are written on the board, and we insist the kids read them, even if haltingly and with the aid of the teacher. We also display corresponding grade-level materials that each kid would be using in normal school. This procedure also applies, although to a much more limited extent, to the programs in social studies, science and English we give our older kids.

Again, instruction in this area is mostly aural. We feel it's ridiculous to ask a non-reader—who may be in the fourth grade chronologically but scarcely academically—to try to read a fourth-grade science text when he can fill in most of his knowledge gaps by listening and doing. Our typical kid would begin dissecting frogs, rather than memorizing body systems in a book. In social studies he will hear endless tapes and engage in plenty of discussion not just with the teacher but with the class. Our kids are great debaters. English consists of listening to stories and acting out plays, along with a lot of Q and A.

We are trying to develop our kids' perceptions and reading and math not only so we can send them back to regular school but send them back without huge gaps in their knowledge of other subjects. But getting them to this point involves a great deal more than mere academic work; it requires almost an equal amount of therapy in other areas.

Our kids, for the most part, do not come to school as middling-nice kids or bratty kids—they come as downright terrible kids. Many of them, like Tim, have been thrown out of school for being "unmanageable." They have done everything from heaving books and tearing up papers in class to kicking and hitting other kids, tossing chairs out the window, even setting fire to the teacher's desk. At home they are equally impossible—biting, shouting, turning the scissors on their baby sister. All of them, at one point or another, have been labeled "behavior problems."

They are also cunning little devils, manipulators who are constantly testing everyone around them. They quickly learn that screams, tantrums and crybaby tears will work every time to get them attention or their own way or relieve the frustration of not being able to do a certain job. They like nothing better than to see their teachers and parents throw up their hands and do the job for them. Which is usually what happens.

For these kids, it's good to be bad. If they're bad, it means they don't have to go to bed on time; it means Mommy or the teacher will pay attention (nobody notices when they're "good"); it means they don't really have to do their homework because, like Betty Wilson, their parents will do it for them—to keep them quiet and to avoid the embarrassment of having the kid turn in a sloppy paper. On the other hand, occasional bursts of harsh discipline, as practiced by Tim's father, only confuse these kids further—and they already have enough trouble making sense out of life.

Before we can even begin to help our kids learn, we have to break through some of this hostility and fear and provide the discipline and structure they so desperately need. You can't teach a kid who won't stay in his seat and pay attention. Even if he does pay attention, you *still* can't teach him if the other kids in his class are tearing the room apart. So to counteract what might be years of reinforced non-learning behavior patterns, we've designed a school environment to fit their needs.

Classes in our school are small—no more than a dozen kids, plus a teacher and an aide. We try to balance personalities: if the class has a strong, authoritarian teacher, the aide will be a motherly type who relies on love and persuasion. If one doesn't reach a child, the other often can. We try to assign our kids to a teacher who suits their personality and whom they can relate to easily. This method also insures that the kids in the class will be a relatively homogeneous bunch.

Our classrooms are kept severely simple to eliminate unnecessary distractions. No fancy posters decorate our walls; no fishbowls, collages or dioramas are on display; there's no decor at all except plain desks and chairs, a chalkboard and walls all painted the same flat color. Though many adults find themselves yawning after a few minutes in this monotonous atmosphere, it helps keep our kids' attention on the important task of learning.

Our kids require not only a simply structured outer environment but a simply structured and consistent inner environment as well. These kids have such a slim hold on the world, perceptually and emotionally, that they have difficulty coping with any kind of change. They need the security of knowing where they'll be and what they'll be doing at any given time, even to the point of refusing to go on a trip if it conflicts with their regular time for math. In school, therefore, we follow a set schedule of activities, with few, if any, disruptions or changes. We leave departmental teaching and classroom switching to the public schools; as much as possible. Our kids are confined to one room, one teacher and one group of peers.

But we also have to keep in mind their re-entry into regular school, so occasionally we shake them up a little. As an antidote to their inflexibility, we sometimes take trips and have parties; and in gym, in the pool and in perceptual training, we try to introduce a sense of abandon and a few surprises. Frankly, I get a kick out of chasing a kid around the pool with a hose or tickling him until he nearly dies laughing. But even with the fun, he knows he'll always return to the security of that humdrum schedule.

All this means placing the burden of education squarely where I believe it belongs—on the school, not the kids. This means a staff that is willing to juggle four or five different reading or math programs per day per kid, willing to make changes when one approach seems better than another, willing to be constantly flexible. This makes a tremendous demand of any teacher, but I insist it be met.

Any staff of mine has to realize that if they have twelve different kids in their class, they can have fifty different learning difficulties; and no one program, or even set of programs—and I have used as many as seventeen different teaching programs and expected my faculty to familiarize themselves with each one—is going to reach all the children. I won't allow any of my teachers to tell me he or she has found the one method; and there are as many "miracle" teaching methods for LD kids as there are "experts." Because I know there is no single approach, just fifty different approaches to fifty different problems. It's up to them, with my help, to find the combination that works best for each individual kid.

I demand that my teachers be able to relate to their kids—that they not only love them like tough, tender, consistent parents, but manage them that way. Each one of my kids cries for both. I've turned down applicants for teaching positions who have PhDs in special education because they couldn't handle questions like: "What do you do when one of your kids says, 'Fuck you, I'm not going to do this stupid homework!' "; "What if he throws a tantrum?"; "What if he starts a fight?" And I've fired teachers who didn't come through with at least some degree of consistency.

Our kids can count on us always to play by the same rules. They know they can expect reasonable demands from us, coupled with the carrot and stick of *consistent* rewards and punishments.

A kid who can't write isn't asked to make perfect letters. But if his homework calls for him to draw ten "C"'s as best he can and he arrives next morning with a blank sheet of paper, he has to make those ten "C"'s in school during a period he likes, such as swimming. If he consistently jumps out of his seat in class and walks around the room, he will have to sit in the room through gym—the period when out-of-seat behavior is permitted. Innumerable punishments are devised on the spot to fit the situation, and in almost every case they involve a loss of privilege.

Rewards for meeting our reasonable demands are equally

consistent. If a distractible, fidgety kid can't seem to sit still or keep quiet, he is asked to try not forever but for ten minutes. If he remains glued to his seat for the interminable ten minutes, he gets a piece of candy and another and another for each additional ten minutes of self-control. If a kid does his assigned work, no matter how badly, his teacher lets him know how pleased she is. If he does it well, he is applauded in class—he gets an A and a gold star and perhaps a piggyback ride.

Sounds like an embroidery on the old-fashioned Little Red Schoolhouse, doesn't it? That's what it is. Nothing is given away in school—not praise, not gym, not swimming, not even lunch. Each kid has to *earn* his way. Tough as that may sound, what these kids need more than anything else is the security of knowing where the line is drawn and what to expect if they step out of bounds. School-haters all when they first arrive, they rapidly become kids who look forward to being in school.

We make no promises, though—to the kids or their parents—about their progress. A great deal depends on how hard both sides are willing to work. Does the out-of-school environment reinforce or tear down the school's efforts? As we constantly remind parents, this is not a residential school or babysitting center. We have the kids five hours a day; they have them the other nineteen. Because of this, we have tried, with some success, to train parents how to handle their kids at home in the same structured, consistent manner they are managed in school.

Another thing we don't promise is to hike a kid's intelligence. We can't *make* geniuses; and we don't try to push kids beyond their developmental limits—they have enough problems as it is. We won't try to teach a five-year-old to read a normal seven-year-old's book. However, we will teach him to tie his shoes, something he should have learned a year ago.

What we do promise—and this is the toughest job of all—is to crack through the incredible shell of failure and self-deceit that has grown up around these kids. Taking shelter behind "I don't want to, because I can't, don't make me"—these kids want desperately to be left alone in the fantasy world where they can play Superman. Since self-deception is an emotional out resorted to even by normal adults, one can imagine how attractive it is to these confused and frustrated kids. If you can't make it in the real world, why not pretend you're the greatest and create your own world with false criteria for success? Who says you'll ever have to face that world anyway? What dummy thinks you have to be able to read, or play ball, or get along with other kids? Just stay off my back, buddy, and leave me alone.

I wish it were that easy. I wish I could buy each of them a desert island and let them make their own rules and reign as king or queen. Unfortunately, tough as they are, their image of themselves as heroes is their last pathetic defense between themselves and a world that tells them they are failures. But since at some point that world is going to come crashing in on them, I'd rather crash in first. Once through those elaborate protective walls, I hope I can buy enough time to give them a quick win—an achievement that will convince them that if they work with us they have every hope of making it in the outside world just like everyone else.

But that calls for the courage to work, to try and try again at the things they've never been able to cope with before. We demand courage in our kids. We refuse to let them give up. More than that, we demand excellence in meeting each de-

117

mand we make. Nine minutes of quiet behavior won't earn the candy if ten minutes was requested. Seven "C"'s won't answer for ten "C"'s asked. And time after time, I've found that once these kids start—I mean just start—to be successful at simple tasks that they formerly found incomprehensible, their hyperactivity and behavior begin to come under control. They're no longer lost so there's no reason to wander aimlessly around. They understand what they're supposed to do so they begin to do it successfully.

Our school provides the testing ground (frequently the battleground) for their sometimes rocky return to normality. It's the scene of much anguish, desperation and bitter frustration. Often it seems that for every step forward we take at least half a step backward, clawing and inching our way toward our goal. Occasionally we don't make it at all. But our successes far outnumber our failures, and when breakthroughs occur they are thrilling, because they've been achieved through such great effort.

I could never demand what I do of my kids if they didn't have so very much to give, and the guts to give it. We meet each other every day in direct confrontation, and we both give it all we have. My teachers and I are no miracle workers, but we must be doing something right; to date, our results have been astoundingly successful (for our return rate, see the Conclusion).

Of course, the proof of the pudding is in the day-to-day give-and-take of life in our school. To give some idea of what happens—and some of it is highly unorthodox—here is a diary of sorts covering a few months in the school I run for learning-disabled kids.

8

The first day of school went quietly, in spite of the usual foul-up with the buses, which meant that most of the kids were at least an hour late. Even without the bus problem, the first day of school is usually murder, since our kids have great difficulty adjusting to any change in environment. The whole staff was prepared for a holocaust.

But when the buses finally pulled in, the returning kids who knew the system formed a line and the new ones quickly fell in too—even Paul Mitchell, a slight, lisping, bespectacled twelve-year-old I was keeping a special eye on. Paul had not only been thrown out of public school but last year was asked to leave another special school like mine for such infractions as running out of class, refusing to show up, throwing chairs, ripping books and even biting his teacher. It was hard to imagine that this blond cherub, with no apparent spunk, could have terrorized two schools, but there was no denying the facts. Still, I felt optimistic. It seemed to me that all Paul needed to make him a winner was some hard work plus a

119

good tough fatherly-type friend to push him. I intended to play just that role myself.

I called the kids' names one by one and sent them to their rooms—all but Paul and a few other new ones—all tough kids with tough backgrounds. Small as he was, Paul looked funny next to them—they were all older and seemed to tower over him. Nevertheless, it was to Paul that I directed my remarks.

"A lot of you kids," I said, "have had histories of running out of school—right, Paul?"

Paul dipped his head slightly in a nod.

"And many of you don't like to come to school. Right, Paul?"

He shuffled his feet.

"Because you think bad things happen in school. Right, Paul?"

This time Paul looked up, inquiringly, interested for the first time. So did the other kids. I could imagine what they were thinking—about the hated teachers who made them do the hated things they couldn't do day after day after day. The mixed-up little kids who had grown up into "I can't, I don't want to, don't make me" teenagers.

"Well, this school is different," I said. "You can't run away from this school because we won't let you. There's no way out—you have to work. And in this school good things are going to happen for you—if you work. It's up to you. You're going to work and we're going to help. But you're the only ones who can make a difference."

After this little pep talk, Coach Cohen sent Paul and his group to their rooms. They filed in quietly and things went like a dream all day. I couldn't believe it. There wasn't even one minor incident. It boded well for the school, but before the day was over I began to wonder if all I'd have to do that year would be sit in my office and shuffle papers. What a bore!

What a laugh!

The next day Audrey, one of my teachers, came to tell me that nine-year-old Kevin Chin had been crying off and on during the morning, not really yowling, just whimpering and sniffling. This disturbed us. Even though he was introverted and had perceptual handicaps that seriously interfered with his reading and slowed his development so that he tested more than two years below his age, Kevin had never before shown any signs of major emotional stress. I sat down and talked with him quietly, first in class and then over a private lunch in my office. I asked if he was sorry the summer was over, if he liked his teacher, if he missed some of the kids in his old class. We talked about his summer and his brand new books and I told him how pleased I was to have him back. I never did find out from him why he was crying, but in a day or two it gradually petered out. He probably was just having difficulty readjusting and needed a little quiet talking to feel more at home.

I went on my rounds, and when I reached Carl Janicki's class, I found that Paul Mitchell was already beginning to show his true colors.

"Dr. Cohen, we have a problem," said Carl, loud enough for all the kids to hear and thus bring peer pressure to bear. "Paul refuses to work. He won't even open his book."

The other kids looked up from their work (most of them are so used to my presence in class they rarely pay any attention to me) and glanced disapprovingly at Paul. Instead of the hoped-for compliance, however, Paul bolted from his seat and made for the door, fortunately brushing right by me. I grabbed him by the seat of his pants and held him struggling, which wasn't much of a job considering his small size.

"Where do you think you're going?" I asked.

"I'm leaving here," Paul snapped back, his face flushed, "and you can't stop me."

"What do you mean I can't stop you, little Paul?" I asked. "I already have."

Paul stopped his feeble struggling. I lifted him high and plunked him back in his seat.

"OK, now, why are you so angry? Why won't you do any work for Mr. Janicki? Why are you so special you feel you can leave? You haven't told anyone, you know."

"I don't have to tell you anything," Paul said.

"Yes, you do," I said. "That's why you're here and that's why we're here."

Paul considered. "I had this book before," he said finally. And then: "I know everything in it. I'm not going to repeat it."

I knew Paul couldn't read the book, at least not well, even though it was only on a second-grade level. He was too far behind. Normally we don't let kids dictate their curriculum, but if Paul's story was true there was no need to bore him with the same material again. Besides, here was a chance to show him that we were friends, on his side, and that the contractual relationship we so emphasize—you do for me and we'll do for you—really existed.

"Fine," I said, "you don't have to repeat anything you've done before. Let me check. If you had this one before, we'll give you a new book."

I went downstairs and went through his records and, sure enough, Paul had had the book last year. I felt I had to do something dramatic to impress him not only with the fact that we were with him but that we meant business.

Arriving back in class, I picked up the book on Paul's desk and tore it up. "Here's a new book," I said, handing him another, while he and the class sat shocked. "Now show me that you can read it." Then I left.

Carl later reported that for the rest of the hour, Paul worked in his new reader, smiling to himself all the while. Apparently he had decided we could be friends—friends on a tightrope but still connecting. After school and before the buses arrived, Paul popped into my office for a chat—nothing involving the incident in class, just some ramblings about his summer activities, but still the beginning to a healthy relationship. Or so it seemed at the time. Who would have dreamed that Paul Mitchell, who looked like an easy win, would end up the least successful of all my kids—one on whom the jury is still out?

After the kids were safely put on their correct buses, and school was over, Mrs. Cowley brought in her seven-year-old daughter Kathy for her first testing session to determine whether we would take her. Mrs. Cowley was understandably nervous. Kathy had been forced to leave public school, just as she had the private school where she had lasted less than a year when they became totally frustrated by all attempts to teach her. She had been diagnosed mbd by her neurologist and a noted child center in the city had found her to be developmentally immature and aphasic—an injury to her brain centers had caused a loss in her powers of written and oral expression, as well as a similar loss of comprehension of written and spoken language. She displayed highly frustrated behavior—not overtly, by lashing out (Kathy was

123

an unusually quiet child) but, even worse, inwardly. She would go rigid or cry at the least setback and a glaze would come over her eyes as soon as the message became too difficult to comprehend. Which could mean with almost everything. Her mother had every right to feel that Kathy might seem hopeless to us.

I asked Mrs. Cowley about the reports, while Kathy sat by quietly, completely tuned out.

"Does she read at all?" I asked.

"Yes," said Mrs. Cowley, "a little. She knows some words. She can recognize them and pick them out. She knows her name and can write it. But she reverses almost everything. She mirror writes."

"Kathy," I said, handing her a piece of paper. "Why don't you write your name for me here, so I'll have it."

Kathy wrote her name perfectly from left to right, ending in the middle of the page. I looked at Mrs. Cowley. There was nothing wrong; the letters were formed perfectly.

"But wait," she said. "Ask her to write her name on the righthand side of the paper."

Kathy immediately complied, carefully mirror-writing it from right to left, totally reversing the letters.

"That's what she does all the time," said Mrs. Cowley miserably. "At the other school, they just gave up and told her to write where she felt comfortable on a page. She wrote all her words on the left side of the page, but if she had to copy more than one or two in order, she'd get them all mixed up."

I took Kathy into another room for gross motor tests.

"Lie down on the floormat, Kathy''' I said. "We're going to play a game called Angels in the Snow."

Kay lay down obediently as I had instructed.

"OK." I said. "Move your right arm up."

Kathy moved her left arm up.

I tapped her right arm. "No, this one, Kathy. Your right arm."

Kathy moved her right leg.

Without further comment, I tapped each leg and arm in turn and asked her to move them. Sometimes, she'd get it right, but only by dumb luck. I'd never seen anything like it. Many directionally disoriented kids can't translate the verbal instruction of left and right without physical tap reinforcement, many get confused if you tap more than one limb at a time—particularly if they're on opposite sides or diagonal— but I'd never before encountered a child who couldn't correctly translate verbal instruction and a tap applied to just one body part.

Maybe she had tactile perceptual problems.

"Kathy, can you feel me tapping you?" I asked.

"Sure," she said.

"Point to where I'm touching you," I said.

Kathy pointed correctly.

Maybe she was playing games, though I didn't think so. But I had to find out. "Kathy," I said, sharply. "The object of this game is for you to move your right arm when I ask you to and tap it. OK?"

Kathy looked at me mutely. I tapped her right arm and asked her to move it. She moved her left arm.

"That's not the right one, Kathy," I said, softly. "Do you know it's not the right one?"

Tears started out of Kathy's eyes. There were no games being played here. I led a more and more rigid and occasionally tearful Kathy through other tests: on the chalkboard (where she couldn't even draw a circle with one hand while I helped her), on the circus puzzle (where she twisted and rotated pieces, trying to fit large ones into small holes, and pressed down so hard that the whole puzzle snapped out from under her hand into my lap), to the walking rail (which she couldn't even stand on), to the balance board (which clunked down in a locked-in forward position). There was no question that this was the most perceptually, directionally disoriented little girl I'd ever seen. Not only didn't she know her left from her right, she couldn't judge up from down, let alone near from far. Her visual judgments were almost non-existent, she did just about everything by feel. She couldn't get anything in sequence. She not only had one of the most pronounced mid-line jumps while tracking from left to right and back again, but also her eyes took on a jerky staircase motion when tracking up and down. She was totally disorganized. How she'd learned to do anything in school, including writing her name, was more than I could comprehend. Each letter, each word, must have been slowly learned and remembered by habit. In fact, it was her habits—her unconscious habit of writing properly on one side of the page and mirror-writing on the other—that we finally realized we had to break. Two years later we were still working on them, although by then we were successful about seventy percent of the time.

I'd noticed one other thing about Kathy in that first meeting that I thought might provide the key to pulling her through completely. No matter how rigid or tearful she would become, no matter how pronounced her fear of failure or her awareness that she had not carried out a task—and you couldn't fool her by saying, "That's all right, we'll do it again tomorrow"; she knew she'd done it wrong because she had to do it over—she wouldn't give up. Even if she tuned out as she saw failure coming, even if she cried, she would always try and try again if only you so much as asked her. With just a little urging, she took every one of my tests, even though she knew she was failing each one miserably and hated every minute of the failure. She was afraid, she couldn't do it, but she would learn; she would do it, she would try, she would fight. A little girl with true grit.

It was this more than anything that made me and the staff accept the challenge of Kathy, even though to this day neither her neurologist nor I has a clear idea of how she got this way or exactly how to handle the problem. It was a case of a student turning on the staff, rather than the other way around.

I led Kathy back to Mrs. Cowley.

"I'm really interested," I said. "We'd like to have Kathy in school. I must tell you, though, that it may take a long time and we may not be successful. She tests some three years younger than her age and she has a great many problems, some of which we may not be able to solve. But we'd like to have her."

"You would?" Mrs. Cowley said, almost shocked. Then, more cautiously, realizing the possibility of another school bouncing her daughter: "But would you be able to keep her?"

"I'm sure we could," I said. "And I really do want her. I think working with her would be challenging." Just how challenging I had yet to find out.

The next morning Jane, my first-grade teacher, came to me about another little one, Jimmy Blake, a new six-year-old black kid and an orphan in an agency home. Jimmy had not only been doing everything he could to get Jane's attention—typical behavior with an mbd kid—but he kept crying and whining continually.

I took Jimmy for one of my walks through all the "secret" rooms in and around school. We "found" the boiler room. We went under the pool and behind the gym and through the kitchen—where we snitched a few goodies. After a few piggy-back rides up and down the stairs, I took Jimmy into my office and discovered he was a ticklish little son of a gun. He was laughing his head off by the time I got him back to class a half hour later. I promised we would take more walks in the next few days.

Friday morning I sat in my office with six-year-old Ellen Carson screaming through all ten fingers stuffed in her mouth. Even that hadn't seemed to stop her tantrum this time.

Ellen's outrageous behavior was no news to me. I had first encountered it a year ago, when her doctor sent her to me hoping I could correct her severe strabismus. Ellen seemed nervous, but I had been prepared for that. Her mother had briefed me on her intense fear of doctors—and warned me not to wear a white coat. But as I examined Ellen I began to feel there was more here than a common childhood fear of doctors or an inward-turning eye, which is often found in innately hyperactive children who tend to overconverge and overfocus their eyes.

Ellen flitted all around the office. I had to physically chase her before I could examine the eye and even then she wouldn't sit still. She salivated excessively, apparently without control. She got as far as the entrance to my training room—an innocent-looking area with some school desks and chairs, chalkboards, pegboards and viewer-training machines—and, planting her feet on the floor, screamed: "*I'm not* going in there!"

Her mother giggled nervously. "What should we do?"

I slung the still screaming girl over my hip and carried her into the training room. There I sat down and placed her firmly on my lap and insisted she look at me. Ellen went right into her spiel, yelling at the staccato pace of a machine gun: "I want my Mommy. I want my Daddy. I have to leave. I have to go to nursery school. I love you. You don't love me. I have to go to the bathroom. Where's my Mommy? I have to go to nursery school. I want to go home. You don't love me. I love you. I have to leave." And so it went for a full hour, that session and the next and the next. Ellen rattling on without looking at me, while I insisted that she couldn't leave until she did look at me—something hyperactive kids find extremely difficult to do but which I find is prerequisite to reaching them.

I also had a heart-to-heart talk with Ellen's parents about her behavior. Everything they told me confirmed my suspicions. For at least two years Ellen's parents had not left the house. They hadn't wanted to expose a sitter to the screams and tantrums, and they were afraid Ellen might actually damage their home. Whenever Ellen wanted anything, she would throw another tantrum; her mother generally gave in, if only to quiet her down. Her father—who was in therapy—would simply walk out of the house, leaving his daughter to rule the roost.

I gave Ellen a perceptual evaluation, and my tests showed that she was operating at a three-year-old level, two years below her actual age. A neurological and psychiatric examination in a clinic revealed that Ellen was mbd, hyperactive,

129

and severely emotionally disturbed, and Ritalin was prescribed. Her first day on Ritalin, Ellen hallucinated, not an uncommon reaction to this powerful drug but a terrifying experience for her parents. The clinic switched her to a small dosage of another drug, which seemed to help calm her down and increased her markedly short attention span.

Meanwhile the Carsons had enrolled Ellen at our school and I was making progress with her, both there and at my office, in a basic structuring, control and perceptual training program.

In my office I started Ellen on basic sequential commands—sit down, stand up, turn around, sit down, be quiet—adding things like hop, jump and a special one just for her: put your fingers in your mouth. I discovered this not only temporarily stopped the salivating, which was most pronounced while she was talking, but also the incessant talking. These commands were intended not only to increase her body organization and help her control herself, but to teach her to listen and learn to follow instructions—a basic problem for many innately hyperactive children. I refused to take No for an answer or listen to any of her staccato string of excuses. The minute they started, Ellen was told: Put your fingers in your mouth and shut it.

Ellen got the same training at school—with matching and other exercises added—all over her strenuous objections. She screamed from the moment she got on the bus to the moment she got to school.

"I love you," she would say, the moment she saw me, trying to get me to make a deal. I made none.

"Well, Ellen," I would say. "I *don't* love you. How can I love a little girl who leaves her house looking neat and pretty and screams all the way to school so that when she gets here she's all messed up? I can't love a little girl like that." Gradually, the screaming stopped.

Taking our lead from that success, we were able to use the reward-punishment system to teach Ellen some pretty good inner controls. During her first year with us, she really learned to behave. Yet this term she had come back to school as a real little pest, talking out of turn, getting out of her seat, bothering the other kids in class with pokes and nudges, running up to her teacher and clawing her, disobeying in every way she could. Whenever she didn't get her way, she would start to scream bloody murder.

Since she seemed to be following instructions well everywhere but in class—and with her mother—we decided this new disobedience was a deliberate act, calculated to win more attention from her teacher, Esther Simms. As Audrey and I had with Joey Rich, Esther and I decided the best way to deal with Ellen was for me to play the villain. I sat in the back of the classroom, and the moment Ellen started her screaming act for that day I took her to my office and stuck her under the desk. "You're going to have to stay there," I said, "until you show me you can be a good girl."

Ellen turned on the scream again. "I want to go to Mrs. Simms!"

The good girl/bad girl concept wasn't getting through. I needed something more material and concrete to make this work. "Put your finger in your mouth," I ordered.

Surprised, Ellen interrupted her yelling long enough to obey, but went right on bellowing as if nothing had happened. "Mrs. Simms! Mrs. Simms, I wanna go!" she belted out, somewhat muffled by the finger.

"Put another finger in," I said. Ellen did and went on screaming. One by one, I had her put three, four, five—until, incredibly, she had managed to put all ten fingers in her mouth. But now everything she said was completely unintelligible—something even she realized—but still she went on screaming. Even with that living gag, the point still wasn't being made.

I left the office, telling Ellen I wasn't coming back until she stopped. "Scream all you like," I said. "You won't be bothering anybody." The minute I left she became quiet. I waited and then opened the door: she started to scream again. We went through this for about twenty minutes, with me walking in and saying, "Oops, sorry to disturb you, you're still crying," and walking out again. Finally Ellen's screaming reduced itself to a thin whine. As she quieted, I let her take one finger out of her mouth after another, reminding her why they were there—to prevent her from disturbing others with her yells. When she started up again briefly, I had her start putting them all back in. Finally she turned completely silent, both hands in her lap.

"Was it fun sitting there screaming?" I now asked.

"No," Ellen said, then quickly added, "I'll be a good girl."

"What does being a 'good girl' mean, Ellen? Does it mean keeping quiet when Mrs. Simms asks you and sitting in your seat when she asks you and doing everything she tells you?"

"Yes," said Ellen.

"Does it mean you don't scream?" I pressed.

"Yes," Ellen said again.

"What's going to happen if you're a bad girl and you scream?"

"Fingers in mouth," said Ellen.

"Can you do all those things? Can you be a good girl?"

"Yes," said Ellen, jumping up and running to the door.

"Wait," I said. "I want you to remember that if you're not a good girl, that if you aren't quiet and do all the things that Mrs. Simms says, I'm going to come and get you again. And I'm going to make you put all your fingers in your mouth. Do you understand?"

"Yes," again and disappeared.

Of course, that wasn't the end of Ellen's screaming or the finger treatment but we finally got her back in control before she wore out both hands.

Friday noon, Bozo, the sad-faced clown, made his first appearance in the school lunchroom, carrying a huge shopping bag. As he walked in, half-blind and stumbling over his big floppy shoes, a hush fell over the kids. They were unsure how to handle this situation. The clown hobbled over to eight-year-old Mary Ann Williams. He took a lollipop out of his bag and dangled it in Mary Ann's face. Mary Ann grabbed and the clown pulled it out of reach. He did the same thing again and finally let Mary Ann have the lollipop, but in return he grabbed her tunafish sandwich and put it in his bag. Mary Ann started screaming for her sandwich. The clown pantomimed that this was a trade, that if she wanted her sandwich she'd have to give back the lollipop. No deal.

By now, kids all over the lunchroom were shouting, "Bozo, come here." We had thought of having a Name the Clown contest, but apparently the kids had already taken care of that. "We want Bozo." "We want lollipops." Bozo shuffled over to some of them with Mary Ann tagging behind, tugging at him and screaming for her sandwich. Bozo gave it back and then played a similar trick on other kids. Each kid got a lollipop while Bozo drank their milk or their juice or stole their dessert. The kids were screaming and laughing.

133

Then Bozo took handfuls of candy and M&Ms and threw them all over the lunchroom tables. Kids scrambled and screamed in pure, joyous havoc. Bozo rubbed heads and tickled and poked and finally he patted chubby Joey Rich's stomach.

"That's Dr. Cohen, that's Dr. Cohen," Joey shouted. "Dr. Cohen's the only one who rubs my stomach," which was true. I did it whenever I teased him about his weight. Fortunately, almost no one heard in the melee and I don't think Joey himself was totally convinced. Bozo followed the kids upstairs after lunch and ran around, giving out Tootsie Rolls and creating even more pandemonium. After I left, the teachers would have to spend some time quieting their revved-up kids, but that was part of the point—teaching the kids that when the fun is over, you calm yourself down and schoolwork resumes as usual. I was glad that Bozo had been a hit. The clown was an idea Lloyd Jensen, the administrator, and I had hatched that summer. To teach self-control to our distractible and often disruptive kids we would reward them with M&Ms for each ten minutes of proper behavior, extending the time as the year went on. The M&Ms were the kids' immediate reinforcement, and now we were introducing Bozo as their ultimate, end-of-the-week reward. The idea was to motivate them to work like demons all week, knowing that on Friday they would get to break loose for an hour or so with Bozo.

Lloyd and I alternated in the role, masking our identities so the kids would believe Bozo was a real clown. The Bozo who appeared that first day really was blind, since I'd peeled off my glasses along with my ring and other identifying objects.

When we had purchased the clown suit, neither Lloyd nor

I had been quite sure that this kind of character would really make it with the kids. Even though this group were all eleven and under, they were pretty sophisticated. Thankfully, it had. Bozo-Jensen was just as effective as a goofy, floppy, smiling clown the next Friday as had been Bozo-Cohen, the sad, silent clown. The new system had gotten off to a flying start. It was also a real gas, Lloyd and I discovered, just being a clown.

Next day, Eddie Daniel's teacher came roaring into my office. "I want Eddie on an increased dosage of Ritalin," she insisted. "Anything to quiet him down."

Five-year-old Eddie Daniel was a tiny black kid who, like Jimmy Blake, was an orphan recently placed in a foster home. He was also one of the most hyperactive kids any of us had ever seen. It was as if he had a coiled-up spring in his bottom. The minute it hit his seat he popped right up again. He went to the teacher's desk and pulled out the drawer. He went to the door, opened it and looked down the hall. He closed it, bounced to the sink and turned on the water. Ordered back to his seat—pow! He was out of it again to fish a piece of paper from the wastebasket, pull a toy out of the closet or grab some erasers and pound them on the blackboard. There was nothing he wasn't into his first week in school.

To most educators and many doctors dealing with this type of hyperactive kid and obvious "behavior problem," his teacher's request for increased dosage of Ritalin would seem perfectly normal. But I distrust using drugs, preferring to teach the kids inner controls to straighten out their perceptions and make sense of their world. Along with many others, I believe this can reduce their hyperactivity—and it lasts a lot longer than drugs.

Besides, Eddie's teacher was something of a tyrant—one of the few teachers I've ever had to fire. She kept making unreasonable demands on her kids, insisting they behave like robots. Worst of all, she hadn't done her homework. She hadn't read any of her kids' histories or submitted a report—something I require each of my teachers to do by the end of second week of school.

"Drugs are for his doctor to decide," I said. "But let's not even talk about drugs until I read your report. Just because you can't contain him doesn't mean he needs more Ritalin."

The disgruntled teacher returned to class. I looked up Eddie's report from the agency, but found almost nothing in his scanty medical and psychological records. His IQ was a little over 100 and he showed signs of potential brain dysfunction. Otherwise he was a healthy kid.

I went down to the pool that afternoon and watched Eddie at his first swimming lesson. He ran around the pool. He got in the water. He got out of the water. He kicked and splashed and burbled and screamed and yelled. He had a hell of a time.

I watched Eddie in class. Anything new he went after with the speed of light. Put a puzzle or a pegboard in front of him and he was into it at once. Play a tape or a film and he'd go wild. What's more, if he liked what he saw or heard, he'd stay with it, unlike most mbd kids with hyperactive tendencies who are generally so distractible they flit from one thing to the next without really taking anything in.

When he won his first M&M—for staying in his seat five whole minutes—Eddie glowed. His second kept him in his seat a full fifteen minutes. I couldn't stop loving this kid. I began to have a hunch about the cause of his problem. A day or so later, I went in with a lollipop. I dangled it in front of him and he grabbed. He stuffed it in his mouth with both hands.

"Do you know what this is?" I asked.

"Canny," he said, somehow smiling and talking and slurping the lollipop around in his mouth all at the same time.

"Have you ever seen one before?"

"No."

Right then I began to hope my hunch was right.

Next I dropped by Marion's room. I had barely stepped inside when eight-year-old Danny Gordon leaped to his feet and threw me out. "Get out of here!" he yelled. "This is my class and you don't belong here. You're not the teacher. *She's* the teacher," he said, pointing at Marion.

I hadn't had time to fully evaluate Danny, but there was no doubt that he had quickly drawn some very correct conclusions. "All right, Mr. Gordon," I said, "you're right," and left. It made you wonder what a kid like this was doing in our school in the first place. Danny had beautiful verbal abilities. When he spoke, no phrase was misplaced or verb omitted, and his enunciation would have made a speech teacher proud. He showed aptitude in math well beyond his age, and his excellent mechanical abilities held up even under emotional strain—he would fix his younger sister's toys even though he was extremely jealous of her. His motor abilities were fine, as was his visual perceptual accuracy. Danny was also a walking storehouse of knowledge. When Marion told the class the earth was round, she was shocked to hear Danny call out: "The earth," he said fiercely, "is *not* round. It is an oblong spheroid, and if you don't know that, you shouldn't be teaching the lesson!" Because he was such a brain, the kids had elected him class president—but they hated him nevertheless, and immediately nicknamed him "The Iceman" because he never smiled. Nothing got through his defenses, nothing made him show sadness, nothing made him fight back, no matter how outrageous the provocation. The wall around him was as solid as his mind was meticulous. Later on I would pick up this clue to Danny's real problem, but as of now the reason for this kid's presence in school seemed a real mystery.

The next day I had my first serious confrontation. Karin Bergstrom came to see me about Elliott Reimer, a wiry, blond eleven-year-old who was diagnosed mbd and hyperactive and so perceptually disoriented he could hardly make sense. Elliott was also emotionally disturbed—though his mother insisted nothing was wrong and had pulled him out of therapy three years before—and extremely hostile. He would caption his drawings of people with poorly lettered words reading "I'm going to kill you" or "I'm going to hang you." Elliott had never acted out his hostility in school before, restricting it to his drawings. But this year he was in a somewhat larger class, which meant he was getting a little less attention, and he had launched a program of forced belching. Every effort by Karin to get him to stop resulted in replies like "fuck off" or "leave me alone, you bitch."

I went into the room and sat quietly behind Elliott, who was seated to one side of the rest of the class. Within minutes he started drawing in great gulps of air and belching them out, one after the other. Then he stood up and started fake gagging as if he was going to throw up. I decided to act fast—and forcefully—so he'd learn his lesson then and there. At the next phony gagging spell, I grabbed his nose with my fingers and he gagged for real. He stopped abruptly.

138

The rest of the class seemingly paid no attention during the exchange that followed:

"Why were you belching?" I asked.

"Because I felt like it," Elliott answered belligerently. "It felt good."

"No, Elliott," I said. "You didn't do it because it felt good. You did it because you wanted Mrs. Bergstrom's attention, and you didn't think you could get it by working. From now on the only person whose attention you're going to get if you belch is mine, and it's going to be the same way as now. Is that clear?"

"Yes," said Elliott.

"And if you work and try working, then Mrs. Bergstrom will pay as much attention to you as she can. Do you understand?"

Elliott nodded.

I started to leave, feeling he had had enough. Suddenly the class woke up. The kids, evidently feeling Elliott hadn't fully got what was coming to him, called for one of our kangaroo courts. This is a device that not only allows classes to air their pent-up feelings but enables the accused to see himself as his peers see him. Punishments run the gamut of suspension from school for fifteen minutes, a half hour or even a day, to skipping lunch. And the vote can go either way. One teacher was suspended for a full half-hour while her aide took over the class.

This time I objected. "Elliott has already been punished."

Protests from all over. The kids pointed out that belching wasn't Elliott's only disturbance. One kid said he had kicked him, another said he had pushed him, another complained that he was taking their pencils and papers. Karin agreed, explaining that was why Elliott was seated apart from the rest of the class. In the face of such logic, I could do nothing but let the class hold their court. Elliott made no objection. The vote was nine to two to suspend Elliott from school.

"How long should we suspend him?" I asked. "Should we send him home? Should we call in Elliott's parents and talk to them about him?"

Kid-to-kid loyalty prevailed and the kids agreed, no, that would be too much. Elliott's parents didn't really need to know about his misbehavior. They took another vote and this time unanimously agreed that Elliott would be suspended from gym and swimming for a full week, one of the harshest punishments ever made. Both the school and Elliott complied.

I sat down with Kathy Cowley, our favorite problem child, for a personal "What do I like?" session. This was less for her benefit than for mine—to try to help me understand her.

From the beginning it had been obvious she didn't like herself much. Little things, such as the way she would constantly ask, "Am I smart?" or say, "I can't," "Don't know how," even while her basic determination saw to it that she attempted some task. But now, in this session, she showed she had other visions of herself propping up what little pride she had left.

"What do you like to do?" I asked.

"Me like to jump rope," she answered in her baby syntax. "It fun." Kathy couldn't even jump, let alone jump a rope.

"What else?" I asked.

"Swim," she answered. "Water is nice. Floating, it fun. Diving." Kathy didn't know how to swim either. When she told me she liked to read, which she could barely do at a pre-primer level, I asked her what stories she liked.

"Cinderella," she said. "My favorite. Read it every night. At bed."

It didn't take much to figure out that Kathy's mother or father read her the story, but I was interested in finding out something else. How well did she remember this story she had obviously heard many times?

Here was Kathy's version: the story began with Cinderella sweeping out the kitchen with her broom, happy that she had married the prince; next the two ugly stepsisters went to the ball and lost all their shoes; Cinderella's slipper came home in a pumpkin and she lost it before she ever got to the ball; and the prince and Cinderella were married, maybe there or in the pumpkin or back in the kitchen. Seven-year-old Kathy's memory for events and their order and logic was about as discombobulated as that of a three-year-old.

Time for Kathy was out of order—she was always coming to school yesterday—in fact, it really didn't exist.

"How long it to lunch?" asked Kathy at the end of our talk.

"About two hours," I replied.

"Then I go lunch now, Doc, right?"

"No, Kathy," I said gently, "two hours from now." How were we going to get into this little girl's mixed-up head some organization, some direction, some basic perception of time, of what was up and what was down, left and right, where things were, and in what order? And at the same time give her gritty little character the confidence she so needed? She had nothing straight and she couldn't do much of anything. She couldn't read. She had completely skewed perceptions. She didn't have the gross motor skills necessary to even begin to walk a rail, try to crawl, try to swim or even put a circle on the chalkboard. About all she *could* do was write her name and a few other words without reversing on the lefthand side of the page only, and pick out a few other words in a book.

I played with Jimmy Blake for ten minutes in my office. He seemed much happier. Then I caught up with my perceptual training class. Gayle, the kindergarten aide who covered for me when I couldn't be there, had taken a class of nine-, ten- and eleven-year-olds through their perceptual exercises and now had launched into one of our cognitive exercises, a question and answer period on "Who am I?" or "What makes me me?" Other exercises in this vein that run throughout the year include "What don't I like about my teacher? (parents, class, Dr. Cohen)," "What do I like about my teacher? (parents, class, Dr. Cohen)," "If I were Dr. Cohen, how would I run the school?" These not only give us a better insight into the kids' minds but help the kids find their self-image and then define it and their roles. "Who am I?" is the most basic, since most of our kids are wandering around with no conception of this at all.

"What makes you you?" Gayle started.

The class of four looked blank.

"Come on," she asked again. "What makes each of you special? What makes each of you different from any other you?"

Giggles. "I don't know," "I don't know," each one said. To themselves, the kids were complete nonentities. Finally, eleven-year-old David Parish took a stab.

"My name?" he said, questioning. The others quickly agreed: "His name."

"OK, David," said Gayle, "your name is David. But there are lots of boys named David. I know a little three-month-old baby named David. How do you know when you get up in the morning that it's the right David in your bed?''

"I don't know," he mumbled almost vacantly. "I know my bed."

"Does your bed make you you?" Gayle asked. "Come now, your bed doesn't make you special. Everybody has a bed. What makes you a special, different you?"

"Me," David said. The others chimed in: "Me," "Me," "Me."

"Now everybody is a me. I'm a me, you're a me. What makes you, Curtis Ziegler," Gayle asked, turning to another child, "different from all the other Curtises in the world?"

"My name," said Curt. "My mother."

"Does your mother make you you?" Gayle pushed on. "Everyone has a mother. Your mother doesn't make you you. What makes you different, other than your name?"

"A big mouth," I catcalled from the back. Curt talked out of turn all the time.

Curt said, "Naw." The kids giggled and then came to his rescue. They all insisted they had big mouths too.

"Sharon," asked Gayle, "what makes you you? Other than your name? There are lots of Sharons in the world." Sharon looked incredulous. "If someone stole your name," said Gayle, "and went around pretending to be Sharon Kealy, how would I know it wasn't you? How would I know the real Sharon Kealy from the phoney Sharon Kealy?"

Sharon appeared stumped. So did the rest of the class. Then they started whispering, "I know, I know." "She has eyes," said one. "Noses, mouths, hair," "She's bad in class," came out in a jumble. They were getting close but still lost in general characteristics.

"Everyone here has eyes and noses and hair," Gayle said,

143

"and you're all bad in class sometimes. Sharon, what makes you different from the other three at the table? How would I know you from a person pretending to be you?"

Sharon was beginning to break through and so was the rest of the class but only with the cues.

"I'm shy," she said.

"Good," said Gayle. "That's one thing that makes you just a little different. Is there anything else?"

"My legs," Sharon replied.

Though there was nothing particularly distinguishing about Sharon's legs, Gayle accepted this because she had included the key word "my."

"You have special legs," Gayle said. "OK, anything else that makes you different from everyone else here?"

"We all have different faces," said Curt. Now the sun had broken through the clouds. From there on, Gayle went through each of their physical characteristics with them, getting them to define as best they could each one—blue eyes, brown hair, the way they walked, etc.—and to a limited extent their personality attributes. As usual, the kids had difficulty describing each of their physical characteristics; they acted as though they had never thought of them before. And yet each of them had gone through the same exercise several times the year before. Even when found, these kids had trouble hanging on to the simplest parts of their identities.

Jimmy Blake came to my office to play. His fears and whining were all but gone, Jane reported, so this would probably be the last visit for a while. He was sitting on my lap giggling when all of a sudden he put his arms around me and started kissing and hugging me.

"I love you," he said, "you're my daddy."

144

Good lord, I thought. This kid, who is mbd and already considered emotionally disturbed with little or no idea of himself or his environment, doesn't need to get things even more mixed up. Jimmy didn't even have a father. He came from a foster home.

"I love you, too, Jimmy, very much," I said, "but I'm not your father. I can't be your father."

"You're my father," Jimmy insisted, hugging me even tighter.

"But I can't be," I said. "I don't live with you. I live in my house with my own children. If I were your father, I'd live with you. I'd be able to tuck you in at night and pat your head."

"Oh, nice, nice," Jimmy said. "I like that."

". . . and I'd eat supper with you. I'd work and come home and be with you. But I don't."

"You're my daddy," said Jimmy staunchly, hugging me again. "Fathers never live in houses anyway." Out of the mouths of babes!

"Look at my skin and look at yours, Jimmy," I said. "You're a little black boy and I'm a white man. If I were your father, I'd be black, but I'm not so I'm not your father."

Jimmy didn't buy that at all and went on calling me Daddy and hugging and kissing me. I tried several other explanations and finally, in desperation, I pointed out that I wore glasses and he did not—a complete irrelevancy but something that Jimmy seemed to buy, at least in part.

"But you can be my father in school," he said.

I agreed, and took Jimmy back to class. I think the kid still really thinks that I'm his father. Two weeks later, I examined Jimmy's eyes and, as luck would have it, found he needed glasses. I got him frames as different from mine as I could find!

Danny Gordon, our intellectual whiz kid, was making all the right connections academically, all right—except one. He couldn't read beyond a pre-primer level. Moreover, it was obvious he'd gotten that far mainly through memory. His great storehouse of knowledge that had awed his classmates and buffaloed his teacher evidently had been attained through observation and listening to spoken material. His parents had inadvertently obliged, too, by supplying him with all the knowledge and experience he could absorb. But not from books—Danny couldn't get to first base with written symbols. In fact, for a while I feared we might have that toughest of all cases on our hands, at least so far as cure is concerned: a true dyslexic.

We had started Danny on the alphabet, using all the flash cards and other methods that have been tried—often successfully, sometimes not—to drive through the faulty connections of a dyslexic brain. We couldn't do much else, since the alphabet was one of the few written tasks Danny could perform pretty well, and he refused to try anything he didn't think he could do. This was one of the first symptoms of what we later discovered to be his major problem: he couldn't stand to make mistakes. But it quickly turned out that Danny's idea of a "mistake" was the slightest deviation from a completely flawless performance.

He wasn't a perfectionist; he was a perfectionist's perfectionist. God forbid an "A" should tilt slightly off center or one leg hang below the other—he would insist on making "A"'s until they looked like those printed on this page. Many of our kids perseverate, but Danny's perseveration seemed to have an aim: absolute perfection.

We decided that this compulsion to be perfect, to be constantly right, may have aggravated his apparent dyslexia. Because he had trouble making out letters and words, because he couldn't read right by *his* standards—i.e., flawlessly, instead of well behind his class—he had blocked those tasks out. That gave us an idea. Why not *use* this perfectionist drive; why not start him off on the alphabet, and let him make "A" after "A" after "A" to his satisfaction, and then "B" after "B," and hope that this repetition would finally get the configurations through the fuzzy connections?

Marion and I decided to make our proposal to Danny together.

"Good morning, Mr. Gordon," I began. "I have a proposition for you—how would you like to be your own teacher?"

Danny looked at me suspiciously. Was I finally coming to share his conviction that no one—but *no one*—was smarter than Daniel Gordon?

I explained that we were going to give his exceptional concentration and determination full rein, and that in such a setup a teacher would be not only superfluous but distracting.

Danny looked pleased, so we walked over to the windows and showed him the "office" we had arranged for him. It was a learning carrel—a three-sided cardboard pen I use not for punishment but as a kind of isolation booth for particularly distractible kids. With Danny's help we filled it with all the books and materials he would need, and Marion set him to work on phonics.

When I returned hours later, just before the final bell,

Danny was hard at work inside his "office," still going over the same material. I would never demand from any kid the perfection that Danny demanded of himself, and any other kid but Danny would have gagged on the repetition. But Danny *wasn't* like any other kid. Maybe our new plan would work.

That afternoon Mrs. Hammack called about Bobby's therapist. A year ago Bobby had been so hyperactive and emotionally disturbed that his therapist, a friend of mine, had given up on out-patient treatment and recommended either hospitalization or a special school. Bobby's parents had chosen the latter alternative and enrolled him with us. After a year in our program he was well enough to benefit from therapy, and his doctor had happily taken him back. Just yesterday I had sent him off to his first appointment, and now Mrs. Hammack was calling to tell me it had been disastrous—not for Bobby, but for the therapist. During the visit Bobby had to go to the bathroom, and afterward flushed down a large wad of toilet paper. The john had overflowed and for the remainder of the hour Mrs. Hammack, sitting outside and growing increasingly upset, had listened to the psychologist, an old friend of mine, bawl her son out just like any parent. "Why did you do that?" he raged at Bobby. "Why did you make a mess of my bathroom? Why?" Bobby just laughed and laughed. Mrs. Hammack wanted to know if I thought Neil was the right therapist for Bobby.

"The kid's hostile," said Neil, hotly defending himself when I asked him about the incident. "He's taking out his aggressions on me." So I explained what Mrs. Hammack had told me: that rather than get anything else on his hands, Bobby always used a huge wad of paper which went down

148

easily in his apartment toilet. If anything was weak that day, it was Neil's john, not Bobby's head.

"Oh my God!" said Neil. "What do I do?"

"I don't know, baby," I said, "but you dropped the ball. You'll have to pick it up." (He did, a few weeks later, though with difficulty.) But I was still chuckling as I got off the phone. We all goof, but for my loony-toon Bobby to get the better of his therapist struck me not only as funny but beautiful. I didn't think then that very shortly I was going to have my own problems with an older, tougher, more alienated version of Bobby—my little, lisping twelve-year-old cherub, Paul Mitchell.

This year wasn't my first encounter with Paul. Some five years earlier, his mother had brought him to me for a perceptual evaluation as a public school "underachiever." I found he had major deficits all along the line and lined him up for a heavy series of perceptual training sessions. We had worked together fairly well, even though Paul seemed to lack almost any motivation at all—an almost spineless kid. But after perhaps two months, Paul's mother pulled him out of training and he disappeared. Now, after proving himself a behavior problem too rough for two schools, she had brought him back to me, claiming I was the only one who could "work with him."

His mother's defeatist attitude—shared by his father— boded ill for Paul since it only reinforced his privately held sense of failure. So did his behavior record in school. And so did my evaluation which not only showed him over three years behind in reading and four in math but still suffering from just about the same perceptual deficits I had found five years before. His age was no help either—he was that much

149

more locked in—and his self-deceit, as shown by the episode with the second-grade reader, was enormous: he knew it all. If that wasn't enough, both his parents worked, and Paul, an only child, had to get to school in the morning by himself and return to an empty house in the afternoon. Lonely and friendless as are many of our kids, he was burdened with responsibilities shared by few normal boys his age. Some load for an LD kid!

On the plus side, however, were some weighty factors. Paul was very bright—even with the perceptual blocks that tended to obscure his IQ. His problems were just those our school was designed to overcome. Finally, it looked as though I was able to get through to him.

The morning after the reading incident, Paul had his first perceptual training session. I handed him a lotto game and asked him to match different sizes and shapes.

He turned up his freckled nose in disgust. "Hey, this is baby stuff! I'm not gonna do it." Not "I can't," which he really couldn't, but "I won't"—the old self-deceptive ego mechanism found in so many of our kids.

"You're not," I answered. "Why not?"

"It's stupid," Paul said adamantly. "It's one of the stupidest things I've ever seen in my life. Besides, I know how."

"Well, maybe you're stupid," I shot back. "So if the work is stupid and you're stupid, things are equal. And I believe in equality. If you know how, prove it to me and then we'll go on to something not so stupid for a not so stupid Paul."

"I'm entitled to an opinion," Paul sniffed, backing off slightly.

"And so am I," said I. "So we're still equal. And as long

as things are equal, you're going to have to do this. So do it and do it now!''

Paul grumpily sat down and did the lotto game, better than I expected but not perfectly. Nevertheless, I thanked him—he had done it, at least—and told him he would have something different the next time. Again he appeared in my office after school for what turned into many such post-schoolroom visits. He would talk about everything but his work and problems in class—his mother, his father, the Boy Scouts, his non-existent playmates—but still we were talking, relating. The forceful attitude I'd taken seemed to be working. I told Carl Janicki, Paul's teacher, to sit on him, hard.

Even after Carl reported a week later that Paul was becoming increasingly hard to handle—turning into a real little Napoleon, talking out of turn, poking the other kids, snickering about everything, and doing just minimal work—I still couldn't believe we had too much of a problem on our hands. All he needed was strong medicine.

I was even more convinced when I dropped into Paul's class during last period to give him a homework assignment to help him learn longhand. The minute he saw me Paul piped up brightly to say he was bored with math—Carl's teaching specialty and the work of the moment. I charged in then and there, marshaling all the information I'd picked up from his mother and teacher in the ten days he'd been in school.

''Oh, you are'' I said, sarcastically. ''Why are you bored with math?''

Paul had no answer.

''I asked you why, Paul?'' I said sharply.

''I'm bored with it,'' Paul answered, as the smile started to fade. He hadn't expected this sudden attention. The class had become deathly quiet.

"Is that all you're bored with?" I pushed on.

"Yes," said Paul in a whisper, his head starting to droop.

"Look at me, Paul," I said. His head came up. "Now I hear you're bored with lots of things. Your teacher tells me you're bored with English. Is that right?"

"No," said the small voice, "just math."

"That's not what I hear. Your mother tells me you're bored with English too, and that you're bored with writing and that you're bored with school. Now I'll tell you what we can do. Just for little Paulie, we'll put on a show so you won't be bored. We'll have a whole act. Cindy here," I said, winking at a twelve-year-old classmate who was really built, "will do a little dance for you and we'll have all kinds of things going on so baby Paulie won't be bored."

The class began to titter, Cindy most of all. Paul's face started to work. You could just feel the kid's humiliation and rage at being singled out in this fashion. I knew all he wanted was for me to just go away and leave him alone. I pounded on.

"Would you like that, Paul?" I asked him. "We'll do it just for you. We wouldn't want you to be bored."

No answer.

"You know what I think," I said, as the class quieted again. "I don't think you're bored at all. I think you're just afraid. You're scared, not bored—just scared, scared to try. Every kid in this room has been right where you are. They all have the same problems you have. If they didn't and you didn't, none of you would be here. Each one of them has been scared just like you, but each one of them has tried. They managed to try and get somewhere and they have. You can too. You can, just as they did, stop all this nonsense and sit still and work. Is that clear? Now you're to take this special assignment home—it will help you learn to write— and get it done tonight. And I don't want to hear one more thing about how you're bored or that you're in any kind of trouble at all." I handed the homework to the teacher and walked out.

Fifteen minutes later, as I was calling off homebound bus numbers, Paul came bouncing up to me. "Bye, Doc," he said with a winning smile, waving the homework at me as he left. The next morning, his teacher reported Paul had done it all. Was it possible the terror of two schools had turned into a cream puff with only a couple of hard lectures?

I had yet to plumb the depths of this kid's sense of failure or test his years-hardened ability to run away from reality and clothe himself in self-deceit. His brief periods of work were only quickly replastered cracks in the surface.

The next day I observed the kids at lunch. The new teachers and a few of the old were off jabbering among themselves and the room very quickly turned into a zoo. Kids were moving from table to table, punching each other and jawing, and the noise level was deafening. They were on such a high that I knew they'd never get down to work in the afternoon, and at this rate would be unmanageable all afternoon at home.

Using an old ploy of mine, I switched off the lights, leaving only the dim glow from a few windows. There was immediate silence. "The noise in this room is splitting my ears," I shouted at the top of my lungs. "I don't see how any of you can eat. Now everyone get back in your seats and shut up." They finished their lunch in the dark, but quietly. They filed back to their rooms, and just as quietly I let each of the teachers have it. Our kind of education is a full-time job.

The next morning I caught nine-year-old Charlie Hoffman as he left gym. He'd been turning up at school in the same unwashed clothes day after day, and in all that time hadn't got within miles of a bath or a shower. He smelled it.

I called Charlie's mother. She was no welfare case, but even if she had been one, like Mrs. Rich, the least she could do was keep Charlie clean. Joey Rich managed to come in scrubbed and shiny every day, dressed in clean if shabby clothes.

When no one answered the telephone at Charlie's house, I made him peel off his clothes, gave him a bar of soap and threw him in one of the pool showers. He protested all the way, but I made him scrub everywhere three or four times and then left him wrapped in a towel while I washed his clothes and put them on the boiler to dry. A half hour later, Charlie walked back to class, in wrinkled clothes but clean for the first time since he'd entered school two weeks before.

Jan Berger's mother had a different problem. She sent six-year-old Jan to school every day immaculately pressed and scrubbed and pleated, with her shoes polished to a high shine and every hair on her head pulled back into a tight pony tail, topped by a crisp bow. But she couldn't face the facts of her child's disability.

Unlike Ellen Carson who, despite her turned eye and excessive salivation, could be described as pretty, Jan was a plain, thick-lipped little girl with large ears that stood out from her head. She walked with a definite lurch and had a habit of winching one eye and one side of her face in a grimace. Like Ellen, however, Jan's perceptual abilities appeared to be on about a three-year-old level. She couldn't distinguish near from far, bigger from smaller, taller from shorter. Her balance was terrible and she was afraid to leave the ground in any kind of jump or hop.

But unlike Ellen, Jan was not a happy child. She was withdrawn and never seemed to want to please. She also rarely relaxed, as we found out one day when we decided to test the kids' sense of abandon. Jan and her classmates were told to take a running leap onto soft mats laid on the gym floor. After a few initial doubts as to the stability of the mats and their softness, Ellen and the rest of the kindergarten kids took turns racing and flinging themselves onto the pads, laughing and having a ball. Jan wouldn't go near them. Finally, after crying and resisting in every way she could, she ran at the mats—only to come to a screeching halt in front of them, screaming. An aide and I flipped her on the pads, still screaming. We had to pick her up and repeat this at least four more times before her howling stopped and she began to join in and enjoy herself.

In spite of all this, we were convinced Jan had potential. During the summer I had started her on some simple sequential commands and physical exercises, particularly those aimed at helping her overcome her fear of leaving the ground. By this time she was jumping and hopping alternately on either foot fairly smoothly, although she still was having her problems. When she hopped on her left foot she didn't seem to know what to do with her right and would hold it awkwardly straight out in front of her. I realized she had to compensate immensely to maintain her balance, using her stomach muscles rather than the weight of the free leg,

155

but this seemed something we would correct in time. What did matter was that she was finally conquering gravity.

Recently I had assigned her some hopping exercises to do at home. About half an hour after I had sent Charlie back to class, I received a visit from Mrs. Berger. She was obviously very upset.

"Jan doesn't look right!" she announced.

"What do you mean?" I asked, thinking of the upheld right foot but also thinking this was a strange reaction from a parent. "You mean when she hops?"

"She doesn't look right. She never looks right," the woman repeated over and over in the same grim, forceful manner.

I explained the training technique and that when Jan had consolidated some of her basic motor abilities I would work on the extended foot.

"But she doesn't look right," her mother persisted.

A few weeks later, she called especially to tell me about Jan's wonderful new hop and how pleased it made her. A week or two after that she called and bawled me out, again with her former ferocity, because Jan had hopped all the way down the aisle in the supermarket. "What is this hopping?" she barked. "Where did she learn this hopping?"

I decided that Mrs. Berger was just one of those parents who didn't understand what we were trying to do for her daughter. But I went ahead and corrected Jan's foot problem anyway.

I was working with one of the kids on left-right exercises when my aide screamed in delight from across the room: "He did it! You did it!"

She hugged and kissed little Stevie Sachs. For the first

time, this seven-year-old had managed to put together all the circles and all the squares and he'd also separated all the black shapes from the white ones. I went over and hugged Stevie myself as he giggled happily. Then we gave him a bunch of M&Ms, Stevie's particular favorite, and a piggy-back ride back to class.

In the hall, Julie, my assistant, stopped to tell me about Maureen, one of my teachers who was being observed by her supervisor in a post-graduate course she was taking at the university. Maureen had been uptight all morning, and had even prepared a special lesson—something I don't permit—to impress her teacher. Julie had gotten nervous, too, when she saw the copious notes the supervisor was taking. I decided to put a stop to it then and there. I bawled Julie out and told her that if these visits from the teachers' teachers (which are fairly frequent) were going to disrupt everyone like this, I'd have to stop them. Later when I spoke to Maureen's supervisor I found the reason for all the notetaking was because she was so impressed with Maureen's work. If only I could get it through my teachers' heads not to worry. It sounds immodest, but I feel if they're good enough for me they're the best around.

In the cafeteria, I noticed that Ellen Carson was refusing to eat her ravioli. Her teacher could not get her to try some, even though the rest of the kids obviously were enjoying it; they were covered with it from head to toe.

"Ellen," I said. "Have you ever had ravioli?"

"No," she said.

"Then how do you know you don't like it? You have to taste it to find out whether you like it or not. Now taste it. You don't have to eat the whole thing, just taste it."

157

Ellen started wailing. "I want peanut butter and jelly."

Remembering a trick my mother used when I wouldn't take my medicine, I gently pinched Ellen's nose shut and waited for her mouth to open to take a breath. When it did, I popped in a nice wad of ravioli.

The crying stopped and she munched away.

"Do you like it?" I asked.

"Yes," she replied (though she didn't eat much more). I rewarded her with a peanut butter and jelly sandwich.

Luckily the next day's lunch was peanut butter and jelly and several other things Ellen liked. Spaghetti appeared the following day, however, and once again she refused to eat. This time there were no preliminaries.

"Ellen," I bellowed, "EAT THE SPAGHETTI—NOW!"

Ellen put a whole fistful of spaghetti in her mouth and gobbled up the rest of it in about two minutes flat. Several days later Ellen, who minds everyone's business but her own, was sitting next to another kid who wouldn't eat her pineapple dessert.

"Feed her the juice," Ellen advised me.

"Mind your own business, Ellen," I said.

"Make her open her mouth," said Ellen, ignoring instructions as usual. I was surprised she didn't tell me to hold the other kid's nose.

I had some unaccustomed time on my hands, and started reading the individual analyses and prescriptive teaching outlines each teacher is required to submit on each kid in his class at the beginning of the school year. I went out and harassed lagging teachers who were late with their reports. I rubbed Joey Rich's tummy and tickled Jimmy Blake in the hall. I looked in on Karin Bergstrom's class and saw that

Elliott Reimer, now on the last day of his gym and swimming ban, was back with the rest of his class. "He seems to be trying to get along better with the others now," Karin whispered to me. Ellen Carson was buried in her work and being a "good girl." Charlie was still relatively clean from his shower though he was dressed in the same clothes. I told his teacher to be sure and call Momma. At lunch, Bozo was another howling success. A good day, a good week.

The following Monday I learned that things weren't going nearly as well as I thought with Paul Mitchell. Again he was refusing to do his math. When I came into class, there he was, smirking, his arms folded contemptuously across his chest, while the other kids looked on with fascination.

I sized up the situation quickly. "What do you mean Paul won't do anything for you?" I said in mock surprise to Carl. "Why, little Paul wants to do everything he can for you, don't you, little Paul?" I had decided to play up Paul's small stature, hoping it might cut him down to size. Apparently it got through to the class, who quickly regained their perspective over his defiance. "Little Paulie, little Paulie," someone said from the back of the room.

"Go on with your lecture, Mr. Janicki," I said. "Little Paul and I are going to show you how much he wants to work for you."

With that, I plunked myself in Paul's lap, held his hand, and guided it into copying down the problems Carl had written on the board. The class went on with its business as if nothing was happening; they had seen such scenes before.

"Hey, get off me," Paul whispered. "Who do you think you are, you fat slob? Are you crazy or something?"

"Yes, I'm crazy," I answered quietly. "And I'm fat. Just how fat you're going to learn if I have to sit here much longer. As a matter of fact, I'm not too comfortable myself, but I'm willing to sit here all day if that's the only way I can help you do your work. Of course, you can always do it yourself, you know." I turned the page in his book.

"OK, OK," Paul whispered in embarrassment. "I'll do it. Just get the hell off me."

I left a redfaced Paul copying away with the rest. But I was already beginning to get the picture of what we were up against. Here was a kid who could barely read, who hardly knew how to add or subtract, who maybe could do a lotto game but not all that well, refusing even to try other tasks, puffing himself up with a phony sense of importance and lies to hide the possibility that he was really a retard, a kid who had given up. As his parents evidently had.

That night Paul went home and told his mother he was having trouble in school and, surprisingly, was quite honest about what had happened to him. That was a real plus—in marked contrast to Mrs. Mitchell's attitude.

"I'm so embarrassed," she said on the phone, expressing the disappointment she—like many of our parents—convey to their children from day one. "How could I have wished him on you! He's no good. Maybe I should send him away where they'll knock him out with drugs. Then he wouldn't be any trouble to anyone. He's always been a problem. I can't handle it."

"Now just wait a minute, Mrs. Mitchell," I said. "Sure, Paul's a problem and sure he's tough, but all my kids have problems and a lot of them are tough. That's no reason to send him away. That's why he's here."

"Well, do anything you want," she replied, adding doubt-fully: "And good luck." As she hung up, I thought how in the world do these people expect their kids to have the gumption to overcome problems when they offer them nothing but defeat and disapproval. And I wondered, as I have on a number of such occasions, whether kids like Paul might not be better off in a residential school after all. And yet I was all the more determined not to give up. Perhaps I saw it as a challenge to my ego, but I was going to penetrate Paul's problems and defenses or know the reason why. If only I had the time . . . out there were so many other kids and they all needed help. As if to prove it, I had two behavior problems to contend with the very next day.

Herbie Goodman, another twelve-year-old, had been acting up for two weeks. Now, his teacher told me, he had just run out of school.

If there is one word to describe Herbie, it's "meek." When he came to us, he was terrified of everyone and everything; his voice was barely audible and he'd blanch at a loud or cross remark. Nevertheless, though he was still exceedingly quiet, he had made excellent academic progress in the two years he'd been with us and had shed most of his fears as well. He had increased his self-confidence, and we were planning to return him to regular school at the end of the year.

Now this had happened. Like his acting up, it was totally out of character and could sabotage our hopes for sending him back. No one, including his mother who had noticed some sign of impending trouble at home, had been able to find out from Herbie what was disturbing him.

I chased after Herbie and found him only a few blocks away. But he was nearly hysterical, almost incoherent through his jitters and tears. I called his mother and asked her to come for him.

161

While we waited for her in my office, Herbie began to calm down and started to talk, jerkily.

"I don't want to," he said.

"What don't you want to?" I asked.

"I'm scared," he said. "I can't."

"What are you scared of?"

Herbie began to cry. Then he calmed down. We went around the circle a couple of times again. Finally, when I asked what was the matter, he wailed, "My bar mitzvah!"

Herbie would be thirteen in a week, and finally we knew what had been bothering the poor kid these last weeks— something we should have all guessed, particularly me. I could remember only too well my own nervousness when I had to get up in the synagogue and perform the simple rites that made me a man. With Herbie, that nervousness must have been magnified a hundredfold.

"Why are you frightened about your bar mitzvah?" I asked, urging him to talk it out.

"There will be strangers there," he blurted out, his words tumbling over each other. "I don't know them. They'll laugh. I'm going to forget what I'm supposed to say. I know I will. Then they'll laugh at me. I can't do it. I can't. I know I can't.

"Wait a second, Herbie," I said. "What makes you think you're going to mess up? What makes you think you can't do this? If I know you, you'll do everything perfectly, just right, the same way you've been doing everything in school. You've studied, haven't you?"

"Yes," said Herbie, starting to dry his tears.

"Then study some more," I said. "But you know, it really doesn't matter if your bar mitzvah doesn't go perfectly. I made a mistake or two at mine and nobody even noticed."

"You did?" asked Herbie incredulously.

162

"Sure I did," I said, "everyone does."

"But what about all those people?" Herbie said. "I don't know them. They don't know me. I'm sure they'll laugh."

"Herbie," I said, "why don't you get me and your teacher an invitation to your bar mitzvah. I promise we'll both come, and if anybody laughs we'll punch them in the nose and shout, 'Yay, Herbie!' at the same time."

Both Herbie's teacher, Carl Janicki, and I received invitations to Herbie's bar mitzvah and we watched with pride as a very tense Herbie did beautifully. He delivered his speech perfectly, and afterwards went on an orgy of cake and punch, basking in all the well-earned attention and admiration. Of course nobody laughed, but if they had I was fully prepared to carry out my end of the bargain. But Herbie Goodman didn't need help from anyone that day.

Next, a sobbing Bobby Hammack trudged into my office. I mean he was really heaving. Someone in his class had spit down the stairwell and it landed on a teacher's head. When Audrey, Bobby's teacher, asked the class who did it, Bobby raised his hand. So here he was, crying his head off in my office. Somehow I knew he hadn't done it—Bobby just isn't the type who spits.

"Did you spit?" I said, glaring at him, "and don't lie to me."

"No," Bobby whimpered.

"Do you know who did?" I asked.

"No," he said, still sobbing.

"Then why are you here?"

"I didn't want them to get in trouble," he managed through his sobs. "I'm always in trouble, so I'll take the blame. They're my friends. I'll take the blame."

"Look," I said, "you're not in trouble with me, because

163

you didn't do it and I'm not going to let you take the blame. The only thing that makes me mad is that you're in here lying to me. That makes me very angry and I'm not going to let you get away with it.''

Taking Bobby by the hand, I marched him back to class. ''Who spit down the stairwell?'' I snapped at them. Five kids turned, and whack! pointed at an eight-year-old in the back row, a tough little new kid named Alan Greenspan, whose father was an attorney.

''Why did you let Bobby take the blame?'' I asked them. ''Why did you let him get so upset? He's your friend. Now treat him like one.'' With that the class was forced to skip gym as a punishment and Alan was sent to my office.

''Did you spit down the stairwell?'' I asked him.

''Sure,'' he said, cockily. ''Did I hit anyone?''

''You hit a teacher.''

''Did she wipe it off?''

''Yes,'' I said quietly.

''So what's the problem?'' he sneered.

So he was one of those! Well, there was one sure way of handling such kids. ''Do you know what's going to happen to you if you spit again?'' He just looked at me. ''This,'' I told him and gave him a dose of his own medicine—right in his face. ''And from the whole school.''

For the next few weeks that kid turned a right angle and did everything except move bricks when I came down the hall. Needless to say, there was no more spitting.

That night Alan's father happened to return a call I had placed the day before about his son's homework. Mr. Greenspan, like most of our parents who had no idea what if anything was wrong with their kids, would hassle Alan about his homework and often as not end up doing it himself. We believe the kid alone is responsible for his homework. This not only relieves the parents of an unwelcome chore but helps us evaluate the kid and teach him to take responsibility for his actions. Also, the teachers know the true capabilities of the kids; the parents generally don't. We've had more than one kid who under parental pressure to do his homework right—when all we've asked is that he do it, period—has got into such a sweat he's been afraid to come to school the next day.

So far, Audrey had been unable to get this message across to attorney Greenspan, who had justifiably high expectations for his son Alan, testing as he did at a 110 IQ. Of course, homework was no longer the only thing Greenspan had in mind when he called me back.

"Did you spit at Alan?" he asked sharply, in his best prosecutor's manner.

"Yes, I did," I said, and told him why. After I explained what had happened, for once the counsellor had nothing to say. Then I launched into a lecture about laying off Alan and his homework. I had expected a big argument—Mr. Greenspan had impressed me as a tough man to change—but before I knew it he agreed to do what I asked and hung up. Maybe he decided I was tough enough on Alan for both of us. Soon after that, Alan's behavior in school improved and he acted a lot less frustrated with his work.

I popped into Jane's class the next morning and found her at the back of the room laughing while her class was taking a test. When I asked in a whisper why she was so cracked up, all she could do was point to Jimmy Blake, the little black kid who was so fearful at the start of the term and wanted me for his daddy. When I saw what she was pointing at, I could hardly keep from laughing too.

We had caught Jimmy in the act. His hand was extended

under the desk, and the kid sitting next to him was just about falling out of his chair trying to squint at it. Jimmy had laboriously written down his answers to the test for the kid to copy. There was only one thing wrong. He had written his answers on the back of his hand in pencil—and against the black skin the black writing was just about impossible to see!

My kids! I thought. If they'd only spend half as much effort trying to learn as they do devising ways to cheat.

As I'd expected, putting Danny Gordon in a learning carrel had been no problem for anyone except Marion. Danny did "A"'s and "B"'s and "C"'s until he was blue in the face. He read and re-read words until he had them memorized and he went through nursery school books the same way. He was clearly no dyslexic, as I had originally thought, but Marion still had a problem—getting him to stop reading and spelling and start on his math. She had worked out a method, which she tried out one day in my presence. What I saw reinforced an idea about Danny that had been building for some time in my mind.

"Danny," Marion shouted, "put down that book and start doing your math." Then she ducked under her desk, but not fast enough—she got caught in the hail of books, erasers and pencils that came flying out of the carrel as an infuriated Danny yelled: "I'm not *finished* yet!"

Why would Danny try to hurt Marion, whom he adored? Not because he wanted to hurt her, certainly. Danny just thought Marion was being "unfair" to him by not letting him finish his work perfectly. The flying missiles were a protest. Punishment was pointless, as we discovered every time we tried it—Danny just sat there in sullen acceptance of one more unfair act directed at him. He never made the connection that what hurt him might hurt others, an immature social perception typical of six- or seven-year-olds, and very common among our LD kids. Without realizing that, Danny couldn't possibly reach the next obvious conclusion that beaning Marion might lead to other consequences —punishment or a fight. That was completely beyond his perceptual limits.

It was all beginning to fit together. Danny, locked into his own world, displayed the social perceptions of a four-year-old. This severe lack of social perceptual maturity just wouldn't do if Danny was ever to progress in learning. Children and adults learn with greatest efficiency by receiving information from the outside. They prevent distortion by comparing with different points of view; only thus can they begin to attain objectivity, flexibility and the ability to generalize from one experience to another. But if the basic *interaction*— or capacity for interaction—doesn't exist, then no matter what the IQ, learning will be an exceedingly slow process blocked by constant perceptual distortions. (This perceptual capacity to relate to other self-centers begins to show itself, many child psychologists feel, around the age of six or seven—the age, remarks Jean Piaget, when most children are considered ready for school.)

Danny could accept no direction other than his own. In his world he was always securely "right" because he wouldn't allow anyone in to challenge or help him—that would be an admission of "wrongness." So he fed his own distortions. "Horse" was "house" because Danny initially had perceived it that way, and since he never learned otherwise, "house" it remained. Correction from the outside was impossible.

We had to find some way to break through Danny's "Iceman'' armor, to open a chink so he could perceive himself in terms of others' actions and reactions, to accept the world and himself as part of it. But first he needed the confidence gained by making real academic progress on his own terms, which, of course, were the only ones he could accept.

I checked on six-year-old Frank Alejo. He had a habit of continually rocking in his seat in class (an infantile form of masturbation). We were less disturbed by his rocking than the fact he wasn't aware he was doing it, so I'd asked the shop teacher to make me a special belt and Frankie agreed to wear it. It was a conventional belt in all respects but one: it had a dinner bell attached to its back. Now every time Frankie would start to rock, the clanger hit his seat and the bell rang. At the same time every time Frankie set off the bell—as he did quite frequently the first few days—all the kids in his class would turn around and shout: "You're rocking again. Stop rocking. Keep quiet." Poor Frankie had put up with this—stopping himself each time the bell sounded—for two weeks, until his rocking had been reduced so dramatically that we could take off the belt. Some kids will go through all kinds of misery to take one step in the right direction.

Not so good old Paul Mitchell. Now he had decided to have no part of gym and swimming—a treat for most of our kids in spite of their general clutziness. Paul wasn't even going to put on his bathing suit or play ball. Yet the evening before, in one of our office chats, he had bragged how much he liked going to the playground and said that he was a great catcher. I walked into his class and found most of the kids still peppy from gym period. All except Paul. In my best tough-guy manner, I called him outside.

"I'd hate to think you missed out on your gym period," I said. "How about coming along with me for a little work-out?"

The anticipated smirk crossed Paul's face at the thought he'd be getting out of class, which he liked even less than gym. He hadn't yet learned that special treatment was nothing to smirk about, at least when it came from me.

We got down to the gym and I picked up one of our volley balls—soft ones that are easier for our kids to catch.

"I'm going to throw this ball at you and you're going to catch it," I announced.

"No," said Paul, smirking away.

"Well, I'm going to throw it anyway, and you'd better catch it."

"Go ahead, fatso," said Paul, calm as you please. He also hadn't learned yet that I do everything I say I'm going to.

I threw the ball and hit Paul in the gut, not hard, but he gave a gasp of surprise anyway.

"You're a real big man," he whined, "throwing balls at little kids."

"You're a real little kid," I retorted. "And little kids need big men's help. Now catch," I said, picking up another ball.

"No, I won't," said Paul.

"What do you mean, you won't. Now catch it," I ordered again, pretending to throw the ball.

Paul flinched. Then he said, "I can't." Another honest admission, and one I intended to exploit, as I had with Joey Rich.

"That's no news," I said. "I know you can't, you know you can't. So we're equal again. But that doesn't mean you can't try. Now try to catch it!"

Paul, however, was no compliant Joey. "I don't have to do what you say!" he said.

"Oh no? Well, catch this ball when I throw it."

"You're a big jerk!" said Paul.

"You're right. Why else would I be wasting so much time with an ungrateful jerk like you?"

"Don't call me names," Paul warned.

"Why not?" I said. "You called me one. So again we're equal. Now catch this!"

"Eat it," Paul said.

"Paul, when I count up to three, I'm going to throw this ball, and if you don't catch it it's going to hit you in the gut again."

"OK, OK, you jerk," Paul mumbled, "throw it. I can catch it. I can catch any ball any time. What do you think I am, an invalid?"

"Aren't you?" I asked, latching on to this new opening. Catching balls, I knew, was hardly Paul's forte—bravado was.

"No," said Paul, hotly. Then, curiously: "What do you mean?"

"I mean your whole attitude," I said. "The way you won't do things for your teacher or for other people who are only trying to help you. You won't even get into your bathing suit for the swimming teacher or work in the gym. Doesn't that sound like an invalid—a mental invalid?"

"Bullshit!" said Paul. But I could see I was getting to him.

"OK, then stop acting as though you're trying to prove you are one."

"Leave me alone," Paul wailed.

"Not until you show me how good a catcher you are. If you make three catches with no drops, then I'll leave you alone and you can go back to class where I'm sure you'd rather be. I'm sure you don't want to be down here with me throwing balls at you."

Tears started rolling down Paul's cheeks.

"C'mon, now," I said as evenly as before. "If you cry, your eyes will get all fogged up and you won't be able to see the ball."

Paul snuffled back his tears. I threw to him three times, very easily; and clutching desperately he managed to catch the ball and hold on to it. He nearly ran back to class, where he buried himself in his work. But a point had been made: here, in this school, Paul had to do what he was asked to do, no matter what. He couldn't hide behind his smirks, his "I won't"s, his know-it-all attitude, his tough little Napoleon image. We were inching closer, poking holes in all his defenses as we did.

Paul still had an escape, however, or so he thought. The next day he didn't come to school. I didn't think too much about it. Sometimes our kids are sick. It crossed my mind that his mother hadn't called and I made a mental note to check into it later.

Ruth's class—the equivalent of a second-grade level in math and reading—was getting its first exposure to two-place addition. They were having trouble with the concept of carrying, to say nothing of adding and counting in general without

171

the use of their fingers. They were becoming more and more frustrated. I got a pack of cards and went in.

"Who here has lunch money or candy money or allowances with him?" I asked. Each of them had a few pennies for lollipops or other candy.

I spread out the cards. "We're going to play a little game," I said. The kids perked up—games and gambling always seem to get to them, which is why we use them so often. I explained the rules of black jack, or twenty-one. I was the dealer.

The kids, of course, were terrible players since they couldn't add. Roger would draw a card, even though his two cards face up added to twenty and he had another face down. Tim would get twenty-one and ask for another card. But like most gamblers, no one would give up even if they were losing. They were totally absorbed. As we went along, Ruth and I explained each of their mistakes in addition and calculation.

By the end of a half hour, I had taken all the kids' money and even their pocket goodies. (I put their losings in separate envelopes and gave them back at the end of the day.) But most of the kids had learned how to add and count to twenty-one in their heads. A game had taught them quicker than any textbook. I risked no more blackjack with them after that. I was afraid I might lose my shirt.

Six-year-old Robin Lasky, who had come to us the year before so perceptually underdeveloped that she couldn't crawl, hop, jump or walk with any coordination, and was so distractible that if her head were on a swivel it would have spun, finally showed us she could pay attention to what she was doing and confine her eyes and hand to doing it. Instead of coloring all over the page, the desk and herself, while she looked at everything except her work, she had just done an almost perfect job of coloring a square, and only the square, red. A week later she would be able to draw straight-line letters, like "A" and "H," by connecting dots.

Robin's breakthrough had come after three weeks of solid exercise. She had dropped a pointer through a straw held at arm's length, picked up rings with a pickup stick and placed them on a pegged wallboard, pushed lighted buttons on a box—all aimed at getting her eyes and hand to track together.

"It's beautiful," Elaine, her teacher, told her, "absolutely beautiful. Isn't it, Dr. Cohen?"

"Marvelous," I answered, hugging Robin. "You do great work. Now be sure and take that home and show it to Mommy."

Unfortunately, not all our kids respond to our program the way Robin did. Brian Murphy, a tiny two-and-a-half-foot five-year-old, was my TV set. When he first arrived in my office for evaluation he kept piping away: "Beep, beep ABC-TV." I thought it was pretty funny; unfortunately, so did the other children in Brian's class.

We found Brian to be quite bright. When I turned off his channel he showed fairly good perceptual and pre-reading skills for his age. But when he wasn't lost announcing his station (his means of warding off a hostile world), we found him afraid of just about everything. His eyes would flutter, and he would shiver when an adult passed him or a child spoke to him. He refused to climb the stairs. Since school started, one teacher or another would have to carry him up and down.

173

Obviously this would never do. I decided to tackle the stair problem first.

I placed Brian at the bottom of the stairs leading to the upstairs classrooms and did everything I could to make him go up on his own. I picked up his feet and placed them on the first step, made up games and tried to bribe him. He refused to budge. I carried him halfway up the first flight and refused to help him either up or down—though I sat nearby and encouraged him. After about an hour of crying and screaming, Brian finally went up the rest of the steps to the landing—on all fours. I rewarded him with candy and a big hug and kiss. But I was a long way from a lasting breakthrough—Brian would walk up and down the stairs, all right, but only when no one was around except his teacher or me. He was still afraid of the other kids, even those in his class, and he had added WPIX to his channels.

As I had with Jimmy Blake and some other small kids who were frightened the first days of school, I decided to give Brian a breather from class, and brought him into my office. He stopped beeping almost immediately and read and played quietly for a few days. In an attempt to break the beeping pattern, I got him a play TV set and told him he had it all wrong—he wasn't a TV set, he was a TV repairman. Together we took apart the TV and put it back together. He worked on this for hours, but the moment he left my office back came the beeping and his extreme fearfulness.

I called Brian's mother and asked why her son was so afraid. She told me that he was an only child who had never been made to do anything at home and no one was allowed to raise their voices with him. His father wouldn't allow it. No wonder this tiny kid couldn't cope with a class and school full of loudmouths.

Even though his neuropsychologist diagnosed his reaction in school as paranoid schizophrenic, Brian's mother pleaded with me not to give up on him. For her sake, we tried one more time. For the next two weeks I kept Brian in my office, with occasional experimental forays into class. Once there, all he did was beep. Worse still, his beeping was reinforced by laughter from all the kids, who were too busy with Brian to pay attention to their own work.

This couldn't continue. Finally I had to call Mrs. Murphy again and explain that it was unfair to the other kids. I recommended to her another school for children more disturbed than ours, who were so far into themselves that they would probably ignore Brian's distracting antics. Reluctantly, Mrs. Murphy agreed to send him there.

Shortly after he started at his new school, Brian's beeping stopped, probably because his new classmates were less threatening and his noise attracted no attention. Evidently this environment was better designed for his needs than ours, for Brian began to make his first academic progress.

Toward the end of the day I dropped into Paula Wolfe's class to see how Amy Friedman was coming along. Amy was an organically brain-injured epileptic child who, when she first came to us two years before, was given to short but violent seizures that often jackknifed her whole body, sending her head crashing into the desk. To prevent possible injury we had rigged up a foam rubber pad on her desk.

Because of her high level of seizure activity, Amy arrived at school each day stoked up with anywhere from five to seven medications—drugs that left her virtually in a complete stupor and snuffed out what little ability she had to pay any attention at all. There were a lot of people, even a few on my staff, who thought Amy belonged in an institution and not in our day school.

I worried about that myself. Though each year we accept a small percentage of kids who are organically brain-injured, as opposed to minimally brain-dysfunctioning, and some who are epileptic, it is normally on condition that their handicap is slight. We're prepared to handle epileptic petit mal seizures as well as the similar-looking psycho-motor "incidents" —detected in blank stares, short loss of memory, fluttering eyelids and even arm-flailing dervish-like behavior—that many of our mbd and emotionally disturbed kids display, especially when extremely frustrated. But Amy, with her grand mal-type seizures—and the drugs used to control them—was almost beyond our pale. We had taken her, along with our other few epileptics, because her parents had rightfully pointed out that there was no place else for her to go: few schools provide special classes for epileptics and the normal classroom is not designed to handle their problems. But as I watched her struggle month after month through basic perceptual training and kindergarten classwork with little success and practically no recall, I'd begun to feel there was little we could do for her unless something changed. Finally, it did.

A few months before, Amy's seizure activity had lessened and her doctor reduced her medication. Immediately she became more alert. So we decided, more or less arbitrarily, that it was time for Amy, now eight, to start in on preliminary academic work, and develop her visual tracking abilities and manual skills so that she could physically handle reading and writing. I say arbitrarily because there is no firm timetable to determine when a child is ready to take this step.

We started Amy on numbers, relating all her other training

to them. After some work with rubber bands to strengthen her fingers so that she could use a writing instrument, we laid large number templates, or stencils, over a big slab of clay and let her gouge them out with a sizable stylus, thus getting the feel of the clay and the sweep of her hand and her arm as she made each number. From there, we switched her to digging lightly drawn numbers in the clay, making the same numbers in plates of sand, drawing them on sandpaper with pastels and finally writing them on a piece of paper with a thick pencil.

In perceptual training class, we started her on sorting and set concepts; we had her separate larger and smaller groups of objects and, as soon as she could count to ten (which we taught, at first, by rote), put her to work placing five red cubes in one box, three blues in another, and so on to every number-type gradient we could devise at her level. She also joined the other kids in hopping and jumping and walking around numbers pasted on the gym floor with masking tape. I gave her the usual tracking exercises, plus a new one devised specially for her. I set up a row of ten large white candles and had her shoot out the flames with a water pistol while I called them out by number position. "Shoot out candle one," I'd call. "Now candle three." Amy loved this, though the janitor didn't appreciate the pools of water all over the floor.

Amy made such astoundingly fast progress that I still wonder if I shouldn't have started her on this phase long before, even given the massive drug dosages: maybe she'd just been bored. Within three weeks she knew her numbers solidly up to ten, she could write them on paper, and she complied with almost all our instructions correctly and quite easily. We started on letters as well as two pre-reading pro-

177

grams and instruction from Sid, our speech therapist in expressive language. (Though we decided at the outset there was no point in trying to correct Amy's constant slurs—caused by the substantial medication she was still taking as well as by her basic impairment—we did want to work on her syntax, her baby-talk speech style and improve her ability to sound out consonants and vowels.)

Here again, Amy blazed away, seeming to grow more alert at each new challenge. A little over a week ago, long before I would have thought possible, Paula had begun giving Amy her first words. Could it be that all this kid needed to get going was an intellectual challenge? Or was this just the expected result from all our hours of developmental training, along with the drop in seizure activity and medication? I'll never know for sure, but one thing was apparent. This was no kid for an institutional zoo, no kid to be swept under the rug just because of her multiple problems.

But now when I walked into Paula's room, I found Amy crying, tears of frustration and anger streaking down her cheeks. She couldn't get the word "street"—her new word for the day. For the first time, Amy was really unhappy with her work, and that wasn't going to help her today or tomorrow. I decided it was time for me to play a game with her.

"Amy, Amy," I said, putting my arms around her, as I had during many of her seizures. "I'm going to have to call off the wedding. We can't get married."

Amy looked up, immediately forgetting about the difficult word in front of her. "Are *we* getting married, Doc?" she asked.

"Sure," I said, "but I'm not going to marry any little girl who is crying. Here you are in a beautiful dress, your shoes are all shined, your hair is combed, with a beautiful bow, you smell so sweet, and you're messing it all up with that crying face. And I feel so bad because I want to get married to you and now I can't because of the way you've made your face. I'm going to have to go back to my office and cry too."

"You're right, Doc," Amy said stoutly, though in the mixed-up terminology that often characterized her speech. "We can't get married if I briding (crying) now." Then, showing she was fully processing the information, she continued, "I supposed to be briding at the wedding and maybe my mother should be briding too."

"OK," I said, "let's go to my office and call your mother and see if she'll bride with you."

Amy fairly danced down the hall with me, full of elaborate plans about the wedding. Once in my office, I asked her to dial her number on the phone.

"You know I don't know how to dial, Doc!" she shot back at me. That gave me an idea.

"Sure you do," I said, "but why don't you dial something you already know?"

"What do I know?" asked Amy.

"You know the word 'street,' " I said. "Here, I'll call out the letters and you dial them."

Amy dialed "street" as I spelled it. Then she listened. Nothing, of course, happened, because the word contained only six letters.

"This phone doesn't work," she stated.

"Try it again," I said.

Amy dialed the word "street" correctly on the phone all by herself. Still getting no ring she did it again. And again. Now she was really annoyed.

"This phone doesn't work right, Doc!" she said, slamming down the receiver.

"I don't think it does," I said, trying to conceal my excitement. "But you know something now that you didn't know before."

"What?" asked Amy.

"You know the word 'street,' don't you?"

Amy charged out of my office and back to her room. On her magic slate Paula had written the word "street."

"Who wrote what I know on my slate?" she demanded crossly. "Who wrote my telephone on my slate?"

"What do you know? What telephone?" Paula was totally confused. But like most of my teachers, she recovered quickly, realizing we must have done something in my office that was connected to the telephone. "Is that what you know?" she asked Amy, pointing at her slate. "Is that your telephone?"

"Yes," said Amy, erasing the word by lifting up the plastic cover. "I know it. It's my telephone." And she proceeded carefully to repencil the word "street" on the slate. "See?" she said, showing Paula. "I know it."

We had many "telephones" after that. Any time Amy had difficulty with a new word, it became a "telephone" and she would come to my office to dial it, almost invariably getting it right from then on. Luckily all the new words were under seven letters or we would have been ringing wrong numbers all over the city. But just like our "marriage" which could quell all tears, this became another element in the mysterious learning process—why, I don't know. The only thing I do know is that it worked.

The next day was Paul Mitchell day. For the second time in a row, he hadn't shown up in school. Early in the morning, I called Mrs. Mitchell at work. She seemed completely surprised at the news. Paul wasn't sick and he'd told her the night before he'd been in school all day and, for all she knew, he was there right now.

I decided it was time to involve Carl, Paul's teacher, in more of the disciplinary process. After all, he was the one who had to deal with Paul daily and to whom I'd have to spin off the kid once we reached him—as I was sure we would, given enough pounding. I also wanted Paul to realize that he was surrounded—that there was no one he could turn to for sympathy or get around with his many ploys.

As I learned later, Carl did an excellent job. His arrival on Paul's doorstep made it a double surprise, since if Paul would have expected anyone it would be me.

Carl rang the bell and a pajamaed Paul answered the door, still half-asleep, even though it was ten o'clock. Carl asked him why he wasn't in school.

Instead of saying he overslept—which would have been an honest answer—Paul exploded: "I don't have to go to school and I'm not going to. You can't make me. Now go away and leave me alone! You're all bullshit there—just bullshit!"

Carl pushed the door open as Paul tried to slam it in his face. He told Paul to put on his clothes and hurry up about it, he was taking him to school.

"No, I won't!" Paul answered fiercely. "I don't have to go to school! I already told you. I didn't have to go to the other school and I don't have to go to yours!"

"Put your clothes on, Paul," Carl continued quietly, "and do it in five minutes or I'll have to take you as you are. This is your last chance."

Paul started to snicker. He cut a funny figure in his red,

baggy, knickered pj's, his skinny legs showing above an old pair of shoes he was wearing as slippers. "You wouldn't do that," he jeered. "I told you—you're all bullshit."

"Yes, I would, Paul," Carl said. "I'm just like Dr. Cohen. I do what I say I will." He picked Paul up, draped him in an old coat, and started out the door.

The next thing Paul knew he was in a cab with Carl on his way to school in this ridiculous outfit.

"Tell him to turn back!" he yelled, struggling and kicking. He even tried to bite Carl. "Tell him to go back! I'll get dressed! I'll come to school!"

"I told you it was your last chance," Carl said quietly.

Paul sat sulking in class in his red pajamas while Carl picked up the lesson where his aide left off. Julie, my assistant, and I took turns looking in on Paul. I must say he looked pretty funny.

Finally Paul pulled out of his sulk long enough to throw an eraser at me, hitting me squarely in the back. I ignored it, pretending I hadn't felt anything at all.

At lunch I sat down directly across from him. But I paid no attention to him.

"You know something, Doc?" he said at last, bridling under The Treatment. "You're a weakling. I threw an eraser at you and I hit you! And you didn't do anything about it."

"You did?" I asked. "I didn't feel anything. Where did you hit me? When?"

Paul sputtered like a firecracker.

"Look," I said, "if you're so strong, why don't you prove it to me? Let's Indian wrestle."

"Here?" asked Paul.

"Here."

182

We locked hands. Paul started straining for all he was worth. He couldn't budge me, of course. I outweighed him by a good seventy pounds. To add to his misery I pretended I wasn't even trying and started up a conversation with the rest of the kids.

"Hey, Pete," I asked one. "What's the spaghetti like? Any good today?"

"Yeh, Doc," answered Pete Connelly, one of our feistiest kids, grinning. Pete had given us a lot of trouble when he first arrived a year before and his temper still got out of hand now and then, but he knew the score so we often made allowances. Besides, his anger had been used to good purpose with many another kid.

"Any time you're ready to start, I'm ready," I said to straining Paul. "Hey, Mike, did your mother drive you to school today? I didn't see you get off the bus."

"Yeh," said Mike Friendly, another kid who'd given us a hard time before he began to live up to his name. "She took me and my father to work this morning."

"Say, Paul," I said. "I thought we were going to arm wrestle. When are you going to start?"

Paul's face was red with pressure. Finally, he said, "I *am* wrestling, you jerk!"

"Paul," I said, giving him my full attention and continuing the one-sided wrestle. "Now I've gotcha. You're just not stronger than I am. You're not physically stronger and you're not as stubborn as I am. No matter what you do, I'm going to be stronger than you are, Mr. Janicki is going to be stronger than you are and you're just going to have to give in whether you want to or not. See?"

I pushed his arm flat on the table and held it there.

I thought Paul was going to try to hit me with his free hand. Instead, he said resignedly: "OK. What do you want me to do?"

"Just what's expected of you, just what we ask you," I answered, "which isn't a lot. Just do your work. And do what we ask you to do in school. OK?"

"OK." said Paul. I let his arm go free. That evening I spared him the embarrassment of taking the bus in his red pajamas and drove him home myself. For once in our after-school sessions, Paul was silent, evidently still impressed by the incident at lunch. Good, I thought, and let him go whisking in the house with just a goodby. Maybe this time the impression would last—that school was not the big joke he tried to make of it. It did—for a week or so.

The next morning I went into Elaine's first-grade class with a couple of large handmade styrofoam dice—one with the numbers from one to six, the other just with four numbers from seven to ten. Just a few weeks ago, seven-year-old Stevie Sachs had finally learned the differences between circles and squares; now I wanted to see whether he could match the shape and sound of a number—2 or 3—with the concept of the number—*one* orange, *two* oranges.

At Elaine's request, I had taken Stevie from class for some one-to-one perceptual training sessions. I'd started him on the button box. I asked him to punch the button on his box to light up the figure 2 that matched the 2 on mine—in this case the second button. In ten days he was punching the right button with little trial and error. So we moved to an abacus and sorting trays, using M&Ms rather than the usual beads and popsticks since Stevie was the school's biggest M&M fan. I would put three orange M&Ms in one of my boxes and he'd have to match them (he had his colors down fairly well). If he did, he could eat them. By the next week he was making such good progress I put him on the pegboard, copying my number designs.

So far, everything was mainly visual motor. Because Stevie rarely spoke, and his lisp and poor syntax made him almost incomprehensible, we decided to simplify all auditory input, so our conversations were basic and, for me, very boring. I would say, "Here, Stevie, make something just like mine" or "Do just what I did." Stevie would lisp "Thure, Doc," and silently proceed to work. But in the week before I showed up in class with my dice, I had begun to casually count out loud, "one, two, three, let's see, four, five" and so on, up to ten as I put the M&Ms in my box or designed numbers on my pegboard. Stevie began copying me with great deliberation, and caught on quickly.

By the end of that week I felt sure he had the concept of numbers—the amounts they stood for and their sequence—fairly firmly in his head. At least they were no longer a complete mystery to him. But I wasn't sure he had grasped the association between the concept, the sound and, especially, each individual number's configuration. The game I was about to play with Stevie and the rest of his classmates—who all had these concepts and associations down pat—would test how far he'd come. Perhaps the competition could force some more verbal expression from him.

I stood there with my huge dice and asked who wanted to play a game. All eight hands in the class went up, including Stevie's. I told them that I would throw one die on the floor and whoever correctly told me what number came up would get an M&M.

The first die came up five.

"That's number five, right, Doc?" cheeky Ellen Carson was the first to pipe up.

"Five! Five! Number five!" chimed in Robin, Eddie Daniel and the others right behind her. They wanted their M&Ms.

"Fife," said Stevie finally. He got his M&M with the rest.

After about twenty minutes, with Stevie always lagging a little behind, I threw a number 6.

"Thix!" Stevie shouted right along with the rest. In the next few throws, he was in a dead heat with the rest of the kids on 3, 7 and 9. His associative powers and verbal expression had caught up with that of the class, though so far he only knew his numbers up to ten while they were past twenty. Good, I thought, the rest would come more easily; this was already more than I expected.

As I made the last roll, once again I saw how competition produces wonders. "Eight!" shouted slow-to-speak, inarticulate Stevie—before anyone else could open their mouth. Eight it was. This time Stevie got a triple M&M reward.

That evening we held our first co-ed parents' conference on behavior management. We usually held these meetings in the morning, which virtually excluded the fathers. Now, with both mothers and fathers, we had a group of sixty-odd people.

I was pleased and surprised. The last time we drew such a crowd was just before the beginning of the school year when I held an orientation meeting. It had turned into a pretty stormy session, featuring some rough interrogation, with me play-acting as teacher and the parents the "dumb" kids (to give them an idea of what it was like for their own kids in regular school).

186

Each parent had been given a sheet of paper as he came in. It contained unintelligible writing (so they could see the words literally through their children's eyes) and jumbled math problems. The exchanges had gone something like this:

ME: "Mr. Miller. Would you stand up and read the first paragraph for me, please?"

MILLER (looking at the gobbledegook): "I can't."

ME: "What do you mean you can't? Can't you read? What were you doing in school for four years, just fooling around, getting into trouble? Or are you just dumb?"

(The atmosphere in the room stiffened suddenly and abruptly.)

ME: "Mrs. Bronson, would you do the fifth math problem for me."

Mrs. Bronson mumbles she can find no fifth math problem on the sheet, and indeed there were only four.

ME: "The fifth one—the one you didn't copy from the blackboard yesterday when I told you to. Can't you follow instructions?"

From the strained looks on the parents' faces, it was obvious this little psycho-drama was getting through. They were all attention.

ME: "This is the situation that every single youngster of every single parent in this room has faced in school. Look around at you. Do you see anyone who looks different? Anyone with webs between his fingers, three sets of hands, two heads? Yet before you signed up your youngster, every single one of you came here to see what the other kids *looked* like. Now, look around at yourselves."

Heads turned selfconsciously.

ME: "That's right. None of you looks any different. And the kids are no different either. They look exactly the same as any other kid. The only trouble is that they haven't been able to learn. And the reason they haven't been able to learn is because they are learning disabled. But another reason they haven't been able to learn is you.''

Heads rose in puzzlement, hurt.

ME: ''Don't look so surprised. Every one of you at some time or another has helped your child cop out. In some way, at some time in the last few years you have made excuses for your child. You've protected him, you've done his homework for him, you've turned on his school and teachers, you've kidded yourselves and said that he'll grow out of it, you've agreed with him that his teacher was no good, you've let him build up this image of himself as a real genius when he can't read or write or even do a puzzle. How often have any of you made your child stand on his own two feet and answer for his deficits? Haven't you hidden the truth from your kid and refused to let him know that anything was wrong?''

I had hit a nerve. Here and there, in the silenced room, came the sound of soft sobs. These parents had suffered right along with their kids; they felt hopeless. Whipped, they were hungry for some miracle cure—but all I could offer them were more hard truths:

ME: ''You've also let your kids manipulate you. After a day of trying to make them behave, all you want is to be left alone. 'Go play outside! Stay up half an hour past your bedtime, watch the stupid television, but just stop screaming!'

''We offer your kids a tremendous amount of structure throughout the school day. They have to earn the right to eat lunch. They have to earn the right to go to gym or to the pool. When they get out of line they're punished, when they're good they get rewards. The kids are taught exactly what's expected of them every moment of every day. But we have your kids only five hours a day, you have them the rest. And what these kids have to earn in school, you're giving away free.

"Who can blame you? These are your kids. You feel for them. They are very difficult kids who seem to defy any kind of control, and you have to be consistent all the time, every day. You've got a job you're not trained for—you don't know how to be consistent (most parents don't)—and you've reached the limits of your endurance. The easiest thing to do is to give up and say, 'OK, have your way. Just leave me alone.'

"But you can't afford to do that anymore—not if you ever want your kids to get anywhere, not if you want them to stay in school. You can't give up. I don't want any parent here to say, 'Here, take him, he's yours,' because I'll throw him right back at you. I don't want him. This school is not a babysitting service, it's not an institution. It's a place where your kids are going to face themselves and learn. Come to us *with* your child and we'll do everything possible we can to help you.

"But remember, changes come slowly. Make sure your goals are reasonable ones, so that when June rolls around you can say, 'Yes, he only made a two-month gain in reading, but it's the first time he's made *any* gain in reading! He didn't show any loss, but it's the first time he didn't show any loss! He likes the other kids in his class and they like him. He's less of a problem at home. He doesn't get into the mischief he used to get into. He hasn't been thrown out of school. He's happy, he's proud of himself, he feels good.'

"Because all these things are important with kids who haven't gotten anywhere in school, kids who have no friends,

189

kids who can't make any kind of sense out of their world, kids who walk around with labels like 'emotionally disturbed' and 'brain-injured' attached to them like a leper's bell, kids other kids whisper about and jeer at and call 'retards.' Your kids have the toughest job. We're asking them to do the impossible. We're asking them to shake all this off and work. We're asking them to learn. We're asking them to do what they never could do before, what they've given up on even trying to do a long time ago. We're not just asking— we're *demanding* this colossal effort from the kids just so that one day they can walk out of here with their heads up, with a smile on their faces, without labels. Well, if we can ask that of them, it seems little enough we're asking of you. If we all pull together I'm convinced we can be successful.''

My pep talk was over. The parents applauded, but I knew many of them had been hurt. Which is why I was surprised— and gratified—to see so many of them here tonight.

Once again I had decided to use dramatic skits to make my points. For the parents' conference I had worked up five different sketches and had asked two dramatically inclined mothers to play child and parent. There were sketches on homework, bedtime, dinnertime and other routines during the day. I hoped each little play would kick off a discussion of different ways to handle each problem.

Instead of a discussion, however, what we got was a war of the sexes. The mothers complained that their husbands weren't home enough and didn't do enough with the kids when they were home. The husbands insisted that their wives couldn't handle the kids and kept laying the burden of discipline on them. We lost track of the kids completely, as wives and husbands went at each other tooth and nail.

"It was a disaster," I later said to Larry Kraus, the school psychologist. "Those people are going to go home and fight all night."

Larry disagreed. "It wasn't exactly great," he said, "but at least they let it all out. That may help them understand their roles with the kids a little better."

Maybe so, but I decided there would be no more co-ed meetings for a while.

We were into October and all the younger kids barreled off in buses for a pre-Halloween trip to a pumpkin farm. They had a ball. Nine-year-old Kevin Chin lost his shoe in the mud and we didn't find it—because he didn't know he'd lost it. Eleven-year-old David Parish started grumping because the trip finished up an hour early—too early for his mother, who lived nearby and wasn't at home, to pick him up at the farm as arranged. So he'd have to traipse back to school and then home again. All common problems.

The only uncommon problem concerned our two seven- and eight-year-old epileptics, little Tami and Jimmy Fox. Julie and I had to bundle them back in the bus to keep warm. Though it was a cold, late October day, with the trip planned long in advance, they had arrived at school in light shirts and nylon windbreakers. Elaine swaddled them in a couple of old undershirts and a sweater, and the tiny kids stuffed their hands up to their elbows in each of Julie's gloves, but still they were blue with cold. This was once too often—the kids had been coming underdressed all year. That afternoon I called Mrs. Fox and let her have it. From then on, they came to school overdressed, but at least you could peel the stuff off.

191

I also gave Charlie Hoffman his second school shower and called his mother and told her so.

"Why did you do that?" she asked.

"Because he needed it. You can smell him through the whole school. I think the least you could do for Charlie, if not for the school, is see that he gets a change of clean clothes each day and some kind of bath."

"I can't do it," she whined. "He won't take baths or showers."

"Well, he's taken two here and we've even washed his clothes," I said. "Don't you think it would be nice if he came to school tomorrow as clean and nice as he's going home today?"

"Sure," she said, huffily.

"Well, if you don't manage to see that he does, I'm going to give him a shower personally each day."

I lost that exchange. Mrs. Hoffman told me that she thought that was the best idea. But Charlie himself seemed to be getting a kick out of the whole new idea of bathing. Maybe he was pleased that after a shower he smelled like a boy instead of smelling, period. Maybe he was pleased that the other kids no longer edged away from him. Whatever the reason, from then on he started to come in a little cleaner.

Some kids are so difficult to reach you have to resort to highly unorthodox methods to get through to them. Even then you need all the luck you can get. About the time I chased Joey Rich into the street I told Lester Geffkin, another ten-year-old in his room, to stand in the hall with a cup and a sign that read: "For a penny, I'll stick my finger up; for three cents, I'll kick you; for a nickel, I'll say a dirty word; for a dime, I'll bite you."

I had placed Les in Joey's class for two reasons. They were both new kids entering after the start of the year and they were both losers. I figured they'd go together like peas in a pod; they did and became friends immediately.

Les was, in many ways, more fortunate than Joey. His IQ was a high normal—120—and although his perceptual deficits were as bad as Joey's, we knew he could read at some level. Although his parents had caught him going through magazines at home, he wouldn't read, at least not out loud, for anyone. And that wasn't his biggest learning problem. Les Geffkin was hardly in this world at all.

Without question, Les was—still is—one of the loopiest kids I have ever met. He would go into the john, take off his shoes and socks and begin flushing and reflushing the toilet, telling himself he was taking a shower. When his teacher started praising other kids for good work, he would get up and say, "Thank you." He'd come back from gym or the pool with his clothes zipped and buttoned perfectly—inside out. When another kid had a birthday party, he'd march around and pick up a party hat, put it on his head and sing "Happy Birthday"—to Les. His intellect, which had helped teach him to read, also gave him the tools to muster up a staggering array of emotional defenses to ward off the real world. Les was an actor and the part he liked to play best was as the toughest little baby around.

If he was upset, he'd bite someone. He'd kick out at another kid or the teacher in the uncoordinated babyish manner of a four-year-old. He'd pass a kid, slap him lightly and whisper, "I'm going to beat you up." When the teacher tried to stop him, and often even if she did not, he would come out with a stream of foul language—"Fuck you, you bastard. Up yours, you bitch"—kick the chair and slap and bite, climaxing with his trademark: giving everyone the finger. Yet Les had so little grasp of reality that he saw no inconsistency between these performances and attempts to buy everything, including friendship. Once he got five dollars' worth of bubble gum baseball cards—enough for almost all the children in school—and went around handing them out to the kids, whispering, ''Here, I'm your friend, have a card.'' The kids just stared, though they took the cards.

I started Les on the early perceptual aspects of ''Who am I?'' Most of our children seem to have trouble with this, but Les had no grasp of it at all. Day after day we plunked him in front of a mirror and made him point out and feel his legs, his arms, his face, his ears—everything he was made of. Gradually Les began to perceive that he was a real person with distinctions all his own and slowly began to relate that real person to the things going on around him.

But only gradually. I realized we needed to find some short-cut to curb Les's outrageous behavior so that he could remain in a class with nine or ten other children with disturbances of their own.

From then on, every time Les stuck up his finger I painted it red. Whenever he went into his cursing, biting, slapping, kicking act, I hung the nickel/penny sign on him, gave him the cup and put him out in the hall.

At first this seemed to work. Les was ashamed to have to stand there while all the kids and teachers passed by, laughing at him and throwing pennies and nickels. His acting-out in the classroom decreased dramatically.

But then the strategy boomeranged. Les started to enjoy his position in center hall. He was collecting all sorts of money and attention and having a ball in the bargain. This just wouldn't do. So, after one of Les's episodes, I walked him and Audrey to the auditorium, placed Les, painted finger and all, on a chair on stage, turned the big spotlight on him and joined Audrey in the audience.

"OK, Les," I called out. "Let's have your show. We want the whole thing, nothing left out. Let's see you kick the chair and bite and curse and stick your finger up. Mrs. Turner and I want to see if you're any good. OK, first act."

Les stared uncertainly into the black void of the auditorium.

"Come on, now. I want to see something really good. Where is it?"

Les hesitated and then proceeded to give one of the funniest half-hour shows I've ever seen. He kicked the chair, he stuck up his finger, he cursed, he ran around and screamed and flailed at imaginary opponents. Audrey and I were doubled-up laughing. "Wait, wait," he said, pausing for breath. "Short intermission now. Then the show will go on." He was organizing like crazy. There was a real ten-year-old boy putting on his own show, and a good one at that. And he was in total control of himself.

The problem, of course, was that all this was only reinforcing his out-of-sight behavior. How in the hell was I going to get him back on the right track?

I clapped my hands and stopped the show. "Les," I said. "That was really great. I mean really great. Mrs. Turner and I really enjoyed it. But it's so good it doesn't seem fair that only your teacher and I get to see it. How about inviting the whole school so they can enjoy themselves too. OK?"

Les was on such a high that he just nodded in agreement. I don't think he too realized that I always do what I say I'm going to do. I rang the bell and ten minutes later every student in the school was seated in the auditorium waiting to see Lester Geffkin put on his show.

It was strong medicine, but it worked. Les froze. I dismissed the audience and took Les back to my office. I told him that from now on if he wanted to make a public spectacle of himself, he'd have to do it in public. If he wanted to perform in class, he'd have to do it for everyone. "So just remember, Les, if you want to stick up your finger, you'll have to do it for the whole school."

That was the last time we had any trouble with Les and his finger. Not that he still wasn't one of the loonier kids in the school, but he got to be fun-loony. You could go on his trips with him, let him sail up there in his balloon and then slowly lead him back to earth.

Elaine had noted that many of her kids could now add single numbers in their heads and even some two-place numbers, though they still needed the help of sorting trays and fingers. A few were even able to work out different combinations of numbers to achieve the same total; using a special counterbalance scale, they would decide to put a 4 and a 1 on one side and balance a 5 on the other. That was tremendous progress in so short a time. Best of all, Elaine told me that Stevie Sachs, who had started out with practically no conception of numbers, could now add single numbers in his head just like the rest of the class. I decided to see for myself.

"Who wants to show me how they can add?" I asked. Once again every hand went up, including Stevie's.

I called on Ellen and gave her a simple problem which she did correctly. I called on another kid. Stevie was getting itchy. I called on another child. Stevie couldn't wait.

196

"Call on me, Doc! Call on me! Call on me!" he shouted out.

"OK, Stevie," I said. "Now, let's see. How much is seven plus five?"

Stevie deliberated and deliberated some more. As he did, I noticed his hand was moving under his rear end. Maybe he's counting out with his fingers, I thought, disappointed but realizing it was better than not adding at all.

"Twelf," said Stevie finally.

"Right," I said, and gave him an M&M. "But why were you cheating?"

"I wath not cheating!" said Stevie indignantly. "I wath not!"

"Yes, you were," I said.

"Wath not!" Stevie replied.

"You were," I said. "I saw you. You were counting with your hand, the one you're sitting on."

"I wath not, Doc!" said Stevie, nearly crying. "My balths itcth!"

I burst out laughing, I couldn't help myself. Then I took Stevie in my arms and hugged him. Best of all, it turns out that he has a real aptitude in math, for he was soon speeding past the kids in his class.

Other good things were happening. My pet pain-in-the-neck, Paul Mitchell, seemed to be coming around. The day before, Carl, his teacher, reported that he'd volunteered for the first time and wrote a math problem on the board. I went home happy.

Apparently I had misjudged Paul again, because the next morning, as I carried another kid, eight-year-old Paul Radano, kicking and squalling into the lunchroom for a calm-

197

down session, who should I find there but big Paul himself. He had his feet up on the table and was whistling and humming to himself, twiddling with a piece of paper. He had again refused to read when called upon, flying into a rage and declaring it was all "baby stuff" that he already knew. Carl had sent him to the lunchroom as punishment; Paul saw it as a great escape, a way to goof off.

"Well, if my two favorite people aren't in trouble at the same time," I said. "Paul the young and Paul the old."

I had an idea. I sat them across from each other.

"Paul," I said to Mr. Mitchell, "look at young Paul. This is just what you used to be, biting, kicking, screaming, five or six years ago. You should be proud of yourself. You haven't changed a bit. You're a little taller, you wear glasses and young Paul doesn't, but when you talk out of turn and you won't do this or that, you're just the same. How does it feel to have five years go right down the drain?"

Paul Mitchell said nothing. Paul Radano was now completely quiet, because he didn't know this twelve-year-old from a hole in the wall and wasn't quite sure what this bigger kid might do.

"Here," I said to Paul Mitchell. "Talk to him. This is you—you the way you were, you the way you are. Tell him what it feels like to be five years older and have nothing changed. Tell him how it feels not to be able to read, to do your math, to write, to work out in gym. Maybe if you get him to be good and go back to his class like a person, you can do the same thing with yourself."

I walked out. A split-second later, Paul Mitchell tried to bolt out after me.

"Where do you think you're going?" I said, stopping him in his tracks. "Now go back and talk to him."

198

"I won't."

"Yes, you will."

After a couple of exchanges, I sent little Paul, completely subdued by now, back to class and then sat down for one more harangue with Paul Mitchell.

"Well, how does it feel to be nowhere after five years? Nowhere, just like the little Paul you were just looking at?"

"Leave me alone, you shit!" Paul screamed. "You're always around, you're always here. You don't give me time to do anything! You're always interfering! Just go away!"

"There's no way I'm going to do that—just no way. This is only the beginning." I decided to hit him with something stronger. I knew one of the things he hated was riding the special bus, the one that said "Handicapped" and carried several kids who were obviously retarded to other schools along our route. I was sure that Paul, as many of our kids, felt deep down that they were the same as the other kids they rode with. "Paul, do you think you're a retard?" I asked bluntly.

Paul bristled. "No!" he shot back with intensity.

"Well, then why are you playing the retarded game? No matter how often we say you *can* learn to read or do math or all these other things, no matter how anyone tries to help you, you won't do it, you won't even try. Sometimes I think you wish you *were* retarded so you'd have a good excuse for being the way you are. But unfortunately, you happen to be kind of bright. You just don't want to change. That's what eats at your gut, the fact that you're going to have to change, that we're going to make you change. But you're so full of self-pity you're afraid that if you change, you won't have anything to pity yourself for. Who will feel sorry for little Paulie when he learns how to read? Am I right?"

199

"I don't care what you do to me," Paul sulked. "I know all about you. You're just going to send a report card home to my mother and . . ."

"Yes, I am," I interrupted, "and I'm going to send a special report card just for you."

"Why do I have to have a special report card?" Paul asked, suddenly interested.

"Because I want to show you that there's at least one course Paul can pass, that he'll get A-plus-plus in. That's self-pity."

"You can write anything you want on it," said Paul. And then he laughed. "It won't matter. I get the mail before my mother. That's why I don't come on trips sometimes because I don't tell her, that's why you don't get the lunch money, that's why . . ."

"Wrong, Paul," I interrupted again. "I *know* when you're not coming on a trip because your mother calls and tells me. I *know* when your mother's sending me the lunch money in the mail and I get it, because she tells me and she sends it. I know everything about you. I talk to your mother all the time."

"How can you!? That's not fair!"

"I told you before, Paul," I said. "I'm going to surround you like a blanket. I'm going to know everything you do— in school, at home, in the Boy Scouts, everything. And the only way you'll get me off your back is to start doing what we want you to do in school. Now get back to your class and work or we'll have to have another workout in the gym. Or maybe you'd like me to come sit on your lap again?"

"No, forget it, I'll do it," Paul said hastily. He went back to class and we'd bought another week. That night his mother told me on the phone that he'd come home talking about how

200

smart Dr. Cohen was, how he couldn't fool him, not like those other "jerks" of teachers. But I had learned my lesson by now. I wasn't breathing any more sighs of relief. This was obviously going to be all uphill, particularly if Paul's teacher couldn't win Paul's respect and if he was going to get no help at home. I could tell that Mrs. Mitchell had all but given up when she remarked: "He's hopeless. I can't do anything with him. You're the only one who can." Paul was my baby, she was saying, and though I didn't have the heart to carry out my orientation session threat—and throw him right back at her—I knew I couldn't be with him all the time. Nor could Carl, one of my best and toughest teachers, even with only ten other kids in his class. Maybe a residential school was the answer, but the Mitchells couldn't afford one, I knew. As with a good many kids we get so late in the game, I was barely hanging on. If only we could get them a couple of years younger before they got so terribly locked in.

Almost as if to prove the point, my first problem the next day was in Dan Shea's "senior class," a group of twelve- to fourteen-year-olds who were doing the most advanced work in their age bracket. Both Dan and I were concerned about thirteen-year-old Louis Kantrow and twelve-year-old Howard Glass. Each had been with us for about three years.

Louis, a mild-mannered type from a middle-class family, had done extremely well in school. He had come in as a kid with many visual perceptual motor deficits and secondary emotional problems but no brain dysfunction, and had progressed to the point where he was less than a year behind grade level in reading and math. As a consequence he had lost almost all his defeatism and was now able to hack it with his peers and had developed a fairly good self-image. Other than an occasional bout of inferiority, he was now a happy, learning, adjusted kid.

Howard was a different sort. When he turned up, he was a hyperkinetic, minimal brain-dysfunctioning, emotionally disturbed child. Perhaps because of his highly academically oriented parents—one a college professor, the other a high school teacher—his progress academically had been much swifter than Louis's. He stood above his grade level in math and only somewhat behind in reading. But despite having overcome most of his hyperkinesis—he had long before been taken off Thorazine—and the worst of his emotional problems, he still tended to be a loner and a fighter. Nevertheless, we felt that Howard and Louis were ready to return to regular school; both were ripe for the experience. So early in the term we'd quietly promoted them to the senior class, and loaded them with extra catch-up homework, mainly in the science and social studies areas we have to slight because of our emphasis on reading and math.

To minimize the pressure on the kids and reduce premature expectations, it's our policy to tell only the parents what we plan for their children. Now both Louis and Howard were complaining about their added workload. Each was being asked to do an hour and a half of homework each night, well over twice as much as the other kids in class, and they weren't exactly hiding their annoyance.

I took the two outside.

"What's the problem?" I asked Louis. "Why are you bugging Mr. Shea?"

"Why do Howard and I have all this extra homework?" Louis said. "It doesn't seem fair. None of the other kids have to do all this work."

Howard nodded his head vigorously. "It's not fair at all,"

he said. "You're picking on me. And if you don't stop, I'm going to tell my father."

"The reason you're getting all this work," I said, aiming my remark at Louis, "is that you and Howard are the only ones in class who have the ability to do it." I hoped they would accept the honor and leave it at that. Our kids are fiercely competitive.

Louis bought it, but not Howard, who had instigated most of the fussing in the first place. "I don't have the time," he said. "I want to play with my friends." What friends? I thought—he hadn't been able to make any close friends even in school. "I won't be able to watch TV. My parents don't like it when I have so much work." He had a whole list of excuses.

"Well, you're just going to have to do it," I said firmly.

"I'm not going to," said Howard as his parting shot, "I'm going to get my father to call you and set you straight on this." (Howard's father, a professed believer in learn-at-your-own-speed education, was also, paradoxically, highly critical of the most minute details of Howard's curriculum and schedule. He expressed reservations about every phase of his son's education. I wasn't looking forward to his inevitable phone call that night—it would probably mean a fight.)

Sure enough, when the call came, it was to report a fight—but with Howard over his homework. Dr. Glass had finally made him do it, he said, and, to prove as much, Howard brought it in complete the next day. Maybe his father had finally realized that we were offering his son a firm chance to return to normal boyhood. At last we had him on our side. Now if only we could get Howard to go along, without blowing this back-to-school program sky-high. His classmates were already suspicious.

About an hour later, I saw little Dennis Sullivan in the kindergarten class jumping up and down out in the hall. I went up and asked him what he was doing there.

"I don't know," Dennis said. "I don't remember."

"Well," I said, following a standard school procedure that each kid must know and say why and for what he's being punished, "you go in and ask Mrs. Wise why you're out in the hall. I can't have you standing out here not knowing why. Then you come back and tell me."

I waited for a minute or so and Dennis didn't reappear. As I started to open the door to his room, he jumped up from his seat and started shouting, "Get out, get out!"

"Mrs. Wise," I said to Elaine, loud enough for the whole class to hear, "did Mr. Sullivan ask you a question for me?"

"No, Dr. Cohen," Elaine responded in the same tone of voice, "Mr. Sullivan didn't ask me anything. He told me that you told him to go back to his room."

"Oh, he did, did he? I told Mr. Sullivan to ask you why he was out in the hall. He said he didn't remember." Dennis was beginning to get the idea that secrets were not safe here.

"Mr. Sullivan," replied Elaine, "was sent to the hall because he was talking out of turn and wouldn't listen."

"Is that right, Mr. Sullivan?" I asked. Mr. Sullivan nodded.

"Are you going to listen, Mr. Sullivan?"

"No," said Mr. Sullivan.

I took Mr. Sullivan to my office and put him under my desk, where he sat, moping and tearful.

"You know, Mr. Sullivan," I called down to him, "you have this big mouth that doesn't do anything but talk out of turn. It gets you in trouble. Now open it wide. I want to see how big it really is."

204

Dennis stuck out his head and opened his mouth and showed his tonsils.

"Why, that's not big enough for me even to put a lollipop in."

"Yes, it is," Dennis asserted quickly, reaching for the lollipop I had fished out of the desk.

"Why are you under my desk, Mr. Sullivan?" I asked, holding the lollipop out of reach. "It's pretty hard to get to this lollipop if you're under the desk. Now, why are you there?"

"I'm here," said Mr. Sullivan, "because my mouth is . . . is . . . uh . . . isn't big."

"No," I said, "your mouth is too big. It's too big."

"Make up your mind," said Mr. Sullivan, and he was right. He started to chuckle and laugh.

"You're dumb, Doc. You're really, really dumb."

"You're right," I agreed, "but at least my mouth is the right size. It's the right size for me to control. How's yours? Is it the right size to control?"

"I can get it to the right size," Dennis replied.

"Can you get it to the right size and keep it to the right size so you can control it?"

"Yeah."

"That means you can keep it shut when you're supposed to keep it shut and listen? And then keep it shut and listen some more and still keep it shut?"

"Yes, I can do that," said Mr. Sullivan.

I said, "OK," gave him the lollipop and sent him back to class.

As Dennis hurried down the hall, David Parish came up. David is an introverted, squirmy kid who had been taken off drugs the year before. He cried at the time and several times after, saying he needed the drugs, fearful that he wouldn't be able to maintain control. He also seemed to fall apart with any kind of criticism. Maureen and I had arranged to make me the villain whenever David got out of line, sending him to me rather than letting her alienate him with punishment. So far this year, David had not been sent to me once.

This time, David, like little Dennis Sullivan, had persisted in talking to a neighbor after Maureen told the class to be quiet. When she asked him to stop, David complained she was being unfair and picking on him. He started crying, then got moody and shifted around in his seat, and resumed talking. Finally, Maureen had sent him to me. This meant David would not only have to face me but skip gym, which he loved.

He came in and sat down brooding by the desk.

"Isn't it about time that you learned to control yourself?" I said.

No answer.

"How does it feel being off medication? Does it make it harder to control yourself?"

"Yeah," he said.

"Well, maybe the thing to do is for you to go back on it."

"No, I don't want that," David said quickly. Good for the kid.

"That makes me very happy. I don't want you to go back on medication either. And I think you can control yourself without it because you have up to this point, except when you get frustrated or forget what you're doing. But now you're going to have to learn much better control of yourself and not even get into these little difficulties. Can you think of some way to really control yourself and learn to keep your mouth shut?"

"Yes, I can," said David. "I'm going to do it."

"How?"

David got very quiet and then said, "It's a secret way."

I grinned. "How am I going to know that your secret method is working?"

"You'll know," David insisted. "You'll know."

"OK," I said, and put David to work straightening shelves. But I kept at him.

"You know secrets can be forgotten," I said, while David was working. "You have a secret on your mind, you get busy, and then, before you know it, you start thinking about something else and suddenly you don't remember the secret anymore. And since you're the only one who knows the secret, it's forgotten forever."

"Why don't you leave me alone?" David said.

"I can't leave you alone, because I'm working on secret orders to help you keep your mouth shut."

"From my father?" David asked, suddenly curious.

"No."

"Who gave you the secret orders?" he asked.

"I can't tell you," I said, "because they're from a secret organization."

"Who's the secret organization?"

"That's a secret," I said, "but I'll trade my secret for your secret."

"No," he said. "I'm not going to tell you."

"OK," I said as I sent him back to his room. "But I want you to do one thing. I want you to let me know when your secret plan for keeping your mouth shut is in effect so that I can see if it's working. If it's in effect, and it's working, then I can tell my secret organization that it's working and they can call off my secret orders and everything will be all right."

David started to laugh. "You'll see," he said, grinning as he left, "you'll see that my secret plan is working."

"OK," I said. "I'll wait."

Lester Geffkin's good behavior couldn't last forever. One day at the end of swimming, when everyone had gone to the lockers to dress, Les reappeared in front of the next class stark naked. He was crying as if his heart would break. The swimming instructor asked him what was wrong.

"They put my underwear down the toilet," Les moaned. "They tried to flush it down the toilet. It's all wet."

"Les was cursing. Les was cursing," the other kids chorused.

I put Les back in his bathing suit while we dried his clothes and decided to let the incident pass without comment—he had already been punished by the kids. But he didn't let it go.

"I guess, Doc," he said in the resigned tones of an adult taking his medicine, "I'll just have to go back on the stage." I had to find another line, quick, and decided to try to reach him at a more mature level.

"Did you enjoy yourself cursing?" I asked.

"Yes," he admitted.

"Then you've had too much fun with it already," I told him. "You don't deserve to go back on the stage." Les looked at me and I saw the lesson had been learned. A basic behavior pattern—making trouble to attract attention—was being uprooted.

Les began to contain himself, and the next few days passed without incident. Then, as Audrey was passing out books for reading, she noticed something curious. Les was ignoring his second-grade book and looking at his neighbor, Kathy's, third-grade book. What's more, he was silently lipping the words.

"Would you like that book?" Audrey asked casually.

"Yes," said Les.

She gave him a book and asked him to read. He read the story straight through in a clear voice.

Audrey rushed out in the hall and grabbed me. "What should I do? What should I do?" she gasped and told me what had happened.

"He took Kathy's book. He's reading. I mean he's *reading* Kathy's book! It's a third-grade book. Should I let him have it? Should I give him the next book?"

Audrey usually goes berserk like this whenever one of her kids does something right, let alone terrific. I told her to let Les have the third-grade book but not the fourth, and to do the homework so he would get it consolidated in his mind.

Two months later, we started him on fourth-grade reading, but not before he had thrown Audrey again. Given a list of words, the class was instructed to "circle all the vowels," nothing more, nothing less. Lester Geffkin, the kid who would never do as he was told, wrote the letters "a," "e," "i," "o" and "u" on his paper and put a circle around each one.

"What mark should I give him?" asked Audrey, showing me Les's paper.

"One hundred percent," I replied, "and A+ for following instructions perfectly."

I was getting as bored as the kids in perceptual training—what with all these metronomes and flashing lights—and was eager to see if the kids could integrate visual and auditory perceptions with such motor perceptions as tapping or tracking. So I decided to try another technique—music. I turned on an operetta and asked the kids to fingerpaint to the various changes in tempo and volume as I recorded their movements on our TV tape camera (which we watch on a monitor).

"OK, kids," I barked in my best director's voice, "this is loud music. Paint loudly." Then, as the music changed, "This is soft music. Oh, it makes me *so* sleepy, we have to paint slowly, very sl-ow-ly." I kept calling their attention to the music: "This is fast! Paint fast, faster, faster! Now, lightly, lightly."

I was having a ball, directing and playing with my mechanical eyeball, zooming in and out on the kids, concentrating on a few kids who had really opened up recently, before I panned to the rest. We were all getting carried away.

What I didn't notice until I swiveled the camera around to the rest of the group was that two kids—Mary Ann Williams and little Jimmy Blake, my "son" of the beginning of the year—had gotten so carried away that they were literally dancing all around, smearing their fingerpaints on the wall—in loud smashing patterns, gentle traces, fast zips—in time to the music.

Suddenly with the camera on them, they stopped, shocked by the realization that they were out of their seats—a breach of firmly established school discipline. I watched them dutifully return to their desks and sit down, while managing to overlook the customary punishment. Still, it was a shame. Not only was the mural they were painting a beauty, but I never really caught their happy, dancing action on our private channel.

Howard Glass wasn't giving up. He was back at it again, complaining about his workload, still unaware that it was being assigned to help prepare him for return to regular school. A three-hour assignment due right after the weekend apparently was the final straw. When he turned up in school, the assignment was unfinished but in its place was a brief that must have taken him several hours more than the assignment to prepare. It listed his beefs in detail—how the extra work was affecting his life, how there weren't enough hours in the day to do it all, how it violated his constitutional rights.

"Why should I have to do this?" he demanded, reciting the whole litany for the benefit of not only me and his teacher and the class, but for Louis, who was also still in the dark as to the reason for the extra work. Though I realized it might well blow Howard's and Louis's cover, I turned the question over to the class to decide as a court. I didn't want to do it, but I really had no choice. I would have preferred to spare the boys the extra pressure once they understood why they were being singled out; on the other hand, the class had become increasingly suspicious about their "special treatment."

It didn't take long for them to arrive at the answer.

"Howard and Louis are going back to regular school, aren't they?" said Pete Connelly as soon as court was convened. "That's why they're getting all this extra homework." I'll never forget the envious look on his face. "That's it, Doc, isn't it?"

The other kids looked at me for confirmation.

"Yes, we hope so," I said. And then, in an attempt to defuse their jealousy, I added: "But they're going to need a lot of help from you too."

I turned to Louis and Howard, to see their reactions. They were dumfounded. Louis giggled; Howard's face froze.

"Well, Howard," I said quietly, "now you know. Does it make you feel any better?"

Once he had absorbed the news, I could tell he was elated, as if he'd scored some big victory over the others.

Louis, on the other hand, was terrified and still giggling nervously. The news for him was a big threat. We had to make sure it didn't become a setback. The next morning he came in with all sorts of questions, none related to any reality except his own fear.

"How will I know where to go for lunch? What if the bus driver doesn't know where I live? Will my mother be able to come to school meetings from her job?"

"Now look, Louis," I said, after reassuring him on each question. "This is all nonsense. Everything is going to be all right. As long as you keep up with this extra work. Did you do your work last night?"

"Yeh!" he answered.

"Was it hard?" I asked.

"Well, it wasn't too bad."

"That's what your new school is going to be like," I said. " 'Not too bad.' It might even be much better than that. In fact, I'm sure it will be. But it's up to you to make it good. It's up to you and the kind of work you do. And so far, you've been doing fine."

Louis brightened considerably. "You think I can do it, then?"

"Louis," I laughed. "I think you can do anything." What a terrible brainwashing these poor kids get! But Louis had finally come through OK—delicate, in constant need of reassurance, but OK. And he did just fine in his new school.

That afternoon, I put Simon Legree to shame. Audrey, perhaps the best teacher I have, which is saying something since all are top-notch, came to tell me she was a few months pregnant. She'd already had two miscarriages, but this time the portents looked favorable. I said I was glad for her sake, but that I'd have to bring in another teacher to handle her class.

Not surprisingly she was angry and hurt. She started to cry. "Here I'm straight with you," she said. "I tell you the truth and you give me the shaft. It's not fair."

"It doesn't look fair," I conceded, "but it is. I know you're doing a great job, they love you like a second mother, and that's just the problem. Think of those kids (when *didn't* Audrey think of those kids!). You know the emotional tightrope they walk. You've already got them tied to your apron strings and it's only October. What will happen to them around February or March when you leave? They'll fall apart and we'll be lucky if some new teacher can paste them together again by June. Well, it just so happens that I have a qualified teacher available now." I did. Eileen Holscher who had a master's degree and good experience in special ed was working as an aide in another class, waiting for the next opening. "Rather than drag it out and risk sending them into a tailspin later in the year, let's make it short and sweet. I'll bring Eileen in now, while it's still early enough for her to get established with the kids."

Audrey reluctantly agreed that the proposal made some sense, but when the news got around to the rest of the staff— a matter of an hour or so—they were up in arms. They felt it was a dirty deal. I wasn't feeling too happy myself. I was particularly upset that it had to happen to Audrey who was born to be a mother and have a clutch of children of her own.

I sat around the rest of the afternoon, trying to come up with some solution. When I finally did, I was so excited I called her at home.

213

"Say, Audrey," I said when she came to the phone, "instead of just working with this one class, what would you think of helping out with all the kids as my permanent aide in perceptual training?" We had been borrowing aides to fill in when I was called away to attend to one crisis or another. "This way I wouldn't have a transition problem, and you could work as long as you and your doctor think feasible."

Audrey was so happy she cried, and I don't mind admitting I felt like joining her. I'm probably a lousy administrator—Audrey was the second teacher I had fired and rehired (the first because the parents came to bat for him and I must say he shaped up beautifully)—but Audrey was someone I really didn't want to lose.

Eileen Holscher turned up the next morning as Audrey's new aide. All the kids eyed her suspiciously, particularly Joey Rich who was perhaps closest of all to Audrey. When Audrey began shifting more and more duties to Eileen, Joey would wait around after Eileen had approved his homework to show it to Audrey, to see if it was *really* all right. But those problems would work out in time.

I took a visitor from a neighboring public special ed system around school and must admit I felt pretty good. David Parish had his secret control system working. Dennis Sullivan was bouncing cheerily along. Bobby Hammack was smiling; and in kindergarten, Robin Lasky had moved on from coloring within the lines to drawing straight-line letters. This really tickled me because it was Robin my visitor had come to observe, since she rightfully belonged in his school system. Ellen Carson was busily working on her alphabet. Academics, once they'd taken hold, had diverted a good deal of her nervous energy and made her calmer and less distractible. She was really enjoying learning: the school work was structuring her instead of vice versa—having to structure herself for the work. A late butterfly flew into the room. Not one of these highly distractible five- and six-year-olds even turned to look. I went over and cupped it in my hands and let it fly out the window. The kids went on with their lesson. Beautiful. My visitor was impressed. So was I. I thought how, with the exception of Paul Mitchell, things had moved along smoothly so far this year, with the incidents few and far between, and those more amusing than serious. The teachers and kids had really taken hold.

After my visitor left, I was called to the pool. Nine-year-old Denise Ingrassia had lined up in her suit with the other kids, but was screaming that she couldn't go in the pool.

I asked her what was the matter.

"I don't want to get my hair wet," she said.

"Why not?"

"I just had it done," she said primly.

"Well, it looks pretty," I said. "If you're concerned, I'll get you a bathing cap."

"I can't wear one," she said.

"Why?"

"Because I can't hear."

"You don't have to hear anything in the pool except Mr. Welch's whistle, and that you can hear through a cap." I went back and got the cap and put it on her. Still Denise didn't want to get wet.

"Don't you want to go swimming?" I asked.

"Yes," she said.

"Do you want to go in the pool?"

"Yes."

"How are you going to do that without getting wet? Do you think you can walk on the water? There's only one person I know of who tried that scene and got away with it."

"I'm going to walk on the water," Denise asserted.

"OK, try it. Walk on the water in the pool."

Denise still refused to go in. All the other kids were waiting now too.

"Denise," I said, going after the hose. "Do you like to take showers?"

"Yes," she said, "I really like showers."

I squirted her with the hose and went chasing around the pool after her, while she giggled and shrieked and finally jumped into the pool. None of the other kids would go in until they were squirted too. I left Denise thrashing around and thoroughly enjoying herself. "Be sure not to get wet," I called to her.

"I won't," she answered. My kooks.

The next day Paul Mitchell didn't turn up for school. I checked with his mother and learned he was sick—he'd complained of a fever the night before and the thermometer showed he actually had one. He was out for two days, including Halloween. I was sorry. That was one time he could really have fun in this "miserable" school.

We had our second parents' meeting that morning and it went a lot better than the last one. Mothers only. This time the subject was the kids'—not the parents'—problems.

The mothers were concerned that their children had no friends to play with after school. Most of them had already been drummed out of the neighborhood groups because of their physical limitations or their inability to understand and follow the rules or their low threshold of frustration which inevitably led to screaming, tantrums and fights. Most were considered such spoiled brats nobody wanted to play with them.

The solution seemed self-evident: Many of the kids had made friends in school and some lived nearby each other. We drew up a list of kids in the school by class, age and address, and the mothers promised to try to get them together.

When we found ourselves getting into the father's role again, I saw that the lesson of the last meeting had been well-learned. The mothers felt the fathers should avail themselves of these school discussions—but suggested they do it alone. We agreed to set up another evening conference—this time, fathers only.

Monday was Halloween, and the kids came to school in their costumes. We had Charlie Chaplin, Superman, a ghost, the works. I was trying to finish up some paperwork so I'd have the afternoon free for the party when Audrey came in to report that Joey Rich wasn't in school, and no one had called in to say he was sick. I told her to phone his house, and she returned to say that after Joey's two older brothers, who also were home from school for some reason, had hung up on her twice, she had finally gotten Joey to the phone. To the accompaniment of sounds more suitable to a zoo than a home—screams, all sorts of racket—Joey gave her a confused story about how his mother didn't have the money for a costume and had made him stay home from school. I said I would take care of Joey.

I called the house. One of his brothers answered. "This is Dr. Cohen," I said in my sternest tone. "I want you to put your mother on the phone."

"Hey, it's Dr. Cohen," the kid yelled out.

"What's he want? Why the hell can't he stop bothering us and leave us alone?" said a male voice in the background.

"I said I want you to get your mother," I barked again, "and don't hang up on me because I'll call back or come over to the house myself."

"She's sleeping," said the kid.

"Well, get her up," I barked. "Tell her I'm on the phone."

A few minutes later, Mrs. Rich, who usually has a soft spot for Joey, came on the line. She explained that last night Joey indeed asked for money for a Halloween costume and apples for dunking and candy, but she'd had only three dollars and told him No. The other two boys had been thrown out of school and put on home study and the place was a madhouse. To make matters worse, Joey's father was out of work, and when Joey kept pestering for the money he'd hit him. Mrs. Rich locked Joey in his room and kept him from school the next day as punishment.

"I guess I really took it out on him," she sighed.

I agreed, but it was certainly understandable under the circumstances. I told her that Joey had been given the same instructions as the rest of the kids—to make a costume and bring only a few pennies' worth of candy or apples to share with the other kids. Joey had probably gotten confused. "But with or without a costume," I said, "I want Joey in school right now. I know your husband's there and I want him to bring Joey to school this minute. I have a costume for him that I think he'll really like."

"Hey, Bill," Mrs. Rich hollered. "The doc wants you to take Joey to school."

"I don't care what he wants," Mr. Rich yelled back. "I'm

not taking that kid to school or anywhere. I'm tired of doing things for him. I'm tired of breaking my back for him.''

"Mrs. Rich," I said. "Put your husband on the line."

More screaming between husband and wife. Finally Mr. Rich picked up the phone.

"What do you want me to do?" he asked in a suddenly ingratiating voice.

For some reason this really set me off, and I lost my temper and went into one of my tirades. Joey had become almost like a son to me.

"Look here, Mr. Rich," I thundered, "I don't care what Joey does. I don't care if he turns your house upside down. Joey is sick. You don't seem to understand that. Now either you're going to get him to school or you're not, but if you don't I'm going to throw him out of school. And that'll be a shame, because the kid has made such great progress. He's really learning, he likes school—and all this is not costing you a penny. [Joey was being subsidized by state aid plus a school scholarship.] Now I want you to bring Joey to school. He's going to have his Halloween party just like every other kid here. And if you're not here in ten minutes, I'm going to send a taxi for him."

"I'll do it for you," Rich answered, "but I won't do it for Joey."

"That's just dandy," I said, "but whoever you're doing it for, get him here." I hung up. I knew I wasn't being at all consistent—one moment saying that if he didn't bring the kid I'd throw him out, the next that I'd come for him in a cab! I didn't even know whether I would throw Joey out. Apparently his father didn't either, because fifteen minutes later, Rich brought his son in to class and went looking for me to

219

apologize. Luckily I was busy elsewhere and missed him. (A few days later he apologized by phone.)

I found Joey and brought him to my office for a short talk to calm him down. Besides, this was my last chance to break a piece of bad news before it was known by everyone: Audrey's switch to her new assignment. Eileen Holscher had worked out as well as we'd expected and Audrey was due to announce her departure that afternoon. But we wanted Joey to hear it from us, so he'd have a bit of advance preparation.

"Joey," I said after we had talked a few minutes, "I'll tell you a big secret." His eyes widened conspiratorially. "Mrs. Turner is pregnant. She's going to have a baby." Joey looked at me suspiciously. "Isn't that wonderful?" I said, trying to involve him. He wasn't buying. "She's going to help me in my class, so you'll see her almost every day, but because she's having a baby and won't be here for the full year, you're going to have a new regular teacher."

Joey started to cry. "Doesn't she like me anymore?" he sobbed.

"Of course she loves you, Joey. That's why she's depending on you to help her until she has to leave."

Joey was miserable. "Will she ever be back again? Doesn't she like us?"

"Yes, Joey," I said. "I'm sure she'll be back. And she does 'like you. She doesn't want to leave—and she really isn't—but you have to help her and help your new teacher, the woman who's been the aide in your room." Joey just kept crying, so to cheer him up I pulled out the one thing I had in reserve.

"Joey," I said, "how would you like to be the clown today?" And then I confided that sometimes I was the clown, sometimes it was Mr. Jensen, the school's administrator. But

220

I thought some of the kids were catching on, and wanted to fool them by having someone else play Bozo. "The costume would be a great costume," I said. "And no one would know who you were. We'd paint your face and everything."

It worked. A smiling Joey went back to class. Maybe it helped that he had a secret that none of the other kids had. Best of all, Joey, who is chubby, made a great clown and managed to distribute two huge bagfuls of candy and cookies and apples to everyone. Though no one could fail to identify the fat kid in the clown suit, somehow it didn't matter.

The party was a great success. The kids dunked apples, played records, marched, drew pumpkins that they said looked like Doc, ate cupcakes and cookies and generally had a ball. One kid, Barry, came in dressed in regular clothes, with no other costume than a loud orange tie. He said he was me. Since I have a reputation for wearing flashy ties, I got a real kick out of it. Yet for all the fun I couldn't help being impressed by the way each of the teachers had their class completely under control.

Audrey, however, really had her work cut out for her, trying to explain to her kids that she wasn't going to be their regular teacher any more. I kept to the back of the room, as she went through it with her nine kids, over and over. Finally, Spencer, a black kid who has been in several foster homes, looked her straight in the eye.

"Mrs. Turner," he said, "I hope the baby dies in your stomach . . ."

Audrey froze. Those two miscarriages . . .

". . . then," Spencer went on, "you won't ever have to leave us anymore."

Audrey halfway recovered and tried to say something comforting about mothers.

221

"I know all about mothers," said Spencer, interrupting. "They give their babies away. I know. I've been given away lots of times . . ."

Audrey ran out of the room, trying to control her tears. For once the big blabbermouth—me—had nothing to say. Thank goodness, Audrey whipped back in with a cheery smile and took her kids down to the party.

Paul Mitchell arrived back fresh from his sick leave, all the more determined to fight school. Within an hour he was squirming in his seat, poking his neighbors, making his pat complaint that the "jerk" teacher was giving him a baby book he already knew. It was true it was another repeat, but only because Paul didn't know it.

This time I didn't waste any time in gab.

"OK, Paul, prove it to me," I ordered. "Prove that you can read that book to me, show me you can read eighty percent of it correctly, and I'll give you another."

Instead of an argument, to my surprise Paul actually tried to read the book. He couldn't make out more than fifty percent of it, but at least he'd tried and made no further fuss. That was some glimmer of progress. I decided to let him make the evaluation.

"Do you think you read eighty percent of that book correctly, Paul?" I asked.

"No, Doc," said Paul, "I guess I didn't. I guess I'll have to repeat it."

Would wonders never cease? All that pounding, that humiliation, coupled with our little after-school chats which had continued off and on—were they at last producing a reasonable, working kid? If so, we could surely meet him halfway.

I glanced at the book—a prominent "Grade 2" on its cover announced it was truly a "baby" book.

"Yes, you will have to repeat the book," I agreed. "But once you do so to my satisfaction, Mr. Janicki is going to give you special material in reading and math and your other subjects."

Paul brightened and concentrated on the book for the next week when he showed me he could get about sixty percent of it right. I accepted that. Then, good as our word, and as we've done with several of our older kids, Carl prepared almost the same schoolwork—at the same level—for Paul on ditto sheets with no identifying ratings. Status is extremely important with our kids.

Howard Glass was again in trouble, this time with Pete Connelly. It wasn't his work—now that he knew he was headed out of the school Howard was going a mile a minute—but he couldn't keep from flaunting his "graduation" in the face of the other kids. Finally, Pete—who has the shortest fuse of any kid in school—had a bellyful; he slipped behind Howard and with a pair of scissors snipped off part of the ponytail Howard had been growing the last few months. Howard, of course, started swinging and they both had to sit out gym.

I had to laugh, in spite of myself. Howard had turned hippie with a vengeance, complete to wearing ragged jeans, a headband, the whole works—as a matter of fact, his disapproval of Howard's appearance was one of the few things I secretly shared with his father—but it took a kid, Pete Connelly, to do what both of us adults had been itching to do. Howard seemed to take it well, however. He permitted his father to give him a haircut and even to wear some reasonable clothes to school. He also learned something.

"Do you know why Pete did that?" I asked him after the incident.

"Sure," he retorted. "He hates me."

"Maybe he does," I said, "but do you know why?"

"Yeah," Howard said. "I'm leaving here and he isn't."

"Is that all?" I asked. "Didn't you make him feel pretty bad about it? After all, Louis Kantrow doesn't talk about what a big man he is just because he's going back, and someday Pete's going back too. So why are you so special?"

"I'm smarter," Howard answered.

"I'm not sure about that," I said, "but one thing's sure. Pete's a lot quicker than you. Otherwise, you wouldn't be standing there without your ponytail. And if you keep on telling everyone how great you are, you're going to end up in a lot more trouble. Don't you think so?"

"Yeah," said Howard. "I guess you're right. I'll keep my mouth shut."

Samson was sheared.

Louis Kantrow, however, was another matter. He had come to dislike Howard as much if not more than the rest of the class—both because of Howard's Superman attitude and because some of the kids' antagonism toward Howard was landing on Louis's head as well, as the only other returnee. That afternoon Louis came into my office to ask about the fight.

"Is Howard still going back?" Louis said, "or does this mean he'll have to stay here?"

"What makes you think that?" I asked, wondering what was really on Louis's mind.

"Well," said Louis, "if Howard gets into a fight and can

still go back, then I think I should stay because I never get into fights."

I began to see we might have a new problem. Obviously, we had made a mistake pairing him and Howard together—in class, in conferences, in status. He was getting locked in, comparing his every action to Howard's and vice versa. I made a mental note to differentiate between the two as much as possible—and there was no better time to start than the present.

"Louis," I said. "Are you and Howard the same person?"

"No," Louis replied.

"Remember all those times we asked what makes you you and how you're different from any other person?"

"Yes," Louis replied slowly, uncertain what I was getting at. For all the exercises, Louis's self-image was still mighty frail.

"You're tall and you've got freckles and blond hair, and Howard is short and he has dark hair and wears glasses, right?"

"Yes."

"And you're not even going back to the same schools, right?" (Louis was scheduled for a private school situation, Howard for public school in another district entirely.)

"No."

"So you're different from Howard in lots of ways," I went on. "And one big way you're different is in the way you behave. You don't get into fights and Howard sometimes does. Of course, if Howard got into lots of fights all the time, then you're right—we would have to keep him here. But if you got into a fight, that wouldn't be like you and I'd be really worried. And if you kept fighting, I don't know if I could keep you here. (I didn't want Louis to get the impression that one way he could stay in school was to start fighting.) But just because he got into one fight doesn't mean that Howard can't go back, any more than because you don't fight you'll be able to stay. *Everybody*, Louis, everybody is different. And they're supposed to be. So, do your own work and stop worrying about Howard.''

Louis looked only partially convinced, but at least it was a start. But like Howard, I had learned a lesson. I made sure we held our conferences with the two returnees separately and Dan Shea did his best to give them different assignments.

Once again I pondered the problem of Kathy Cowley. We had decided to start her perceptual training with the most basic gross motor tasks, but she was making little or no progress, constantly frustrated, constantly trying again. We had expected that. Joyce, her speech teacher, was also making little headway with her almost overpowering language and syntax problems. We had expected that too. I decided to work on her handwriting, since she could form letters and words, at least on the left side of the page with few or no reversals. I thought this might give her the confidence she needed. But so far in all this time we had made almost no headway there either.

To get her to write all the way across the page properly, without reversing, we had first tried using smaller and smaller pieces of paper. Kathy just bisected the paper and wrote smaller. Then we had tried color coding, drawing different-colored blocks across the page and asking her to fill in the proper letters in the appropriate color with her magic markers. She still stopped in the middle; and then, more often than not, moved to the far right edge, reversing her way back. And this in spite of the fact that by then she could easily connect dots in straight, wavy or crooked lines all the way across the page—one of the basic exercises we use to correct this tendency to stop in the middle. We had also been working on her pronounced mid-line jump in tracking exercises, and the basic directional training at the gross motor level should have helped too, even though she couldn't do much of it.

One of the early things we discovered was that she was using her nose as a kind of guide. If you tilted her head to the right, she would write farther to the right of the page. But you couldn't hold her head all the time. Let go, and she'd be back to her old habits. All she could say, when asked why, was, "I don't know." Something was stuck there; exactly what nobody knew for certain. Her neurologist's best guess: apparently the left and right hemispheres of her brain would not act in concert and she was unable to negotiate the mid-line.

In the past few weeks, however, we had had some small success with masks that created different-sized oblong and rectangular areas across the paper she was using. With these, she had broken the mid-line sound barrier more than once. This gave me the first solid clue to what might be Kathy's main problem, not just in writing but in other areas.

We have said that all of us make use of the cues we perceive in our environment to prompt a perceptual response—whether it's that water is wet, Mommy is love, or the large holes in the shaker mean it's the salt. The more cues we can process and interpret correctly—Mommy is the one with the round face and brown hair—the more satisfied and secure we feel. We have our bearings.

My kids, particularly those as disoriented as Kathy, can get their bearings only fuzzily, if at all. Yet they need points

227

of reference just as badly as other children, and can't feel safe without them. In their desperate insecurity, they often latch on to something they do perceive—usually some stable, unchanging thing in their environment—and use it as a cue for response, even though it may be inappropriate. This pattern is the source of many of the bad habits we so often have to eliminate in our kids.

Kathy, I decided, had misread the square-angled desk and square-angled paper as the cues for her special writing. Every time we allowed her to use them as cues, the pattern became only that much more ingrained. Perhaps if we changed the cue, we could break the orientation pattern that caused her to perform in what *she* thought was a proper manner.

The next morning I called Kathy into my office. I handed her a round piece of construction paper and a magic marker. I sat her at a round table. At that moment I wished I had a round room.

"Look, Kathy," I said. "We're going on a trip soon and everyone will need nametags. I want you to write down your name so I can take you on the trip and find you if you get lost."

Kathy wrote "KATHY," perfectly, right across the piece of paper with no hesitation.

I hugged her. "That's great," I said, "just right. Now do another to show your mother." Kathy did it again.

We had finally found the key. A square-angled paper was a cue that meant writing; and writing, as Kathy had developed it, meant writing in the crazy way she did. A round table and a round piece of paper gave her no such familiar cues or guidelines, so the new learning had a chance to get through. Almost as if to prove the point, after weeks of writing everything properly on round paper, triangular paper, paper in animal shapes, polygons, red ovals, any queer shape we could devise, when we went back to square or rectangular paper, she started her old tricks again. Old habits and ingrained cues are not soon forgotten and it took months to reach the point where this particular one was erased from Kathy's mind.

From then on we took no chances. Every time we had anything new to teach Kathy, we did our best to change her environment and keep changing it. We moved her seat around the room. We sat her at a round table. We sat her at a long oval table. We sat her on the floor. We gave her a learning booth one day and none the next—a blue one one week and a yellow the next. We played every different game we could dream up to teach her in an unconventional way—to make sure there was nothing she could rely on regularly in her environment that might create a new hang-up or evoke an old, skewed association. And though we haven't had complete success unraveling Kathy's habits and matching the proper perceptions to the proper cues and may never (I doubt, for instance, that she will ever drive a car safely), she managed to complete first-grade reading after another year in school.

Parent-teacher night. Report cards on the kids had been sent out, and there was the usual gaggle of pleased and not-so-pleased parents, although most of the kids had made some progress, if only slight, either academically, behaviorally or both. The high point of the evening for me was to see Mrs. Chase, whose eight-year-old daughter, Andrea, had entered school last year with a performance IQ testing at seventy-five—a borderline retardate. We had made an exception and accepted Andy because we suspected that her condition and perceptual handicaps were obscuring her actual mental abilities and pushing down her IQ to that low level.

We had put Andy through every conceivable perceptual training exercise, and pre-reading and math programs. Recently, we had started her on both subjects and she was progressing with a will, if slowly. A few days before, however, Andy's mother had gotten her best news in years—a new test recorded Andy's IQ at 90, hardly genius level but well above the retardation cut-off of 80. Mrs. Chase and I just sat there together while tears rolled down her face.

Joey Rich's mother came in enthused about how much better things were going for Joey and herself at home. Her husband, she said, was really laying off him and she wanted to know if his brothers could be admitted too. I couldn't be very encouraging about that. Though both had the earmarks of learning disabled kids, at ages fourteen and sixteen they would both be too old for us by the beginning of the next school year. What a shame to let these kids just go along, unnoticed and unhelped, until it was too late.

Jan Berger's mother also appeared and asked if she could speak to me in private. In one of the empty classrooms she told me she was upset with her daughter's report, which ran ten pages in length and was as honest as we could make it. Outside of learning to hop, which is only a small part of perceptual training, she had made almost no progress in perceptual or academic learning, or in social behavior. Mrs. Berger had brought the report along with her, covered with her own comments and those of the leaders of a Saturday play group to which she had taken Jan the weekend before. She went over each of her points and comments, all of which refuted anything in the report that indicated Jan might have problems. I pointed out to her that one day at a Saturday play group which made no demands scarcely could be compared to an entire school term.

Without acknowledging my argument, Mrs. Berger continued discussing her own comments. Finally, I felt that as a professional I had no alternative but to suggest that if she was convinced the school was not helping Jan, perhaps she should take her out. We aren't the answer for every child, I told her, and we would do everything possible to help her find another school.

Mrs. Berger exploded.

"No! No!" she practically shouted. "I can't do that. I am going to get a gun and shoot her and then I'll take the same gun and shoot myself. Then there will be no more problems with Jan."

As I held my breath, shocked, she suddenly burst into tears.

Slowly, carefully, I began to explore the home situation with her. As she went on and on, still in her heavy, fierce voice, I began to get my first real picture of Jan's home life.

"Jan doesn't look right. I send her to school clean and she comes home all messed up. Her dress is wrinkled." Before I could explain that even a normal child could not maintain such an immaculate appearance through an active school day, she was hurrying on. "My husband doesn't think she is sick, but she is. She is not normal and it is my fault. She doesn't walk right. She doesn't eat right. She embarrasses me in the restaurant. I do not think I'll let her eat at the table any more. She is always winking her eyes and she looks crazy. She is sick. She doesn't talk right. She is not right . . ."

I interrupted to ask how she managed Jan at home. "Does Jan do what you ask? Does she mind you?"

"There are times," cried Mrs. Berger, almost hissing, "when I hit her with a stick because I cannot stand her!"

Ye gods, I thought, first she wants to shoot the child and now she admits she beats her with sticks!

As Mrs. Berger talked on, it became apparent Jan was the family shame, and as such was made to suffer for their resentment. Because of her unpleasant table manners (which *were* bad, though no worse than many of our other kids), Jan was often locked in the basement for her meals. To be sure, her behavior at home apparently was far from perfect. She did little her mother asked of her (constant criticism and punishments had taken their toll), and more than her share of misbehaving (anything she did was wrong anyway). When Mr. Berger made any move to intervene he took Jan's side, overprotecting her even when she deserved some punishment.

What soon became evident to me was that Mrs. Berger's impassioned outburst was a thinly disguised plea for help; otherwise, she never would have painted such a derogatory picture of herself as a mother. She knew she was too harsh on Jan, but didn't know how else to deal with her. Somehow we would have to get her to see Jan as a kid with problems—problems that could be dealt with—not as a shameful reflection on herself as a mother. But this would require a lot more than just jawboning and letting her blow off steam. I assured her we would keep Jan with us, and sent her home, promising to think over an approach to her problem.

The next day there were all sorts of mysterious goings on. Teachers and kids seemed to be sharing some kind of secret. Larry Kraus dragged me to his floor to work out some problem, and I was annoyed because it was something he was perfectly able to handle. I was relieved when Lloyd Jensen called me down to his office, claiming a real emergency.

As I entered the lobby, every single kid and teacher was waiting. On Julie's cue they started singing "Happy Birthday."

When they were finished, Julie told them to start counting and asked me to stop them when they reached the right age. Almost all of them made it up to thirty-three. It was the best birthday present in the world.

Later, after school, the staff brought in a huge cake and a birthday card made by one of the kids. Lettered boldly across the front was the greeting: "Bets Wishə, Doc."

I'd need it. The following morning, Paul Mitchell, in spite of the special material he'd been given and his encouraging progress, again refused to come to school. He'd even announced as much to his mother before she left for work. She called from there in a tizzy.

"He's hopeless," she cried. "He got up and told me he wasn't going to go to that crazy school any more with its jerk teachers and its crazy kids. What am I going to do?"

God, I thought, couldn't Paul's family give him any support at all—his mother gave up at the first resistance and his father wouldn't even try. Instead, I said, "Nothing, but you should have called us earlier. *We'll* do something—the same thing we did before."

I sent Carl for Paul a second time—as I would on several later occasions. Paul could not tell us anything specific that had set him off; the only difference was that this time he arrived at school fully dressed. He sat sulking all through that day and the next; and when Nick, the gym teacher, assigned him twenty laps around the track as punishment for not going

233

to gym, he had to run behind Paul pushing every step. That brought Paul around—but only in gym. On again, off again—one step forward, one step back.

That same morning ten-year-old Kenny Meyer burst in to see me, howling: "They took my glasses! They took my glasses!" Sure enough, standing behind him was the teacher, Karin Bergstrom, holding nearsighted Kenny's most valuable possession—his eyeglasses.

The story, as I finally was able to piece it together, had begun in the gym. Kenny had been playing dodgeball and was one of the last remaining players in the game when Eleanor, the gym teacher, blew him out. She said he had been touched by the ball. Kenny immediately went into one of his famous tantrums, screaming that it was unfair, that the ball hadn't touched him, that everyone hated him, that he was always first out because everybody threw the ball at him and nobody else. When he began kicking and throwing the ball at the wall, Karin had appropriated his glasses so they wouldn't get broken. (I had just fixed them the week before after he'd broken them in another temper fit.) This, of course, had only infuriated Kenny, who began to bite and kick and fuss in full performance, until he was sent to my office.

The minute he came in crying and screaming, I started to laugh.

"Well, well, if it isn't my old friend," I said, "the old cry-baby. Welcome home." Kenny had spent a lot of time in my office, screaming.

"They took my glasses," he kept yelling. "It's unfair. I won't stand for it."

"Look Kenny," I said, "if you don't stop screaming,

234

you're going to break Mrs. Bergstrom's eardrums and mine. So stop screaming and start talking.''

Much to my surprise, Kenny's yelling subsided at once, but he fought on.

"They stole my glasses!" he charged. "Mrs. Bergstrom stole my glasses!"

Now Kenny was one of my more disoriented kids as well as one of the most infantile. He had come to school two years before, diagnosed as an mbd, emotionally disturbed kid. His large-and-fine-muscle coordination tested at two to three years below age level and he was equally lagging in his ability to match sizes, forms and shapes. In organizational abilities he tested four years behind. For instance, when he came he couldn't tie his shoes, but worst of all, he lacked the sound reasoning processes which build on good perceptual foundations, among other things, and had a pitifully weak self-image. He had made progress in all areas in the past two years, but so far we'd seen nothing like a real breakthrough. More often, we'd encountered in Kenny a screaming kid making little or no sense out of whatever incident touched him off.

Still, I was pleased with the way he had controlled his tantrum this time, and I picked up on his accusation. "So she's a thief, is she? Now, you know no one steals anything in this school. What were you doing to make Mrs. Bergstrom here take your glasses?"

"I wasn't doing nothin', nothin' at all," Kenny asserted. "And she stole my glasses! The school stole my glasses!"

This line wasn't getting very far, but Kenny wasn't finished.

"I'm going to sue you!" he cried. "I'm going to sue the whole school! You stole my glasses!"

I don't know what made me do it—maybe the feeling that I was getting to Kenny's reasoning processes and could push them a little further—but I rolled a piece of paper into the typewriter, reading aloud as I banged out:

"Class Action Suit. The party of the first part—that's the school, Kenny—is being sued by one Kenneth Meyer for . . ."

I looked at him. "How much do you want to sue us for?"

"Twenty million dollars," came the swift reply.

"Quick, Kenny," said Karin. "How many zeros in a million?" They had just had the lesson the day before.

"Six."

Karin smiled.

"OK," I went on, "that's one twenty and six zeros. One, two, three, four, five, six. There. Any cents, Kenny?"

Kenny started to laugh. "No, no cents, just twenty million dollars."

"There will be a trial," I went on, writing up the suit. "The trial will be held in a courtroom, which will be the classroom. If he loses the suit, Mr. Meyer will be responsible for all court costs and attorneys' fees. If the school loses, it will be responsible for all damages, court costs and attorneys' fees. Do you understand that, Kenny?" I asked.

"Yes," he said. I doubt if he did, but he'd seen enough TV to be able to answer the next question.

"Kenny, you know you're going to need a lawyer. Where are you going to find a lawyer?"

"I'll get one. I'll get F. Lee Bailey, I'll get William Kunstler, I'll get . . ."

"Now, Kenny," I said. "This is real life. You know you're not going to get any of those people to be your law-

236

yer. You can discuss it with your parents, maybe they can help. And I'll be the lawyer for the school. OK?"

"OK," said Kenny.

Karin and Julie, my assistant, witnessed the paper and we all went down to the administrator's office and had it notarized. I got some red ribbon and melted some wax from a candle and sealed it on.

I hadn't really thought much about what would happen, but it began to occur to me that this might be a good lesson for everyone in the everyday workings of the legal system.

"There's just one thing, Kenny," I said. "We may have to keep your glasses."

"Why?" he said, suddenly suspicious.

"Because they're evidence and the court will need them as an exhibit for the trial," I said, briefly explaining about evidence and exhibits. Dear as his glasses were to him, Kenny surprised me again by agreeing quickly and without any fuss. He was even prepared to do his homework without them— but I thought that was going too far. So I returned them to him with the stern warning that they were only a loan, they no longer belonged to him but to the court.

Kenny just nodded. He was already planning his case.

When I called his mother that night to tell her what had happened, I asked her not to come in and represent him (Kenny's father had his own business and couldn't take time off), to let Kenny carry this through on his own, although she and her husband could help him as much as they wanted.

The next day Kenny appeared, loaded for bear. "When is the trial?" he asked, "This morning?"

"How can you have a trial now?" I said. "You don't have any witnesses."

"I'll get them," said Kenny stoutly.

He buzzed around all morning trying to collect witnesses. Every time I passed his class he was going in or out, making a list, talking to kids. He went inside and did some work, then he'd be out again looking for someone. Late in the morning he came into my office to tell me that Eleanor, the gym teacher, felt Karin had been wrong in taking his glasses and had agreed to be a witness for him. This boosted Kenny's ego a thousand percent; up to then he thought that everyone in the school was against him.

"OK," I said, "you've got Eleanor, but you've got to have a character witness—someone who will say that you're an honest person, and when you say something you can be trusted."

Kenny came back that afternoon with his character witness—Sarah, our secretary. He was flying high.

"Do you think these are enough witnesses?" I asked him. He thought about it and said, "Yes." We set the trial for Thursday at noon in his classroom. "We'll get six kids from your class and six kids from Mrs. Halpern's class, and Mrs. Halpern can be the judge," I said. "She'll be fair because she doesn't know you and she wasn't there when any of this happened."

Kenny couldn't wait.

Ellen Carson was turning out to be a major little manipulator, which I hadn't realized at first. One day she flipped Jan Berger into a hedge while the class was out for a walk. All the teacher saw, however, was Jan's retaliation, and punished her for hitting Ellen. That night I had to calm down Mrs. Carson, who wanted to know what kind of students I had in my school. I got off the phone convinced that Ellen was one of those kids who can wind adults around her finger, but can't get to first base with her peers. I decided to observe her in class.

It didn't take long for me to wise up. Within the space of an hour, Ellen had brushed past one kid at his desk, slyly knocking his puzzle to the floor, given another girl a tiny pinch, poked her finger in a kid's back and hugged someone else. Ellen was getting exactly what she deserved from her class. But it wasn't until later, when I called her in with her mother for a quick conference, that I found Ellen still really had no notion of the meaning or even the consequences of being bad.

"I'll be a good little girl, I'll be good," she told me. I asked what happened at home when she was bad.

"My Mommy spanks me," Ellen replied complacently.

"What happens when you're good?" I asked.

"Nothing," said Ellen.

"Does it hurt you when your Mommy spanks you?"

"No," said Ellen, "it's fun. I like it."

I sent Ellen back to class and turned to her astonished mother.

"Listen, Mommy," I said, "you've got a little girl here who gets nothing when she's good and something she likes when she's bad." I could just imagine the light tap on the rear Mrs. Carson must regard as a spanking. "I think Mommy better start doing something to make her realize that it's bad to be bad. Otherwise you're going to have a very confused little girl on your hands."

Like many of my parents, Mrs. Carson just wasn't tough enough to be consistent with Ellen. One day she would put her foot down and insist that her daughter dress herself. This took a lot of time and crying and screaming, so the next day when Mommy might be tired or in a hurry to go shopping, she would find it easier to dress Ellen herself.

The same thing happened at meals. One day Mrs. Carson would force Ellen to eat all her food. The next, fearing a scene, she would let the girl run out and play without taking more than a bite. As for bedtime, that was rigidly observed—whenever there was no danger of a tantrum.

All this was only confusing the youngster, who didn't know what was expected of her, something that is important to any child but particularly to my kids. And it worked directly against the careful structure we had set up in school that was already channeling Ellen's bright little mind into academics at a rapid pace. Both her teacher Esther and I felt that Ellen would be moving along a lot faster if her mother could get it together.

Mrs. Carson finally agreed to work with us, and we began weekly and twice weekly sessions over the telephone. Patiently we explained everything that Ellen did, then suggested different ways of handling her at home. Finally, though Mrs. Carson proved almost as hard to train as Ellen was—and had just as many regressions—she's become a fairly model parent who has made life easier for both Ellen and herself. And it has paid off.

Ellen was completely off drugs within a year. She's still overtalkative and overactive—and probably always will be—but she's concentrating most of that energy now on learning. Best of all, she's made another big jump: instead of the five or six years we anticipated, it now seems that in only three Ellen Carson will be returning to regular school.

Howard Glass, his father and I went to check out the public school in Howard's district. I had already been to see the director of the small private school where Louis Kantrow was headed, and was pleased with the whole setup. Not all its kids were college bound, and so it was free of excessive pressure. The director was delighted with the prospect of getting Louis, promised the school would provide him with extra tutorial help, and was so warm and friendly when he met Louis directly that I was afraid he wouldn't finish out the term with us. I made a note to add this school to our list of those we recommend for our kids. Not so the school the Glasses and I visited that afternoon.

It didn't take more than a stroll through the halls to realize this junior high school was a zoo. The halls were teeming with unruly kids, the girls were walking around with jeans so tight that absolutely nothing was left to the imagination, and Howard returned from the lavatory to report that quite a few kids were smoking. We asked him to wait outside while Mr. Glass and I spoke to the principal. The man did nothing to reassure us that things were better than they first appeared.

"We've got a twelve-year-old boy here," I began, "who is pretty much on top of his schoolwork and in fairly good shape. He's still got some mild emotional problems, but most of them are behind him. It would help, though, if he could get a sympathetic teacher and a little special treatment, at least for a while. He's not used to a departmental schedule and I'd like to avoid giving him a full dose at first if it's possible. Also I see in the curriculum that he'd have to take a foreign language right off the bat." I asked if we could modify some of the regulations a bit—maybe hold off on the foreign language until next semester and arrange for him not to have to change classes too much the first month or so. "Also, he'll probably need some tutoring in his reading. He's about six months behind. Can he get that?"

The principal looked at me as if I were from outer space. "What do you think this is," he asked, "one of your country clubs? The departmental setup and the foreign language are Board of Ed requirements and we can't change anything there. As for his emotional problems, he'll see the guidance counselor regularly just like all the other children. And I don't see why he needs any help in his reading if he's only a few months behind. We have lots of kids here who are a year or more behind in reading, but they're all going to make it through anyway."

The guy obviously didn't really give a damn, but I kept on, more for Glass's edification than my own. "Is there any way then," I asked, "that we can give Howard any additional preparation over the summer? Perhaps one of your teachers could give him some tutoring?"

"Well," said the principal, "you could ask them but I don't see where it's really necessary. And why are you sending him back anyway if he's still got all these problems? You know what I think, I think you people don't know what you're doing. The public school shouldn't have let these kids go in the first place. If everyone would just leave them alone, they'd be fine. We don't have any problems with the kids we have here."

"What about the smoking in the lavatories?" Glass asked suddenly.

The principal looked startled. "OK," he said, "so they're smoking in the bathroom. Some of these kids have their parents' permission to smoke."

"But they're not supposed to be smoking in school, are they?" Glass persisted.

"If they're not doing it there, they'd be doing it somewhere else. We can't go in and check on them all the time."

"What about drugs?" Glass pressed. "How do you know they're not taking drugs in there?"

"We don't have a drug problem," the principal shot back.

"That's no answer," said Glass. "How do you know you don't have a drug problem if you don't even check on the smoking?" Glass was a thorough person, as I had often learned to my own chagrin. It was a relief to see him go after someone else for a change.

Suddenly the principal changed attitude abruptly. "What do you want us to do," he cried, "go in there after them and get killed? These kids are no sweethearts, you know."

With that, Glass and I said goodbye, picked up Howard and left. This obviously wasn't where Glass was going to send his son to school.

When I got back to school, Marion and I prepared to mobilize what we hoped would be a conclusive confrontation in the Danny Gordon campaign. For months now we'd been letting Danny grind on by himself in and out of his learning carrel, giving him almost nothing but his materials for schooling—four different reading and math programs, plus all the reinforcements of a full course in perceptual training even though he really didn't need much in those areas. Answerable only to himself, his severest critic, meeting his own incredible demands, he taught himself the alphabet and a fair vocabulary of words; he put himself through kindergarten, he charged through first grade and now he had made it solidly into second. As his successes mounted, and he abandoned his isolation booth for good, Marion and I decided that Danny now had enough solid academic success under his belt, and

243

had developed enough trust in us, so that we could begin to attack his central problem—his lamentable social perceptions, his inability to interact.

Marion started with little things. Instead of her previous policy of almost totally ignoring Danny, she now began noticing him. She began calling on him, remarking that he looked as though he had something to say, even though Danny never had anything to say, particularly in class. He would reply, indignantly and correctly, that he hadn't volunteered. She began to remark on his clothes—which were always neat and immaculate—and try to tussle his hair. She would tease him, playfully. Nothing worked. Danny would either ignore her or pull away.

Then I started on him. In perceptual training classes I'd play poker with him, cheating, deliberately trying to make him angry enough to protest.

I'd deal him five cards and then give myself six, laughing at him as he drew the prescribed two and I took three or four for myself and kept on drawing until I had a perfect hand.

"Ha, ha," I'd laugh. "See, I'm the boss. You're just a kid. The boss gets five cards, and the kid only gets two." Any of my other kids would have exploded in my face, accusing me of cheating and insisting on their rights—probably to cheat too. Danny just sat there expressionless and furiously tried to beat me.

We tried other ways to make Danny react. He had to see himself as a human being surrounded by other human beings and not some kind of robot, operating in a vacuum. Nothing cracked the ice. We decided Danny needed something drastic to shake him out of his single-minded concern with himself. And again we lit on using Danny's perfectionism.

244

This particular afternoon Marion asked him to come up to her desk.

"Here," she said. "You're the smartest kid in the class, smarter than I am. You be the teacher for the rest of the day. Get the kids to do anything you want. Here's my lesson plan. You can read it if you want to."

Marion walked out and joined me in the hall. No sooner had she closed the door than all hell broke loose. Erasers, books, chalk went flying. Kids started chasing each other around the room. They were shouting; you could hear them all over the school. Marion and I peeked through the door.

"You listen to me," Danny was saying, his hands indignantly on hips, but still his precise self. "I am the teacher. You must listen to me." Nobody listened.

Danny picked up a book and slammed it on Marion's desk with such force that it skated off into the adjacent window. There was no visible effect on the kids who were now on their own trip to the moon.

"YOU PEOPLE MUST LISTEN TO ME!" Danny shouted above the din. "IT IS IMPOSSIBLE FOR ME TO UNDERSTAND HOW YOU CAN'T COMPREHEND WHAT I AM TRYING TO SAY! NOW BE QUIET!" Still no response. Here, for once, entering his personal closeted self into the fray, Danny had to bear the full brunt of the realization he wasn't perfect—if he had been, the class would have obeyed him the same way they did Marion. A comparison had finally come home in his mind and, with it, a blinding light: there were other systems and people—the kids running around, Marion and me outside—that he had to contend with. Suddenly and without warning, Danny ran from Marion's desk to the one safe place left—a narrow empty closet. Locking the door from the outside, he pulled it shut behind him.

Marion and I walked in and within seconds she had the class in order. I went to the closet and knocked on the door.

"Is anyone in there?" I asked.

No answer.

"Is Mr. Gordon in there?"

Still no answer.

"You can come out now, Mr. Gordon. The class is quiet now. It's in order, the way you wanted it and couldn't get it. Do you want to come out?"

"No," from the closet.

"Well then, if that's the way things are, then you're going to have to stay there."

I couldn't spend any more time coaxing him—Kenny Meyer's trial was scheduled to start.

At twelve-thirty Kenny's trial started, late as usual. I knocked one kid off the jury and replaced him with Mr. Kane, our janitor, explaining to Freddie that the school ought to be represented, too. He let that pass.

The trial began and right away Kenny yelled out an objection. It nearly sent us flat on our faces.

"Mrs. Halpern, judge," he shouted, "I want a change of venue!"

Whoops! This was a lot better prepared, organized Kenny than I'd anticipated. I thought quickly. "Wait a minute," I said. "You can only have a change of venue if the circumstances are exactly the same from courtroom to courtroom. Since we agreed to use the classroom as a courtroom, you'll have to find another classroom to hold your trial. Until then, I will ask the court to postpone your trial."

Kenny went through the roof. "No! I want my trial! I want my trial! I'm entitled to my trial! I'm a taxpayer! I'm a citizen!"

"OK, Kenny," I said, "you can have your trial now but then forget about a change of venue." Kenny conceded.

"Let's hear your opening statement . . ." I started to say.

"Wait a minute," Kenny interrupted. "I want a chance to question the jurors!"

Dear God, I thought, what have I got myself into?

Kenny started on the jury. "Are you in my class?" he asked, rhetorically.

"Yes," the kid answered.

"That's unfair," he said. "Off the jury."

Boom, boom, boom—Kenny kicked off the five kids in his class and put on kids he liked from the other classes. I began to sweat. Suppose he got this jury stacked and set it up so that he won? The kids know I keep my promises, and carry out all agreements—that lies at the heart of our relationship together. How was I going to explain that I didn't really owe him twenty million dollars?

Kenny opened his case.

"They stole my glasses and it's unfair. I don't want anyone to steal things from me. The school can't steal my glasses from me. It's unfair. It's unconstitutional. They should be put in jail for stealing . . ."

"Wait a minute, your honor," I said to Mrs. Halpern. "There's a difference between stealing and taking. If Kenny is suing the school for stealing his glasses, as the suit says, then I think the whole thing should be thrown out of court."

Judge Halpern asked me, as the defense lawyer, to give my definition of stealing.

"Stealing, as I understand it, is taking something from

247

someone without their knowledge or taking something even if they know it without any intention of giving it back.''

We got out the Webster's dictionary and confirmed that this was essentially the definition, except that the dictionary also mentioned taking something without another person's permission. I ducked that.

''Kenny,'' I asked. ''Are you wearing your glasses?''

Kenny grumbled, ''Yes.''

''Then we gave them back to you. How can you prove we didn't intend to give them back?''

''But you stole them, you took them!'' Kenny insisted.

''Kenny,'' I went on, ''did you know it when Mrs. Bergstrom was taking your glasses?''

''Naw, I didn't know. You stole them.''

''Kenny, weren't you wearing your glasses when Mrs. Bergstrom took them away? If you didn't know she took them, then how come you were in my office screaming that she did?''

''That's different! That's different!''

''So you did know she took them?''

''Yeah, yeah,'' Kenny said. ''But you still stole them and the school owes me twenty million dollars.''

Judge Halpern intervened.

''I agree with the defense lawyer that no one stole Kenny's glasses. Therefore, the way this suit is written I think we should throw it out of court. I pronounce it null and void and the school owes Kenny no money. However,'' the judge said, suddenly throwing in her own Mickey, ''I would like to know if the school had any right to *take* Kenny's glasses away from him in the first place.''

This shows how much control *I* have over my staff!

The trial proceeded along these lines. Eleanor got up and

testified that she felt Karin had been wrong in taking Kenny's glasses. He needed them to do his work. Then she felt there were better ways to handle the situation, such as telling Kenny she was going to take his glasses unless he calmed down and giving Kenny her reasons before she acted. At that point she could have taken his glasses and given them back as a reward once he quieted. A good argument and one along the lines of the contractual student/teacher relationship that we preach.

Karin tried to defend herself, but didn't do too well. Yes, she said, she had acted in haste, but she'd really been afraid Kenny would break his glasses. Then, when he kept on yelling and gyrating, she felt she couldn't give them back. She admitted she'd gotten herself into a disciplinary bind that could have been avoided if she'd followed Eleanor's line of thinking.

Sarah took the stand. She mentioned that she'd heard Kenny could be a crybaby, but that she'd never seen this herself. Otherwise, Kenny had always seemed quite polite to her, basically a nice boy who'd never done many of the more outrageous things that ''some'' children in the school were known for. All true.

I kept quiet. The jury went out in the hall for a secret ballot. After several minutes of murmuring and scuffling, they came in with a verdict of ten to two in favor of the school. Not too bad for Kenny's case, considering that all the odds and the Establishment stood against him. Two kids had the courage to stand up for him.

Kenny, however, was downcast. He'd really thought he had a chance. He left the class and plodded down the hall, and I ran after him and asked him to lunch. As we ate together, I told him that he had tried a hopeless case but had

249

done very well at it, that at one point I was really afraid I was going to have to ante up twenty million dollars, that under the circumstances it was really great two kids had come up on *his* side, and how surprised and pleased I was that he'd handled the case so well. He grew more talkative with each compliment and soon looked a lot happier. I told him I thought he was going to make a great lawyer some day. I truly believed he might. One thing had always been certain: Kenny was no dumbie. For another, many of our kids, as disorganized and illogical as they are at the start, leave us even more organized and logical in their thinking than many normal children, since these disciplines are constantly drummed into them. The self-confidence, maturity and organized reasoning ability he had displayed during his trial and its preparation were a quantum jump beyond anything we'd seen from Kenny before. If he'd done it once, he could do it again.

Next morning Danny got off the bus, walked into Marion's classroom, and headed straight for the closet. Marion fed him his lunch there and, when I came in to talk to him, did her best to teach class while Danny and I shouted at each other through the door.

Luckily, I could communicate with Danny on a fairly high level. "This is obviously the best place for you, Mr. Gordon," I pointed out throught the door. "Everything in that closet is perfect, in order, the way you like it. That's because it's empty. The only thing in that closet that is out of order is Daniel Gordon."

"I am not," came the reply. "Drop dead. Get out of here. If I want to be in this closet, I have every right to be. This closet is part of my room and part of the school and if I want to be here, I can. Now go away and leave me alone."

I did—for the time being.

250

Eddie Daniel's teacher came smiling into my office. With the help of a tape recorder, her entire class had composed oral essays about their trip to the Museum of Natural History, but nobody's report could compare in detail and clarity with Eddie's:

"It was a big place. I saw a bear there. It was a big bear and all brown. It wasn't a live bear but a stuffed one. We had lunch there. We went on a bus and the bus was yellow and there were lots of kids on it and it was noisy. I liked it. And I saw an elephant." On and on, verbalizing fully and perfectly everything he had taken in.

I was pleased, but not too surprised.

Eddie had gotten so many M&Ms and lollipops and trips and toys and puzzles and books and games and training exercises from us it's a wonder he didn't get sick or explode. We stuffed him with all the new experiences we could think of—and still it wasn't enough. Before long we began to notice dramatic changes. Rapidly he had quieted down to the still maddening, but now healthy, level of a normally intelligent child who is trying to make up for lost years of life and experience. He went off Ritalin after the first few weeks. By the end of his kindergarten year he knew his alphabet, read and worked at the first-grade level and reacted to everything—like the Museum—like crazy.

We kept Eddie for another year, promoting him to first grade right on schedule, to make sure his gains would be consolidated and that he'd be mature enough to handle second grade in public school. I didn't bother to test his IQ again, but I'm sure if we had we could have chalked up a minor miracle.

In my mind, there was none. For an agency kid like Eddie—and this also applies to ghetto-raised kids—entering school is often equivalent to entering a foreign country. Not only do these kids often have a language problem—they've been raised speaking virtually a different language, dialect or lingo—but they haven't experienced most of the things middle-class white kids take for granted. I see red when I look at some of the standard evaluation tests that are used by our schools. One of them asks these kids to identify an electric can opener and a covered bridge. What agency or ghetto kid has ever seen such things? No wonder many agency- and slum-raised children are considered backward and become outstanding "behavior problems." What they need is good teaching, geared to their knowledge level. Instead, many of them are erroneously labeled mbd and immediately put on drugs to keep them zonked out in their seats. Luckily—for us and for him—Eddie Daniel was just too bright to keep down.

The incident that finally made me realize I was losing my battle to save Paul Mitchell began the next day. It wasn't much of an incident—not much worse than many we had seen before—it seemed more like the last straw. Carl Janicki stopped me in the hall as classes were about to begin to tell me that Paul, who had arrived on the bus that morning, couldn't be found anywhere. We checked the gym, the pool, even the boiler room and the kitchen. As I went to my office to grab my coat and scour the neighborhood, I found Mr. Mitchell sitting in my chair behind my desk, his feet perched on the top, glowering. I quelled my impulse to bawl him out and instead pretended that his presence in this, of all places, was no surprise.

"Why, Paul," I said, "what brings you here with such an ugly face on such a terrific day like this? [It was a terrible day—cold, raining and windy.] I feel great, just terrific, don't you?"

252

"It's not a good day," Paul growled. "It's a terrible day. And I feel terrible. Every time I come to this school, I feel terrible. I get one block from here and I get this ticking in my head. And the closer I get the louder the ticking gets." He grinned. It was probably true that Paul got bad vibes about school—he'd certainly acted and said as much many times before—but he'd obviously thought up this story as his latest argument against school. I decided to play along.

"Let's see, Paul. Is the ticking like a bomb—a time bomb?"

"Yeh," he said, with a crafty look. "Just like that, like a time bomb."

"Well, I guess if you have a bomb in your head, we're either going to have to defuse it or let it explode. Which do we do?"

Paul's grin faded.

I started busying myself with the mail. "Paul, I don't think you have a bomb in your head—you just feel a little crummy. That's all. That's all. There isn't any bomb—just the one you're making up out of all your self-pity. Poor little Paul—he's got a bomb in his head. Right?"

"What do you care how I feel," said Paul.

"I care a lot," I said, seizing the opening as I had so many before. "If I didn't, I wouldn't make you come to school, I wouldn't send Carl after you and I wouldn't make you do your work. I care enough for both of us. Now why don't you help me and start caring, too, and forget about bombs."

Paul wasn't buying that approach. "You don't care about my attitudes on things. Why should you?"

"You're right," I said. "I don't give one damn about your attitudes. All I care about is you. I know that if you try you manage to get your work done. You even surprise yourself.

253

And you get all that help and attention from your teacher. Nice things happen, right?''

"Yeh," said Paul, grudgingly.

"You feel good and I feel good, right?"

"Yeh, yeh," Paul answered.

"Paul," I asked, "do you know what a punk is?"

"Yeh—a punk is a pisspot."

I laughed. "OK. That's a good enough definition at least of the way you're acting right now. Here you are sitting in my office with your feet up on my desk [Paul still hadn't removed them] telling me about some imaginary bomb that you've made up out of self-pity because you can't do anything in school and Mr. Janicki is sitting there in class waiting to help you learn to do something in school and defuse that bomb. That's a pisspot if I ever saw one, and a punk."

Paul began to laugh, but it faded as I went on. "It's also stupid, because if you went to the dictionary and tried to look up punk or pisspot I don't think you could find them because you don't know how to read. That's why you have a bomb in your head, because you know when you walk in here you're going to be asked to do things you can't do and no matter how much we tell you you can do them, you're afraid to try. Yet all you have to do is go back to class and you'll find you can do just about everything we ask and there are no bombs."

I went back to the mail, suddenly weary of repeating the same words, fighting the same battles again and again. We can't *drag* our kids across the finish line. They have to want to do something themselves. We'd done better with Paul than anyone else ever had, but I began to suspect it wasn't enough. Nothing would ever be enough. Almost as if sensing what was going through my mind, Paul suddenly jumped

254

up and went to class, where he put in a few good days' work. The next morning, I made him a school monitor and let him take attendance—he arrived among the first kids and the responsibility gave a great boost to his ego. But I found little to encourage me either in his response that morning or in the months to come, even though the incidents were fewer and more easily handled and his number of school and working days gradually increased. The mold had been set, as it has been with so many of these older LD kids, and we weren't really winning, just marking time between incidents and frustrations.

Paul is still virtually at the same academic level we found him. Sometimes he comes to school, sometimes he doesn't; every once in a while he works—usually only after I've pounded on him—and when he does, he is consistently rewarded. Most of the time, however, he just messes around, resisting and making little or no progress. Even so, there's always the possibility of dramatic change—even with a dead-end kid like Paul. All I can do right now is grit my teeth—and hope.

I felt as depressed on this cold, raining winter day as I'm sure Kenny did over losing his case. I really thought we had a good chance with bright Paul Mitchell. I desperately needed something to cheer me up. I got it the next morning.

Paula Wolfe invited me to her class at ten-thirty when her kids were scheduled to work on their reading. She said she had a surprise. I wondered what it could be.

Paula saw me as I wandered in and turned to a little girl. "Amy, would you please read your story out loud?"

Amy Friedman, our little epileptic whom I had once offered to marry and who had taught herself some of her first words on my telephone, opened the beginning Bank Street primer. "House, one," she said. "House many. Houses. Many houses." She turned the page. "Street, one . . . Street many . . . Streets . . . Many streets." She read straight through the whole story perfectly and then looked at me.

It was all I could do to keep from bawling. Here was a kid who six months ago didn't even know the alphabet or how to count to ten. I wrapped my arms around her, lifted her high and kissed her. "Now, Amy," I said, "we can really get married."

Marion and I met in the hall and exchanged shakes of the head. Danny Gordon was still in the closet.

Jan Berger had suddenly emerged from her ordinary withdrawn, fidgety, behavior pattern—and regressed to nursery school. She began running around hugging and kissing everyone—kids and teachers—saying, "I love you, I love you," but at the same time shoving and kicking and hitting anyone who approached *her*. Like a nursery schooler, she obviously was trying to attract some love and attention, but in all the wrong ways, and when she was rejected, she became overtly hostile.

During my next conference with Mrs. Berger, I found out why. Jan's older sister, who was a few months pregnant, had come home for a long visit. Jan had been all excited; her sister had been the only one who really cared for her. But this time she refused to have anything to do with Jan. This seemed perfectly justifiable to Mrs. Berger. "She is afraid she will have a child like Jan," she explained. "She is embarrassed by her." I could understand that, but I couldn't un-

256

derstand the Bergers making Jan wait outside a restaurant while they ate dinner inside. When they finally came out she began to cry, so they pretended to drive off and leave her behind.

Right after Mrs. Berger's visit at mid-term I had contacted a psychologist friend of mine for advice. He warned me to stop sending home reports on Jan's behavior that her mother could use against her, and recommended that the whole family enroll for intensive therapy. Mrs. Berger had refused, but now I felt I had to insist. With the help of Jan's teacher, Esther, I convinced her to agree to therapy for the whole family at a state mental hospital outpatient clinic where there would be no trouble about finances. Within months, we had some surpising findings.

Jan's learning problems—her hyperactivity and habit of tuning out people—were found to be caused purely by emotional disturbance. She wasn't organically brain injured or even mbd; in fact, as we had suspected from the few times we could get her to cooperate in school, she was quite bright. She had "learned" her learning blocks—hostility and fear— only too well. So much for Mrs. Berger's hopelessly abnormal child, some kind of "Bad Seed."

More important, as all three Bergers got help Jan began to make her first real progress in school and out. She tuned into us and the other kids, making friends in class and even getting invited to other kids' homes. In a visit to Ellen's home, Jan scared Mrs. Carson out of her wits by scooping up the new Carson baby and hugging him almost to death. And Esther came to me complaining that Jan had done a couple of uncalled for turns around the room—hopping first on one foot and then the other. It was all she could do to get her to stop.

I grinned.

"Did she do it well?" I asked.

Back to Howard Glass. After dispensing with the notion of public school, at least the one in his district, Glass had applied at a private school nearby for his son—one with a very good reputation but with a little too much pressure about college for my taste. That wasn't the biggest problem, however.

If the public school principal didn't give a damn about his pupils, this headmaster seemed all too acutely aware of Howard—as a problem and little else. The guy had requested all Howard's clinical and school records, which we had turned over with permission from his parents, and he kept going over and over them, particularly the psychological. His questions were endless. Why wasn't Howard in therapy? We explained that for all practical purposes Howard was in therapy all day long and that his therapist had long since decided he didn't need additional sessions. Why wasn't he taking drugs? He didn't need them. Was he destructive? Not any longer. Wasn't Howard brain-injured, hyperactive? Yes and no. He could be a handful on occasion, we said; but most of his problems had been resolved, otherwise we wouldn't be returning him. All the questions, as is often the case, were mainly concerned with Howard's past, not how he was at present or what he would become in the future. I had just about had it when the director phoned me one last time.

"Look," he said, "Howard is always going to be a social rebel, isn't he?"

"Yes," I said, "along with Winston Churchill and Mahatma Gandhi. And someday he may become a great leader, too, because he's that good a thinker!"

Howard was accepted. With outside tutorial help—the school never did provide it—he quickly caught up and is maintaining college entrance grades. So, interestingly, is Louis Kantrow in the softer environment and with the extra tutoring provided by his less pushy private school.

The next morning when Kenny Meyer's class marched into perceptual training, I asked each of them whether they had done their homework—extra exercises, puzzles, etc.—and all except Kenny, who had been exempted to prepare his trial, said they had. But I was particularly interested in the response of eleven-year-old Dominic Monaro who had entered just this year.

Dominic had almost no bilateral skills at all. He waddle-walked, couldn't crawl or even creep, couldn't balance on a board or walk a rail, and showed a definite mid-line jump in tracking from left to right—that is, once you got him to unlock his eyes from their stationary position and allow them to track instead of just turning his head. With all this, he was also very fearful of anything even remotely athletic. To prevent his humiliation in front of the older boys, I had started him working on chalkboard circles with both hands simultaneously.

Trouble was, Dominic couldn't make a decent circle with one hand, let alone two. So we had worked weeks and weeks, eradicating squiggly spirals, oval shapes and even linear, square-like shapes—until he could make a decent circle with one hand and then the other. After a while, I started him with two hands and we were back to total confusion. Asked to make two circles clockwise, he would make a circle with one hand and a straight line, or reverse and make a circle counterclockwise with the other.

Then I had a new idea. I brought in a ball of twine and told him I wanted to connect his wrists with a short string, so that when he moved one hand the other would automatically follow suit.

Dominic had reacted in fear. "What are you tying me up for, Doc?"

"I'm not tying you up," I'd replied. "I just want to show you a way to move your hands together."

"I don't wanna be tied up! I don't wanna be tied up!" Dominic had yelled.

"I'm not," I insisted, explaining my reasons once again. "It will help you in your work, really—now calm down."

Dominic had finally submitted and went to the chalkboard. Lo and behold, it worked. "Keep the string taut," I'd called out as he started to reverse and the line slackened.

"I am, Doc, I am." And he'd straightened out the string and corrected himself. By the end of that day's session, he'd been going along by himself quite smoothly. I'd given him the ball of string to take home to his parents and told him to work on the chalkboard with them for twenty minutes.

Early the next morning, I'd gotten a call from Dominic's father, a detective on the city police force and a very easy guy.

"We got a very peculiar request from Dominic last night," began Detective Monaro. "He said it was homework from perceptual training."

"Yes," I answered, "he did have homework. He was supposed to draw circles on the chalkboard."

"Well," said Monaro, "he didn't say anything about circles. He just told us that we were supposed to tie his hands together and that he was supposed to stay that way for twenty minutes."

I started to chuckle. "Well, what did you do?"

"I tied his hands together and let him sit in a chair that way for twenty minutes," Monaro replied, beginning to chuckle himself as the realization came through that something had been garbled. "We didn't know what you were up to, but we figured it couldn't hurt him. It *was* kind of strange, though."

I explained to Monaro what Dominic had been meant to do and we both had a good laugh. I also said I'd ask him about it when he came into class that morning, which I did.

"Did you do your homework last night, Dominic?" I asked.

Dominic looked a little jolted but quickly answered: "Yeh, Doc, I did it. I did just what you told me. I had my father tie my hands, I did. And I sat like that in a chair for twenty minutes. I looked at the clock, Doc. It was a full twenty minutes. I wouldn't lie to you, Doc. No, I wouldn't."

I nodded. "But what else did you do?"

"Nothing," said Dominic in embarrassment. Obviously he hadn't completed his homework as he had hoped.

"Why?" I asked.

"I thought there was something else you wanted," said Dominic. "I thought you said something else. But I couldn't remember what it was and I didn't want to ask my father because I didn't think he knew either, so I just did what I could remember. But I remembered that you wanted my hands tied for twenty minutes, Doc. That was right, wasn't it?"

"Yes, Dominic," I said, "that was right."

Poor Dominic. The string tying evidently had made such an impression that he had completely forgotten the purpose of the whole exercise. No matter. We soon got over that hump

261

and he was making circles—and doing many other exercises—without the aid of string or any crutch. But it was just one more reminder of how difficult it is for my kids to learn, particularly when more than one thing has to be remembered, related and processed at the same time.

I went to Marion's classroom for my daily through-the-door conference with Danny. He'd been in the closet several days now, and nothing I'd said would make him come out, except for brief visits to the bathroom. But I had to try again. Marion quietly led the rest of the class out. Although Danny didn't realize this, she'd gotten into the habit of taking them to the lunchroom during our daily shouting matches so their work wouldn't be disturbed.

"Okay, Danny," I began. "I think you've made your point. You can come out now."

"No," from inside the closet. "This closet is part of *my* classroom. I can stay here if I want."

"Right, Mr. Gordon," I said, "you have every right to be in the closet. But if Daniel Gordon were the way he should be, then he wouldn't have to stay in the closet disturbing the class. If he really was as ordered, as perfect as Daniel Gordon thinks he is and everything else should be, then he wouldn't have to hide in the closet. But Daniel Gordon is *not* perfect."

"I am too!"

"No, you're not. You'd like to play ball with the rest of the kids. But you're afraid you might throw it and miss the basket. Other kids can make a mistake, but not Daniel Gordon. So the best way is to hide from everything in your work, just like in this closet. That's the only place you're in order."

"Get out of here." By this time we were shouting.

"You don't do anything right. You shouldn't be class president. You refuse to answer questions when you're asked unless you are perfectly sure you have the right answer, and that's not right. The class president is supposed to care about other people and you don't care about anyone except Danny Gordon, and that's not right. The class president is supposed to be responsible. He's supposed to get along with the teacher and help her and you don't, and that's not right. The only place you're right and careful is at your desk, and that's not right. In fact, you're not even careful there."

"How dare you say that! I am careful!" Then Danny gave out with his favorite and famous phrase. "When you treat me like this," he bellowed, "you are like a pregnant cockroach crawling on its stomach in a pool of vomit!"

We had been over and over this with little variation each day. Then, as I had every day, I asked him the final question: "Do you want to come out of the closet now, Mr. Gordon?"

This time he stepped out. There was no one else there but me, though Danny hadn't known that.

"How do you feel about things now?" I asked him.

"I don't want to talk to you," he said, but looked pleased with himself as he sat down at his desk. When Marion and the class returned, I left and called Mrs. Gordon, whom we had kept informed all week and who had been as determined as I to complete this phase of Danny's education. I told her Danny had finally come out of the closet.

At noon Danny ate in the lunchroom for the first time in days. When I came by to check on him that afternoon, he marched right up and met me at the door.

In his precise fashion he said, "I am very ashamed of all

263

my actions." Then he walked over to Marion and asked permission to speak to the class. She granted it.

Danny turned and made a speech to the whole class. He apologized for throwing things, he apologized for not playing games, he apologized for not caring for Marion and the other kids, he apologized for everything. Then he asked if he still could be class president. The other kids yelled and applauded their approval. Daniel Gordon looked as close to tears as he probably ever will be.

Danny began to join in class activities and Marion gave him new responsibilities. He tutored some of the other kids for a while, but when the going got rough Danny couldn't understand why the other kids couldn't learn! So Marion dropped that tactic fairly quickly. But at least Danny was interacting. Two years later, Danny returned to sixth grade in public school, reading at an eighth-grade level and doing math just below that grade. Within months Danny's parents and his new school were asking us whether Danny should be put in a class for the intellectually gifted. (We advised, "Yes, but not for another year.")

Though he will always probably be introverted and overly precise Daniel Gordon seems to have stepped out of his closet once and for all.

In February I started my first weekly conference with Herbie Goodman, Jay Koch and Gregory Porter, who were all slated to return to regular public school. I had asked them to discuss their reactions with their parents. Now I was curious to find out those reactions myself.

Greg, a tiny black eight-year-old we were sending back to second grade to allow him an extra year to grow up, was the first to reply.

"Good!" he said, but with such emphasis that I pursued it further.

"Why good?" I said.

"I'm gonna kick his ass!" Greg replied.

"What are you talking about?"

"I'm gonna kick his ass!" Greg repeated.

"Whose ass?" I asked.

"That principal's!" Greg said. "I'm gonna get him. I'm gonna kick his ass!"

Now this was ludicrous not only because of Greg's size but because he had spent such a short time in public school before coming to us. He couldn't possibly know the principal in his district or have had any personal experience with him.

"What principal are you talking about?" I probed.

"The principal at that school," Greg said.

"Why?" I asked. "What do you know about that principal?"

"My friends tell me he's mean," said Greg. "They say he beats on kids. That way I'll do good for me and my friends. I'll show 'em who I am. I'll show that principal too."

"Great, Greg, just great," I said. "You're going to go in and see the principal and then kick his ass. First thing you know you'll be right back here. Do you want that? You *can* stay here, you know."

"No," Greg said.

"Well, then you better stop thinking about beating up the principal. I happen to know that your principal is a very nice guy, as nice as anybody here."

That shut Greg up and I turned to Herbie, who had invited me to his bar mitzvah and whom we were sending back to junior high.

"How do you feel about it?"

265

"I'm afraid," said Herbie, honestly.

"Why are you afraid?" I asked.

Out poured the excuses, the same ones common to any of our more fearful kids, like Louis Kantrow, but Herbie added some of his own: "Well, I won't know anyone. I won't know the teachers."

"When you first came here," I pointed out, "you didn't know the teachers either."

"Well," said Herbie, "I don't wanna walk to school when it gets cold." (All our kids come by bus.)

"Your mother will dress you in a nice warm coat," I countered.

Herbie listed at least a half dozen other things he wouldn't like about public school—the bathrooms would be dirty, they wouldn't have doors, people would look at him, he wouldn't have friends—all of which I managed to put down quickly. Then he said, "I'll have to take drugs."

This threw me for a loop. "What do you mean?" I asked, incredulous.

"Because all the kids in public school are taking drugs," he said. "You hear it on the news. They give it out on the playgrounds."

"That's right," piped up Jay, a twelve-year-old. "They're all on them. All the kids are taking drugs."

"Does that mean you have to take them?" I asked the group.

Greg said, "No." Jay said, "No." Herbie said, "They'll make me."

Obviously Herbie was uptight and getting more so. The whole thought of leaving school terrified him, the same way his bar mitzvah had. "Maybe you're not ready," I said, as gently as I could, but in complete seriousness. "Maybe you should stay here for another year."

Herbie started to cry. Jay said, "Stop crying." Little Greg said, "Make him stop crying, please!" Both were embarrassed. I ignored them.

"Why are you crying?" I asked Herbie.

"I want to go back to school," he finally blubbered through his tears.

"Then you're going to have to stop being afraid of all these things that aren't really worth being afraid of anyway. Remember the bar mitzvah, and how worried you were beforehand? Everything was fine. It's the same here, now. You've learned to do everything. You can read and write and do arithmetic. You've learned your social studies and your science. Now you've got to learn not to be afraid."

Herbie shaped up for the moment, but I realized he would still need a lot of support—something we worked on successfully for the rest of the year. I also called his mother that night and suggested that he go to private, not public, school. That was where he ended up the next September with a small class and a teacher who related to him as well or better than many of ours. Like many of our kids, he couldn't have stood a direct plunge into public school.

Twelve-year-old Jay was next. Here was an extremely bright kid whose main problem was not in learning to read or write but in behavior. He had been thrown out of public school because he was extremely hyperkinetic and a real beaut of a control problem (complete to throwing chairs out windows). We had had little or no trouble with him once we got to him—which was very quickly—and he began to control himself and behave. He was soon reading above grade level and handling his other subjects nicely. But he still had a big chip on his shoulder.

"I'm going to show 'em," he said grimly when I asked what he would do when he got back to public school.

"I'm going to show 'em that I'm the best. I'm going to show 'em I can do everything they ask me to, everything they want me to. I'm going to get every answer right. I'm going to show 'em they shouldn't have thrown me out of that place. They don't know what they're doing."

"What are you going to do when you can't show 'em?" I asked. "What happens when something goes wrong? Are you going to throw a chair out the window?"

"I'm going to show 'em," Jay just repeated.

"But what if you can't show 'em?" I kept on. "You know you can't get everything right all the time. You learned that lesson here." (Jay was one of the few kids on whom we had made totally unreasonable academic demands, just to *show* him that he couldn't always be right and to get him to deal with that fact without going berserk.)

"Yeah, yeah," said Jay. "I know. I know I can't. I remember. I learned my lesson. Sometimes I'm wrong."

"So?"

"So," Jay said, "I guess I'll show 'em by being the very best I can be."

After a few more sessions taming his belligerence, Jay went back to public school that fall. Except for some initial problems which were quickly mended by a tough-minded teacher who knew us and Jay's problems, he adjusted very well.

It was Greg's turn again. He said that when he went back to school he was "gonna do his reading."

268

"What if you don't like the book?" I asked. "What if you don't like the stories in it?"

"Then I'm gonna tell the teacher she doesn't know her ass from her elbow," said Greg with all his earlier bravado. I gulped. We encourage our kids to be straightforward and to express their feelings and frustrations, partly as an antidote to acting them out and partly because I believe that this is the way a school relationship should be handled. But such honesty often throws teachers and parents on the outside, and Greg would be in for a rough time if he didn't learn to curb his tongue.

"Look, Greg," I said. "First, you're going to kick the principal in the ass and then you're going to tell the teacher that she doesn't know her ass from her elbow. How long do you think you're going to last back in public school? I'd say about ten days."

Greg corrected himself. "No, man! I'm not gonna do it that way! I'm not gonna say it that way! I'm gonna *feel* that way! Feel! Feel!"

"What are you going to do when you feel that way?" I asked.

"I'm going to have to talk to the woman," Greg said.

"That's fine, you know," I said. "But how are you going to talk to her?"

There was a gleam in his eye. "After school!" he nearly shouted, "After school! I don't have to run down to a bus anymore, right?"

"Right," I said.

"I won't have to ride one, so I'll have lots of extra time, right?"

"Right," I said.

"And I won't be special any more, right?"

"Right," I answered again, grinning with him now.

"I'll talk to the woman after school," Greg said decisively.

"Great!" I said and I meant it. But Greg wasn't really listening. He was already back in his district school with his old friends—as one of them, no retard—and with plenty of time to play after school, or talk to the woman if he so chose.

9

It's this sad, sidesplitting merry-go-round that I get on each day as I tease, push, paddle and poke our kids to reach for the brass ring: the moment they are finally ready for regular school. We expect most of our kids to leave us within three years, five years at most—a goal made possible by careful screening upon admission. Like Greg Porter, Herbie Goodman and Louis Kantrow, most of our kids will finish out their school days functioning at grade level in a regular classroom with no one the wiser about their earlier problems. Our experience with these students has been encouraging, and the statistics have been even more so.

Of the first group of forty-seven children I worked with, we had the following results: Ten dropped out, mostly in the first few months, because of inadequate screening; these children turned out to be just too tough to fit into our program, and we don't believe in kidding parents along. But twenty of the remaining thirty-seven have successfully returned to regular schools, both public and private—three within one year, eight within two years and nine in three and a half years. The second group of fifty-seven did even better. Stricter screening reduced the number of dropouts to only six (the present rate is even lower—only one or two a year). Of the remaining fifty-one, five "graduated" in one year and ten in two. Statistics on a third group were not available at the time of this book's writing.

Of the kids who have completed our program, not one has regressed academically or has failed to make less than eighteen months' progress in reading and math in an average three-year stay. Though at first glance this may not sound so spectacular, remember that heretofore these same kids not only had made little or no progress but had been losing ground, falling behind as failure built on failure. With them any progress at all is substantial just because it exists.

We even have had considerable success with kids like Kathy Cowley and Amy Friedman, whom we soon saw never would be able to reenter regular school. Severely learning-disabled when they first arrived, they now function almost as well as most children in some areas; and while their lives always will be circumscribed to a degree, at least they no longer will have to be institutionalized—which once seemed their only future.

One of the key elements in our program, of course, is our emphasis on perceptual and vision training. Recently we decided to test the correlation between this training and academic progress, which we did under a Federal grant. Even I was startled by the results.

We broke up our students into two groups: 124 who had been with us for at least a year, and another group of 47 who had just entered school. The base group of 124 received our normal schedule of perceptual training—three hours a week in class groups with occasional individual sessions. The new group was bombarded daily, in individual and group sessions, with all the perceptual and vision training we could provide.

The study lasted seven months. At the end of that time, the base group had made a mean gain of seven months in reading, nine months in mathematics—respectable in any public school and very good for LD children. But since our children test two to three years behind on the average in reading and one and a half to two years behind in math, this would not constitute a sufficient gain to enable them to reenter regular school. We got these gains with our second experimental group. After seven months of intensified perceptual training, their mean progress in reading performance was a full fifteen months—more than twice the rate of the base test group *and* the normal child. And they equalled those gains in math, with a mean gain of 2.1 months for every chronological month spent in the intensive program.

Perhaps even more important, as far as teachers of LD children are concerned: the study confirmed the close relationship between perceptual training and academic improvement, especially in reading. We found an almost exact correlation between perceptual development and growth in language as measured by the Illinois Test of Psycholinguistic Abilities (I.T.P.A.). These language abilities have long been considered the basis for reading. So while perceptual training in itself will not teach a kid to read (that requires a fully staffed reading program), it does seem to greatly enhance the processes upon which reading depends.

Exciting as our findings are, we do not suggest they provide a final answer for an LD child beset by neurological, emotional and perceptual problems. Forty-seven children do not comprise a comprehensive study of the LD population—measured as it is in millions—and obviously some children did better and some worse, though we were encouraged to find most of the ratings clustered around the mid-point. And for all the demonstrations that perceptual training seems to give most of our kids a big boost, there are no miracle cures to LD. Perceptual training is not the solution for every child—any more than are the many other approaches that seem to work for some kids and not for others.

The megavitamin people, who recommend massive doses of vitamins to change an LD child's chemical balance, have had their successes and failures. Other doctors have recommended food free of chemical additives to relieve hyperactivity, while still others believe a couple of cups of coffee can be just as tranquilizing as a dose of Ritalin. While I have already decried the abuse of chemotherapy in treating our children, there are times when only drugs seem to work, particularly with our more seriously disturbed kids. Psychological therapy has been helpful; but so, too, has been just plain remedial work in reading and math. Apparently, no one model will fit every LD child and, for an unlucky few, no approach seems to work.

Our reaction to such conflicting results is not to continue to search for any one single answer, but to bombard our kids from all sides with whatever seems to help. We've increased the perceptual and vision training for all our kids and, to make sure we haven't overlooked anything, we keep it broad—going well beyond the specific deficits found in testing. For the same reason, we saturate them with four or five different reading and math programs and keep our classes small so the kids can receive the maximum individual attention. Another reason for so many different math and reading programs is to provide the kids with all the experience they can get. Any child needs experience, redundant experience, to be able to learn; but this is especially important for our LD kids, who have blocked out experience all their lives. Everything we do is designed to expose a child to different approaches, constantly overlapping and reinforcing weak or non-existent impressions and, once the material is learned, encouraging generalization. It's not enough if a kid just walks rails—he must hop, jump, play Angels in the Snow, Johnny on the Pony, Balloon, and any other exercise we can dream up. He learns visual matching and selectivity skills by working with beads, blocks, paper cutouts, black squares, circles and seven or eight different types of puzzles. We use touch, sight, sound and even smell to teach him the alphabet.

In addition, learning requires something that sounds elementary but is often overlooked, especially by parents: the child must *work* with the experience, he must "take it in." Jean Piaget has found that if a child doesn't play with his toy, he's not learning from it. Experience without reciprocal action, particularly in the case of children who are building their world from scratch, is virtually worthless.

Finally, we structure the kids' school life, remove physical distractions, and teach them inner controls, all so they can conquer their hyperactivity and get down to learning. Despite intermittent disruptions, ours is an astoundingly *quiet* school.

Of course, we make adaptations in our overall approach, based on each child's clinical profile and our evaluation of him. At the beginning of the year every teacher is required to study all the material available on each of her children, make observations in class, and submit a prescriptive teaching program for each student. This program is revised every month, based on the daily performance log we keep on every student. In this way we try to tailor everything—from reading and math to motivation—to each child's particular deficits.

Even though our return rate is twice as high as the average school in New York, I'd be the first to admit that little in our program is completely new. Perceptual and vision training techniques have been in use for years and have proved successful with many learning handicapped kids. So have many of the reading programs we use. Until the recent onslaught of the "open-classroom," well-structured classrooms were the norm; few of us learned our A, B, C's by running around the room, lying on the floor or doing just what we pleased. Lots of classroom discipline and teacher prodding were called for, not only to push us academically but to develop acceptable social behavior. And the idea that distractible children such as ours should have as little distraction as possible has been applied time and again and just makes common sense.

What is new and, I think, unique about our program is that we have chosen not just one approach or method, but remain flexible enough to utilize anything that will help. As I said earlier, I frankly don't care what gets to our kids as long as it does get to them. That is our secret, if it is one, and there is nothing in our program that couldn't benefit normal children, any of whom may develop a hitch somewhere along the line. What if these comprehensive and intensive programs were built into our public school system—is it possible we might cut down the number of learning-disabled kids? It's an intriguing thought. Certainly many of the marginally handicapped might not become the frustrated behavior problems they are now.

Barring this unlikely event, special classes and schools like mine are a necessity. And there are far too few of them. The Fleischmann Committee's comprehensive report in 1972 found that in New York State, only fifty-three percent of handicapped children were receiving the education they needed. Even worse, only fourteen percent of those who had been designated "learning-disabled" (and we still don't know how many have yet to be diagnosed) were receiving any special educational assistance. And that's a real shame, for many LD children can be remediated and sent back to regular school, and make a worthwhile contribution to society, especially if they are spotted in time.

Unfortunately, some of our kids enter school too late for us to eradicate their blocks, eliminate their self-image problems and fill in the gaps fast enough to make up the difference by the time they leave us. Even if we do succeed in motivating him, how much can a twelve-year-old accomplish if he comes to us as a second-grade reader with years of frustration behind him? What if he's a Paul Mitchell who refuses to get going? A twelve-year-old diagnosed too late can improve enormously in several years, but probably not enough to put him in a winning position in the outside world.

For the younger ones, however, particularly the five- to eight-year olds, the prognosis should be dramatically different. But no matter when we get them, from the moment they arrive, we begin to program them for that day they will return to regular school.

Academically, all our kids are presented with the conventional reading and math curricula they will encounter in their local schools. If they show signs of progress, we increase the exposure every day until eventually these programs are about all they are using, with some reinforcement from our other curriculums and perceptual training.

Structurally, we try to approximate as closely as we can the routine in conventional school. Our kids go on trips, recite the Pledge of Allegiance, put on plays and skits for the rest of the school in assembly. Even though we know any break in routine may threaten the kids' fragile sense of control, we stage occasional disruptions (such as fire drills) which they will encounter on the outside.

Long before our kids begin to look outward-bound, we are closely monitoring their social maturity. How well do they endure pressure? How well can they take criticism? Or face surprise situations? After all, our school is a hothouse. Once they leave us they will probably have a much larger school to contend with, and bewildering masses of kids. The environment will be much less structured, often "open classroom" or departmental teaching with shifting classes and different teachers. They may have teachers with little understanding of their problems, even if these problems are now sharply reduced, and who will make the same unreasonable demands of them they would of any kid. Their parents will have much less communication with the school, certainly not the minimum two calls a month they all receive from our teachers. And some teachers who know the past history will go overboard one way or another, either smothering our kids with pity for problems they have largely overcome or writing them off at the first disturbance.

Anticipating these changes—which are most apparent in public school but also can occur in private school, especially college preps—we may recommend that returning kids go the "soft" route taken by Herbie Goodman and Louis Kantrow, at least for a year or so. This means a private school with small, structured classes of no more than twenty.

Wherever our kids go, we run interference for them. Once the parents have chosen a school—something we ask them to do at least six months before their child will be enrolled—we arrange to visit the school. We present the child as he is now, not as he was before, and try to get him placed with a teacher we feel would be a good match for him. This doesn't always work. Many times a principal or headmaster will insist the kid take pot luck. And often, particularly when the child has attended that school before, which is usually the case when our kids return to public school, the principal doesn't want any part of him at all. We have to go into a big sales pitch, pointing out the changes in the kid's behavior and academics. We also keep in touch with our kids' parents and teachers, for years if necessary, to provide what guidance we can.

With the kid himself, we go through a different procedure. Once his school is chosen, we begin to overprogram him. We increase his homework along the lines of the curriculum in his new school, and often recommend to his parents special tutors in various subjects. Whenever possible we advance him *beyond* his classmates in the new school to give him a much-needed head start.

Finally, we get to the trickiest part—telling the kid. Some are overjoyed, some are afraid, and most fall somewhere in between. All need a lot of questions answered and a tremendous amount of reassurance that the people in their new school will like them as much as we do. That's something we can't guarantee, but one thing we can promise is that we're not dumping them forever. From the time we break the news, usually in February, we meet with them weekly, either alone or in groups of two or three, and run through the differences they can expect at the new school. Suppose other kids misbehave in the lunchroom? Or try to get them in trouble? Suppose the teacher doesn't recognize them when they raise their hand, even though they have the right answer? Suppose he's unfair, or they don't like him? We want them to understand

279

that not only will there be differences, but that they'll have to *overcome* them and behave in the controlled, quiet manner they've been taught by us.

These are the same pressures they were unable to handle before, and haven't had to face all the time they were with us. But these meetings evidently get results: so far all our returnees have managed to make the adjustment with only one exception—a kid whose mother sent him to regular school even though we told her he wasn't ready. We had to take him back.

What kind of future can our kids expect after they leave us? Though it lies beyond the scope of this book, the subject of our kids' prospects is an intriguing and important one. So, without pretending to be exhaustive, let me sketch our kids' futures, as we visualize them. Statistics are hard to come by, but there's every reason to believe they can work up to their full innate potential—as long as certain things are kept in mind.

These kids will probably always retain traces of their learning disability. Their concentration and attention span, though adequate for most tasks, probably will be shorter than normal. They will need more time to process information and consequently are not suited for jobs requiring fast on-your-feet decision making. Though we try to make them more adaptable, our kids probably never will feel comfortable with constantly changing situations or heavy pressure.

For those who are college-bound, the longer the program, the better. Five or six years makes better sense than four. Junior college is a good compromise. There's no need to pile stress and competition on a steadily improving kid and turn the clock back so he reemerges as a frustrated failure.

But let's not overlook their strengths. All our kids have learned to stretch themselves and accept the fact that they must work longer and harder to keep up with others. Academically, they do quite well in math; their verbal abilities, on which they've had to rely for much of their learning, are usually well developed. Highly sensitive toward other people, they can also be very articulate, as Kenny Meyer showed at his trial. While a written thesis might be a real struggle, an oral examination would be just their meat.

As for a career, there are a great many jobs they can do, and do well—whether they go to college or not. With their intuition, they can make fine social workers, guidance counselors, teachers. They can also be good managers, especially if they have a secretary to handle correspondence. Lately we've been exploring accountancy, banking and computer programming. Those not so gifted or inclined can aim for a whole raft of high-paying jobs in trades ranging from carpentry to auto mechanics.

Our older, more locked-in kids will be able to get along too, though the future may not be so rosy. Most of them should have no difficulty handling such widely divergent jobs as construction workers, file clerks, farm workers or forest rangers. The list is long and limited only by their particular deficits—and strengths.

For many of our parents, however, these prospects represent a sharp comedown from their initial high hopes. As always in the world of LD, there are heartbreak and heavy burdens to bear. And for the parents of older children, the ones we discovered late—sometimes too late—the "if only"'s multiply. "If only I had known sooner," "If only I had done this," "If only things were different" race through each parent's mind. In hopes of lessening these bitter second thoughts, and perhaps helping others avoid some of these pitfalls, here is some general advice for parents of LD children.

10

Most parents don't have a learning-disabled child. They have a child who is sometimes more of a pest than they can bear; who, like most kids, never seems to listen or pay attention; who never walks but runs everywhere; who can't seem to sit still long enough to finish dinner; who is continually bumping his head or scraping his knee. In other words, they have a normal, active child who progresses with more or less difficulty up the learning and development scale.

But some parents *do* have learning-disabled kids and almost all who do only find out the hard way Betty and Ed Wilson did, usually long after the child could have been helped. Moreover, most of them have no idea how to handle their impossible kids or how they should behave with them. And yet, if my kids hope to have a prayer of hacking it in the outside world, they need the help of their parents as much as, if not more than, that of any professional therapist. That's why the first people we try to educate are the parents. And the way we begin is with a kick-in-the-pants—a deliberately shocking orientation session, followed by meetings where groups of parents can discuss among themselves and with teachers the problems of living with and caring for an LD child. The general guidelines that follow represent the sum of countless such meetings, thoughts that should be helpful to you if you have—or *suspect* you have—an LD child:

Pay attention to your child. Early detection is the surest guarantee that he won't turn up at my school at eight, ten or twelve in Paul Mitchell's predicament: with hang-up piled on hang-up and so far behind academically, emotionally and socially that he may never catch up. Observe your child. Early detection is the parents' job; they are the only ones familiar with pre-schoolers every day. After all, it is the parents who must provide case histories for the neurologists and psychologists. And in spite of their lack of expertise, I believe they can detect early symptoms and bring their suspicions to a qualified professional—*if* they will only take a careful look.

From the moment of birth, the typical mbd LD child starts sending out signals. (If his learning disability derives from emotional causes or environmental deprivation, the signals will show up somewhat later.) By the time he is three, those signals will have increased sufficiently to produce a suspicious profile; by the age of five or six, his condition is usually quite clear.

One of the main signs of an mbd child are difficulties in his behavioral progress, which often swings to extremes. As a small baby, he may be unnaturally lethargic for the first several months—hardly seeming to be interested in anything, much less exploring his body or the objects in his limited environment. If this kind of listless (often considered "well-behaved") child suddenly turns 180 degrees and becomes ex-

283

tremely active and curious—usually around the age of six months—then there is reason to suspect you may have a Joey Rich or Lester Geffkin on your hands.

Or he simply may be highly distractible from birth. A distractible baby looks everywhere without focusing on anything; overreacts—often with a scream—to any minor change in his environment; grabs and immediately throws away anything near him; is frenetic but, again, has no real focus to his activity.

Lethargic or distractible, these babies are displaying non-learning behavior characteristic of mbd children.

By the age of two or three, each of these children—the innately hyperactive or the developed hyperactive—will be a toy-snatcher and smasher, roving from object to object with much the same lack of sustained interest he showed as a baby. When he isn't daydreaming, he'll constantly be on the run, buzzing, fidgeting, pestering to a degree unusual even for his age group. His attention span is nil. A screamer and a bully, he will quickly be classified by neighbors as a spoiled brat.

At five or six, he is still bombing around, uninterested as ever in studying the world and making sense of it. He never questions, always reacts. Perseveration—which he should have outgrown long ago—is still one of his trademarks, and any change in schedule or shift in his surroundings—being left with a babysitter, going on a trip, entering school—will most likely provoke tantrums. Younger children attract him, partly because they're easier to bully, and partly because he can't understand or engage in the activities of his own age group. He also likes to spend time with easily-charmed adults, who tend to be more manipulative and less demanding than his peers.

By five, too, the LD child is displaying personality extremes. His mood can swing violently and rapidly from being excessively introverted or excessively extroverted. One minute he will be unreachable, locked into his frenetic or daydreaming world; the next he may be demanding total attention, even clawing and biting grown-ups if they don't respond immediately to his infantile demands, providing him with instant gratification of his slightest wish.

Another clue to the LD child is his developmental progress, which may be slow and erratic. The LD baby is often late in learning to sit, roll over, crawl or walk. Sometimes he skips certain stages entirely, suddenly pulling himself up on his playpen and walking without ever having crawled. Poor eye control is also typical, and many innate mbd hyperactives are noticeably strabismic, even at the age of a couple of months.

Although most LD kids eventually learn some muscle control (to the unwarranted relief of their parents), they're still pretty klutzy. Bombing around, a three-year-old LD kid bumps into things more often than other children, trips and falls down more, never learning from yesterday's experience. (Often he doesn't seem to notice physical pain.) He has other difficulties in development at this stage. Toilet training though eventually successful, is a major ordeal. And, unlike normal three-year-olds, the LD kid still hasn't decided which hand he's going to rely on for eating, reaching and guiding his actions.

Developmental lags become most apparent at ages four, five and six. Generally as slow to talk as to walk, LD kids often lisp and stutter, but the clincher is their immature speech patterns. A five-, six- or even seven-year-old LD child is often still using the jumbled, primitive syntax of baby talk.

285

Though by now most LD kids will have learned to compensate for—and thus conceal—their most flagrant motor difficulties, an alert parent can spot telltale giveaways: poor balance, skewed posture and inflexible patterns of movement in the same exercise (he may be able to keep his balance while riding a bike, but not while walking a rail). A very common symptom of motor difficulty—one displayed by most of my students—is the waddle-walk, the inability to integrate both sides of the body in a reciprocal motion.

At five or six, fine motor coordination is also noticeably underdeveloped. The kid spills his milk and manipulates a pencil poorly, if at all. He tends to press too hard on a pen or the pieces of a puzzle. He can't throw or catch a ball, or master buttons and shoestrings, which makes dressing himself almost impossible.

In nursery school, kindergarten and first grade, the LD child displays his lack of development in other ways. He has so much trouble playing games, to say nothing of catching on to the rules, that he'll avoid games altogether—if his peers haven't already excluded him. In kindergarten he can't fit puzzles, color within the lines, build with blocks, and he shows more than average confusion between left and right. His drawings are either asymmetrically confined to one area of the page, or so random that they have no interpretable shape or meaning.

Even as late as the age of six, the LD child still persistently reverses letters and words—a sign he lacks left-right orientation. His paperwork continues to be sloppy, full of crowded letters, frequent erasures and words climbing above or below the line.

In reading, the LD child misplaces or omits words regularly and is always losing his place. More likely, he isn't able to read at all. His still poorly coordinated eyes strain easily, leading to excessive eye rubbing and reddening. His memory, never good, will appear nonexistent compared to the memories of his peers.

Every one of these symptoms is apparent in an LD child before the age of six. You don't have to be an expert to spot them—just an interested, observant parent. But having said that, allow me one major qualification:

Don't jump to conclusions. Whether it's your child or someone else's, remember that no one or several of these signals necessarily implies learning-disability. Most of the problems noted are characteristic of any normal child at one age or another. As mentioned, a certain amount of perseveration is normal in a three- or four-year-old. Persistent reversals are certainly common up to the age of five. Distractibility, sloppiness, disorganization and inability to pay attention are natural in any young child, and where is there a three-year-old who hasn't thrown a tantrum or two?

What's more, no child breezes through every stage of development or schoolwork precisely on schedule. Even a child who generally learns faster than his classmates is likely to progress in some areas at a normal or even below-average pace. What is normal for your son at age five may be six months or even a year in the future for your five-year-old nephew.

What *should* parents look for then? An *excessive* number of signs that their child is having difficulty growing up and adjusting in many areas at once. Parents should be on the alert not for just one, but a number of major lags and lapses. A stray tantrum at age five is no excuse to pack the kid off to a doctor. But a number of tantrums may be a tipoff, especially if the child displays many other behavioral and developmental symptoms of LD. Similarly, an irritable, constantly screaming baby may just be hungry, or suffering from a tummy-ache. But if the same baby continues to yell, even when nothing is physically wrong, then it's time to be suspicious. If he is allergic and strabismic as well, an early evaluation should be made. The trouble with LD is that its symptoms are non-symptoms. But far better to err on the side of caution than to wake up long afterward—as the Wilsons did and as countless parents and teachers of LD kids still do—and ask: How could I have failed to see what was in front of my eyes; how could I have failed to help my kid when so obviously he needed my help?

So much for the qualifications.

Once you begin to have suspicions about your child's development, *question yourself and others familiar with his history.*

Many experts think that LD—or a tendency toward it—is genetic in origin. (This theory gets some support from statistics—eighty percent of kids diagnosed mbd are boys.) Consequently, family history is sometimes helpful. Did either parent have difficulties in development or schoolwork as he or she was growing up? Was either parent hyperactive? Grandparents can help here, but generally the value of such information is questionable, memories differing as they will so many years afterward.

On the other hand, there are signs that mbd arises not just from genes, but from problems encountered during pregnancy or birth. Here the facts are matters of medical record, and can easily be ascertained—though few people bother to take the trouble. Was the mother healthy during pregnancy, and did she require any special medications? Ask your obstetrician whether labor was unduly long, whether the baby was a breech presentation, whether forceps were used in delivery, whether everything proceeded normally. Find out if your baby had good oxygen intake at birth, and if there was unusual staining and bleeding. Check on the amount of anesthesia administered during delivery. Get the details of just how your baby arrived, including those small hitches that the doctors may feel were "no real problem."

Don't hesitate to question the pediatrician about your child's development and about the possible effect of illnesses during infancy. Was the fever he contracted when he was a month or two old severe enough to affect brain function? See how many checkpoints he passed on schedule. Ask teachers to talk honestly about how his progress and behavior compare with his classmates'.

Whatever you do, don't accept "He'll grow out of it," "He's just a little slow" or "He seems a bit immature"— either from a doctor or teacher. Dig a little, particularly if you suspect they're being evasive. If the doctor or teacher can't or won't be more specific, find one who will. The answers may hurt your parental ego, but they'll save a lot of grief later on. Remember: The younger an LD child is recognized and treated, the fewer compensatory patterns and emotional hang-ups he'll have, and the more easily his problems can be overcome.

Have your child's health and development thoroughly evaluated—soon. Most parents wait until the child is six before testing his hearing and sight, but these tests can—and should—be made four years earlier. I once examined a seven-year-old child who was about to be classified learning-disabled. He was frenetic and distractible as any I've ever encountered, and his schooldays had been pure hell, for him and his teachers. It turned out that his sight was so poor he was almost legally blind, a disability that must have been holding him back since birth. Poor hearing can have an equally deleterious effect. Don't depend on your child to report these problems—children don't suspect that they are anything but normal. If you've never seen or heard well, how do you discover that other kids see or hear better? But that can produce a lot of frustration when you try to match their achievements.

For eye evaluations, find a thorough doctor who will determine whether your child is focusing properly, whether he is over- or underconverging, how well he is tracking and whether this seems normal for his age. Vision training can overcome many of these reading-related difficulties—but the earlier, the better.

Test your child's speech, language and visual perceptions, especially if you have suspicions about his progress. This can be done quite early, too, at the age of three or four, and will give a much clearer picture of his developmental problems than your own unprofessional observation. If you have a suspect child, a neurological examination is certainly in order, and a psychological evaluation is also a must if things have reached this "red alert" stage.

Finally, although most pediatricians tend to a child's general health, few pay attention to such important aspects of a kid's development as whether he is walking, sitting or moving properly. An orthopedist should check to make sure your child is using his basic equipment effectively.

If all this sounds like a big expenditure, it *is*. But compared to the tab for *treating* an LD child, it's one of the best bargains around.

Make sure your child experiences. Whether your child is environmentally deprived, mbd, emotionally disturbed or just plain normal, he needs all the experience he can get as early as he can get it.

By this I mean experience exploring his world and getting the kind of information a child needs in order to fully develop his basic perceptual abilities. Unfortunately, many contemporary child-rearing practices are geared to the mother's convenience, not the child's needs.

Most mothers, for instance, place the child's crib against an inside wall in a position convenient to their dominant hand. The same happens with the bassinet. Consequently, the baby is invariably picked up from the same side of the crib, and given his bottle from the same side and by the same hand. Even in the highchair his food always arrives at the same angle. How will this child get the stimulus to explore the *other* side of his body and the spaces and objects there?

He advances to playpen, carriage and stroller, but the situation doesn't improve: he's still confined to one small area—very convenient for keeping him safe, but cramping his ability to move around his environment and get the wealth of perceptions it affords.

My advice is to put crib and bassinet in the middle of the room. Approach the baby from both sides for feeding and other activities. Whenever possible, skip the playpen, carriage and other confinements altogether, and let the kid crawl around on the rug or grass. As often as you can, give him the freedom to experience the angle, substance and feel of the objects surrounding him—not only his crib, but your desk, the chair with its legs and arms, the grass and shrubs and flowers that he finds outside. And let him move. Interaction with the things that make up his world contributes to his basic perceptions at least as much as his experience with rattles and conventional toys.

Finally, make sure your baby exercises so that he can build the kind of muscles necessary for widening his experience and environment. As we knock ourselves out running from diaper-changing to feeding, bathing and clean-up, it's easy to forget that *we're* the ones getting a workout, while Baby lies there gurgling and doing nothing. As soon as possible, start playing with him, making him exercise his arms and legs.

Don't confuse your child. Be as creative as you like in finding ways to teach your baby, but don't overdo: first he has to learn basics. Try to look at the world and its raft of unknowns through his infant eyes, and keep it simple for him.

One of the best toys for a small baby couldn't be simpler: just a piece of paper dangling from a string above his crib. He will sight on it (practicing binocular vision), reach for it (coordinating hands with eyes), and struggle to achieve some sort of balance over his body's mid-line—all of which train many basic aspects of perception. But what do most of us do? Instead of a single piece of paper on a string, we hang a colorful mobile, with each of its different shapes swaying in a different direction. And to keep the baby from ruining it, we hang the mobile too far out of reach for him even to bother stretching for it. *We* find this toy much prettier and more fascinating than a simple piece of paper, and can't figure out why the kid seems uninterested, confused or unduly distracted.

The same goes for his surroundings and the rest of his toys. A small baby is confused, *not* stimulated, by the wild shapes and angles of a busy wallpaper, and a mesh playpen makes the world look like a crazy quilt. One pot or pan can teach him more about form than ten educational toys chocked into the playpen so he can't move.

A normal child won't learn much in these circumstances,

but the worst he will suffer is mild confusion and boredom. For an LD child, however, such an overstimulating environment can be a disaster. Any baby who seems at all hyperkinetic should be placed in the *least* stimulating environment possible. Somber as it seems, his room should be painted a neutral color, furnished sparsely, stripped of any knickknacks that might distract him. He can play with simple toys, but only one at a time. Far from retarding his progress, this boring environment may enable him to concentrate on the one or two items at hand and learn something from them. A similar environment is recommended even for older LD kids of seven, eight and nine, and we provide these surroundings in our school. Adults may yawn, but it is in this environment that LD kids learn best.

Try to provide a normal daily life for yourself and your child. One major problem for our LD kids is that they have no friends. Neighborhood kids will rarely put up with an LD child's bratty, crybaby, bullying ways and are quick to brand him a retard as soon as he falls behind in games or schoolwork. Most sisters and brothers are even worse. As impatient as their friends, they are also ashamed that he is "different" and are jealous of the special adult attention he rates. Try to give equal attention to each child—a difficult job when one kid demands so much himself—and draw on the sibling's understanding. Remind him that the LD child has problems, and try to enlist his help. Tap the older kid's pride and sense of responsibility by suggesting that he help Billy with his homework because he always gets A's in math and you've forgotten most of it by now. Children love to teach—it makes them feel important—and in our school many of the older ones do it quite well.

Even parents have a tendency to give up on their child as a

293

social being, becoming either overprotective or ashamed, and thereby further isolating him from normal society. But this is where parents can make the greatest contribution. If he has no friends, you play with him. Include him in on all family affairs and try to give him as much responsibility as he can handle. He can and should learn to make beds, shine shoes, clear the table and wash dishes. (Just don't expect him to do it as neatly and quickly as the other kids.) Cooking, sewing, caring for pets—there are lots of possibilities, as long as the task is clearly explained and not too complicated. Hobbies and games—catch, jacks, checkers—are OK too, as long as they meet these same criteria. Not only may you be surprised by his willingness to pitch in, but his success with you will have a direct bearing on his chances of returning whole to society.

The last people who should give up are the child's parents. But none of this is easy, and one place to turn for help—for you and your child—is therapy. Whether or not the root of their learning block is emotional, all our kids have emotional problems, stemming from their failure to learn. In addition, parents themselves develop emotional problems arising from their own inability to deal with the daily hassles this outwardly normal child creates. When this happens I often recommend that parents and child get into therapy either with a private practitioner or at a good clinic. Hopefully, they will learn not only to accept their child's sickness, but how to cope with it effectively.

Our kids should also have friends and social activities outside the family. Unfortunately, most of them are usually too alienated from the other kids to join in normal neighborhood play, but there are other possibilities. Many of our kids' parents have looked into such organizations as the church-affiliated play groups, the Scouts, even day camp if the child can handle the activity—which can provide a few friends as well as the kind of structured situation our kids need. Find out what each group is offering. Some have special groupings for children with similar problems. Research an organization carefully before committing your child to it. And once you've decided to enroll him, be honest with his supervisors. It will do the kid no good to "flunk out" of yet another scene because his parents have lied about his behavior, or the person in charge isn't equipped to handle him, or the group is too large or unstructured for his needs.

Structure your child's day. Even a normal child needs structure—to hang his plans on, to give him the security of knowing what to expect, or to rebel against. The more immature the kid, the more structure he needs—and our highly immature LD kids need it most of all though their screams and yells seem to be saying just the opposite. Once they internalize a regular daily pattern, they become happier, quieter and more productive.

After consulting with us, the parents of our six- to ten-year-olds worked out a master daily schedule for their general guidance. It goes like this:

After school the child bursts off the bus and is allowed to run around letting off steam for a while. Mother has juice and cookies ready in the house and sits down prepared to listen to the child's pell-mell account of his exploits, problems and feelings during the day.

After about half an hour, the child is returned to a more controlled situation. The next half hour should be homework time, with Mother at his elbow ready to ask and answer questions. Distractions are minimized: friends and relatives are asked not to telephone during homework hour and visitors are banned. No family interruptions are permitted, either, and brothers and sisters home during this time have to play quietly or do their own homework. Because of the LD kid's short attention span, tackle only half an hour of studying at a stretch.

After homework the child goes out with his mother or a responsible older child to play in the park, shop or just go for a walk. This is also a good time to schedule an after-school play group, dancing or swimming lessons, or Scouts. But for approximately an hour and a half, the child should be provided a controlled situation in which to indulge his need for physical activity.

The child has to come home, however, at least half an hour before dinner so he has time to settle down; dashing in at the last minute is likely to disrupt him as well as the family. This half hour should be another quiet time and we recommend TV (no shoot-'em-ups, please!).

Mealtime should be as organized as possible. The family eats together, at the same time every night. Everyone takes his regular seat at the table. The appetizer, meat, vegetables and dessert are not served all at once, so the child doesn't know where to look or what to taste; each arrives separately, and is cleared away before the next course arrives.

The half hour after dinner is another homework period, this time with Daddy helping. If there is no homework, the father plays with the child in some constructive way, reading a story to or with him, playing checkers, or helping him build a model airplane. This is a quiet time for father and child to be together, away from telephones, radios, and family interruptions.

After that, the child is free until bedtime to watch TV and

do pretty much what he wants, short of creating bedlam. If homework has taken up his time with Dad, this is a good chance for his reading or checkers.

At least fifteen minutes before bedtime—an hour as fixed as dinnertime—the child is sent off to get ready. If he undresses quickly and without fuss, his father rewards him with another story. Before he falls asleep, one of his parents questions him about the next day at school—is his homework done to his satisfaction, is he ready for tomorrow's trip or reading class, does he have his schoolbooks together? The kid's mind is thus prepared for what he'll experience when he wakes up.

Work together as a team. Today most parent-child relationships are dominated by the mother. Always present, always nagging (though usually manipulable), she is by far the stronger parental influence—except when, because of some offense the kid never clearly understands, the father is dragged in to discipline him. Bad as this imbalance is for normal children, it's much worse for the LD kid. If he is ever going to organize his discombobulated perceptions and break through his learning blocks, an LD child needs more continuous, concentrated help than any one parent can be expect to provide. What's more, if parents don't team up they are likely to be played off against each other (our kids are great little manipulators). Mommy and Daddy must *both* discipline and they must both encourage and reward. Each parent must agree to the rules the other has set up, so there is no arguing at the last minute over whether the kid goes to bed at eight-thirty or gets to stay up half an hour later. Last-minute rule changes will only further confuse their already-confused child.

297

Be consistent. Once you've gotten together on rules, procedures, punishments and rewards, explain them to your child and stick to them.

Insist on your household schedule. If your child understands what time dinner is served, but shows up late anyway, he should be sent to his room with no food and allowed no snacks until the next meal. (Believe it or not, your child will not starve if he misses one meal . . . though he will probably complain at the top of his lungs.)

If the child makes it to the table on time and without a fuss, but refuses to eat all or part of his meal, make him sit at the table until he has finished each course. Don't relent, even if he sits there until bedtime, missing his hour with Daddy or his favorite TV show. Try to impress on him that once he's eaten, he will get to do the things he likes.

Here again, though, you don't have to be unreasonable. If you are serving something new, or something the child dislikes, make his portion a small one. And never serve him more than you know he can possibly eat.

This doesn't mean that the structure can never be varied. But if the kid wants to eat dinner at a friend's house or stay up late for a special TV show, see that he understands in advance that this is a special occasion.

Consult your child, too. Rules and procedures don't have to be presented flatly, without explanation or discussion, for children to understand or respect them. In fact, it's usually just the opposite.

An LD child needs to have school and household rules firmly planted in his mind. But he is much more likely to remember and cooperate if he has participated in the rule-making procedure. Once our kids understand that rules and schedules are intended to help them learn, they often devise

298

stricter systems for themselves than any adult would have dreamed of setting up. So sit down together and get your child's views on how his life should run. Reason things out with him until all of you are clear on just what his behavior and schedule should be.

Again, make sure your rules are simple and consistent with his level of maturity. Don't expect him never to get angry with his sister. Just agree that when he does, he will take his case to a parent instead of pounding on her first. And then keep to the procedures and rules you've all agreed on. You'll have to remind him a dozen times a day for the first few weeks, but after a while he'll catch on.

Make reasonable demands on this kid. So his homework is messy. Your first response shouldn't be "Do it over." Instead, appreciate his making an effort to do it at all. If he hasn't completed the entire assignment, perhaps he's done as much as he could. If he is *rarely* able to finish, the school may be making inordinate demands that should be discussed with his teacher. More often, however, we find parents expecting two or three times more than our teachers would ever ask from a child. If your eight-year-old son is drawing his first shaky circles, be proud of that—don't be ashamed because they aren't perfectly round. There's no harm in challenging an LD child—we do it all the time. But make sure that what you demand isn't more than your child can give in return.

Give yourself and your child a chance. Too many times we suggest to our parents ways of handling a situation, only to hear from them three days later that it doesn't work. Of course it hasn't—yet. Expecting an unruly, undisciplined child to reform overnight is unreasonable. Give your efforts at control some time to get through. And even after he's begun to respond, expect occasional lapses, just as you would with any child.

Help *us* be understanding with your child. In an LD child's home, family life should be as organized as possible—but life has a way of fouling up schedules. If a parent has to work overtime, or perhaps rush one of the other kids to a doctor, the disruption of routine will affect the LD child. If he is going to turn up at his Scout meeting disturbed and anxious, prepare the group leader ahead of time. If he is too upset to do homework, call his teacher in the morning and explain it isn't his fault. Each morning before school I get at least a dozen calls from parents in regard to such matters, and the good it does their children and us is immeasurable.

Raising an LD child is a superhuman job and always will be. We encourage our kids' parents to draw on each other and work on problems together, trying new approaches until they find some that work. We contribute what we can, but it is the parents who have to implement our suggestions and solutions. I've watched parents try, and experience has made me an optimist. If they put their minds to it, most parents *can* come up with the strength and skill they need to help their kids and be happy themselves.

SUGGESTED READING LIST

Anderson, Paul S. *Language Skills in Elementary Education*. New York: Macmillan, Inc., 1972.

Ayres, A. J. "Patterns of Perceptual-Motor Dysfunction in Children, A Factor Analytic Study." *Perceptual Motor Skills,* 20 (1965): 335–68.

———. "Tactile Functions: Their Relation to Hyperactive and Perceptual-Motor Behavior." *American Journal of Occupational Therapy* 18 (1964): 6–11.

Ayres, W. Stewart, ed. *Behavior Modification: Principles and Clinical Approaches*. Boston: Little, Brown and Company, 1972.

Back, Kurt W. *Beyond Words*. New York: Russell Sage Foundation, 1972.

Bartley, S. Howard. *The Human Organism As a Person*. New York: Chilton Book Co., 1967.

———. *Principles of Perception*. New York: Harper & Brothers, 1958.

Birch, H. G. *Brain Damage in Children: The Biological and*

Social Aspects. New York: The Williams & Wilkins Co., 1964.

————, and Belmont, L. "Auditory-Visual Integration in Brain-Damaged and Normal Children." *Developmental Medicine and Child Neurology* 7: 135–44.

Blumenthal, A. L. *Language and Psychology: Historical Aspects of Psycholinguistics*. New York: John Wiley, 1970.

Borish, Irwin M. *Clinical Refraction*. Chicago: The Professional Press, Inc., 1954.

Bradfield, Robert H., ed. *Behavior Modification: The Human Effort*. San Rafael, California: Dimensions Publishing Co., 1970.

Brutten, Milton; Richardson, Sylvia O.; and Mangel, Charles. *Something's Wrong With My Child*. New York: Harcourt Brace Jovanovich, Inc., 1973.

Burks, H. F. "The Hyperkinetic Child." *The Exceptional Child* 27 (1960): 18–26.

Carter, Daniel B., ed. *Interdisciplinary Approaches to Learning Disorders*. New York: Chilton Book Co., 1970.

Clark, Margaret M. *Reading Difficulties in Schools*. New York: Penguin Books, Inc., 1970.

Cole, Michael; Gay, John; Glick, Joseph A.; and Sharp, Donald W. *The Cultural Context of Learning and Thinking*. New York: Basic Books, 1971.

Copel, Sidney L., ed. *Behavior Pathology of Childhood and Adolescence*. New York: Basic Books, Inc., 1973.

Cronbach, Lee J. *Essentials of Psychological Testing*. 3rd ed. New York: Harper & Row, 1970.

Cruickshank, W. M.; Bentzen, F. A.; Ratzeburg, F. H.; and Tannhauser, M. T. *A Teaching Method for Brain-In-*

jured and Hyperactive Children. Syracuse, New York: University of Syracuse Press, 1961.

Ekstein, Rudolf, and Motto, Rocco L. *From Learning for Love to Love of Learning: Essays on Psychoanalysis and Education*. New York: Brunner/Mazel, Inc., 1969.

Ellingson, Careth. *The Shadow Children*. Chicago: Topaz Press, 1969.

Evans, Richard I. *Jean Piaget: The Man and His Ideas*. New York: E. P. Dutton & Co., Inc., 1973.

Gesell, Arnold. *The First Five Years of Life*. New York: Harper & Row, 1940.

——, and Amatruda, C. S. *Developmental Diagnosis: Normal and Abnormal Child Development*. New York: Paul B. Hoeser, 1948.

Glasser, William. *Schools Without Failure*. New York: Harper & Row, 1969.

Haley, Jay, ed. *Changing Families: A Family Therapy Reader*. New York: Grune & Stratton, 1971.

Hall, Mary Anne. *Teaching Reading as a Language Experience*. Columbus, Ohio: C. E. Merrill Publishing Co., 1970.

Hammill, Donald. "Training Visual Perceptual Processes." *Journal of Learning Disabilities* 5 (November 1972): 552–59.

Hanison, Saul I., and McDermott, John J., eds. *Childhood Psychopathology: An Anthology of Basic Readings*. New York: International Universities Press, 1972.

Haworth, Mary R., ed. *Child Psychotherapy*. New York: Basic Books, Inc., 1964.

Hewett, Frank M. *The Emotionally Disturbed Child in the Classroom*. Boston: Allyn & Bacon, Inc., 1968.

Jones, Reginald L. *New Directions in Special Education.* Boston: Allyn & Bacon, Inc., 1970.

Kanner, Leo. "The Place of the Exceptional Child in the Family Structure." In *The Exceptional Child: A Book of Readings,* edited by James F. Magary and John R. Eichorn, pp. 33–42. New York: Holt, Rinehart and Winston, 1962.

Kephart, N. C. *The Slow Learner in the Classroom.* Columbus, Ohio: C. E. Merrill Books, 1960.

Levy, Harold B. *Square Pegs Round Holes.* Boston: Little, Brown and Company, 1973.

Lewis, Helen Block. *Shame and Guilt in Neurosis.* New York: International Universities Press, 1971.

McNeill, David. *The Acquisition of Language: The Study of Developmental Psycholinguistics.* New York: Harper & Row, 1970.

Minahin, Patricia; Biber, Barbara; Shapiro, Edna; and Zimiles, Herbert. *The Psychological Impact of School Experience.* New York: Basic Books, Inc., 1969.

Myklebust, Helmer R., ed. *Progress in Learning Disabilities,* vols. I and II. New York: Grune & Stratton, Inc., 1971.

Nielsen, J. M. *Agnosia, Apraxia, Aphasia: Their Value in Cerebral Localization.* New York: Paul B. Hoeser, Inc., 1946.

Orson, S. T. *Reading, Writing and Speech Problems in Children.* New York: W. W. Norton, 1937.

Paul, I. H. *Letters to Simon: On the Conduct of Psychotherapy.* New York: International Universities Press, 1973.

Piaget, Jean. *The Construction of Reality in the Child.* New York: Basic Books, Inc., 1954.

304

————. *The Language and Thought of the Child*. New York: Harcourt Brace, 1926.

————. *The Origins of Intelligence in Children*. New York: International Universities Press, 1952.

————, and Inhelder, Barkel. *Memory and Intelligence*. New York: Basic Books, Inc., 1973.

Schefler, Albert E. *Communicational Structure: Analysis of a Psychotherapy Transaction*. Bloomington and London: Indiana University Press, 1973.

Siegel, Ernest. *The Exceptional Child Grows Up*. New York: E. P. Dutton & Co., Inc., 1974.

————. "The Real Problem of Minimal Brain Dysfunction." In *Learning Disabilities: Its Implications to a Responsible Society*, edited by Doreen Kronick, pp. 53–67. Chicago: Developmental Learning Materials, 1969.

Strauss, Alfred, and Lehtinen, Laura. *Psychopathology and Education of the Brain-Injured Child*. vol. 1. New York: Grune & Stratton, 1947.

Taft, Lawrence T. "Brain-Injury—Its Definition, Diagnosis, Cause and Treatment." New York: New York Association for Brain-Injured Children, n. d.

Valzelli, Luigi. *Psychopharmacology: An Introduction to Experimental and Clinical Principles*. New York: Spectrum Publications, Inc., 1973.

ABOUT THE AUTHOR

Dr. Martin E. Cohen, O.D., is now Director of The Buckingham School in Queens, New York, a private school for learning disabled children, age five to seventeen. A graduate of Hobart College, he earned his doctorate at the Massachusetts College of Optometry, where he first became interested in perceptual disorders. Before establishing the Queens Buckingham School, he served as Director of Child Development at The Horizon School for Perceptual Development, also in New York City. Dr. Cohen has written several articles on the role of optometry in education, and lectures frequently on the subject of learning disabilities. He is an active member of the New York Association for Brain-Injured Children and the Association for Children with Learning Disorders. Dr. Cohen resides, with his wife and four sons, in Greenlawn, Long Island. *Bets Wishz Doc* is his first book.